TRASH
TALK

Gregg—

You're welcome!

11·20·23

Greg -

You're welcome!

11-30-23

RAFI KOHAN
TRASH
TALK

The Only Book About Destroying Your Rivals That Isn't Total Garbage

PUBLICAFFAIRS

New York

PublicAffairs
Hachette Book Group
1290 Avenue of the Americas, New York, NY 10104
www.publicaffairsbooks.com
@Public_Affairs

Printed in Canada

First Edition: December 2023

Published by PublicAffairs, an imprint of Perseus Books, LLC, a subsidiary of Hachette Book Group, Inc. The PublicAffairs name and logo is a registered trademark of the Hachette Book Group.

The Hachette Speakers Bureau provides a wide range of authors for speaking events. To find out more, go to hachettespeakersbureau.com or email HachetteSpeakers@hbgusa.com.

PublicAffairs books may be purchased in bulk for business, educational, or promotional use. For more information, please contact your local bookseller or the Hachette Book Group Special Markets Department at special.markets@hbgusa.com.

The publisher is not responsible for websites (or their content) that are not owned by the publisher.

Print book interior design by Bart Dawson.

Library of Congress Cataloging-in-Publication Data

Names: Kohan, Rafi, author.
Title: Trash talk : the only book about destroying your rivals that isn't total garbage / Rafi Kohan.
Description: First edition. | New York : PublicAffairs, 2023.
Identifiers: LCCN 2023018367 | ISBN 9781541788916 (hardcover) | ISBN 9781541788930 (ebook)
Subjects: LCSH: Invective—Political aspects | Invective—Psychological aspects.
Classification: LCC BF463.I58 K64 2023 | DDC 179—dc23/eng/20230623
LC record available at https://lccn.loc.gov/2023018367

ISBNs: 9781541788916 (hardcover), 9781541788930 (ebook)

MRQ

Printing 1, 2023

*For Azalea and Elliott, who live rent-free
in my head (and house).*

And for Arielle, as ever.

**Art, like morality, consists of
drawing the line somewhere.**

—G.K. Chesterton

Sportsmanship is overrated.

—Malcolm Jenkins

CONTENTS

Section IV
THE PROBLEM WITH THE LINE

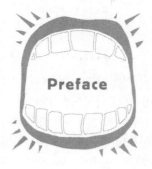

HOW CONOR GOT HIS RUDE BACK

JULY 8, 2021

"FUCK THAT SAUCE! Fuck that sauce! Fuck that sauce!"

It's not every day that people jeer a condiment.

But today is not every day. Today is the official press conference for Ultimate Fighting Championship (UFC) 264, a mixed martial arts event that will feature, at the top of its card, a trilogy bout between Conor McGregor, the brash Irish brawler whose meteoric rise to superstardom began in 2013 when he introduced the world to his aggressive striking style and antagonizing mental gamesmanship, and Dustin Poirier, a quiet lunch-pail type from Lafayette, Louisiana, for whom nothing seems to come easy. At thirty-two years old, Poirier has never had more celebrity than he does right now, coming off arguably the biggest and most stunning victory of his career, a second-round upset of McGregor, avenging his 2014 loss at the hands of the Irishman. This fight will be something of a tiebreaker between them, but Conor isn't one to willingly share the spotlight.

McGregor makes his entrance first. With a languid, almost bowlegged strut, he climbs onto the stage of T-Mobile Arena, just off the Las Vegas Strip, careful not to crease his immaculately tailored purple tartan suit, and installs himself on the front edge of the platform. "This is the notorious Conor McGregor," says the PA announcer. From behind a pair of oversized aviator sunglasses, McGregor turns his expressionless face from one side of the twenty-thousand-seat venue to the other, taking in the spectacle of a frenzied American crowd overwhelmingly dressed in the colors of the Irish flag. Slowly, McGregor raises his arms, palms upturned, in acceptance of the room's adulation.

As the PA announcer comes back on the mic to introduce his opponent—"winner of six of his last seven fights, including a January knockout win over McGregor"—the Irish fighter snaps out of this reverie. Beneath the puckering smile of Dana White, the UFC's president and emcee for these press events, McGregor shows off the fast twitch that has made him a world-class athlete. He snatches two bottles of hot sauce—Poirier's Louisiana Style Hot Sauce—from atop the dais and proceeds to dump them on the floor as Poirier, in a tropical shirt and shades, takes the stage to a chorus of boos. It's vintage McGregor, this brand of insulting provocation, this in-your-face attempt to make your blood boil.

What happens next is a kind of inaudible if not wordless dance, as White blocks Poirier's path and security rushes in from both sides of the stage, as the fighters try—or at least feign trying—to get at one another. McGregor screams through his beard. Poirier rips off his sunglasses. But they are held apart. The brawny presence of security would typically signal the end of such an episode. Poirier recognizes this and relaxes, ready to sit. But McGregor is far from finished. Practically vibrating with hostility, McGregor dances again in Poirier's direction, his movements coiled with violent intentions. He hip-thrusts and finger-points his way around the dais, where Poirier is now on edge again, reacting to everything McGregor is doing as if strung to a psychic tether. The crowd chants *oléeee, olé-olé-olé, oléeee, olé*, as McGregor crosses to the other side of the stage, breaching an invisible threshold of sorts, and more explicitly invading Poirier's space. There, with Poirier restrained, McGregor swipes another bottle of hot sauce, which he throws into the crowd.

"Fuck that sauce! Fuck that sauce!"

Before finally, mercifully, taking a seat, to Dana White's great relief, McGregor stops directly in front of Poirier. He lingers for a beat, until their eyes meet. With his back to the crowd, McGregor offers his opponent a shrug, the purple cloth of his suit jacket rising and falling on the thick ropes of his battle-ready shoulders. But it is hardly the sheepish shrug of apology. It is instead the gesture of a transgressing drunk man after midnight—the raised eyebrow of invitation, of a gauntlet thrown, and it says, unmistakably: *Whatcha gonna do about it?*

SINCE THE MOMENT TV cameras caught a glimpse of his sinewy, tattooed frame, McGregor has been known as much for his mouth and attention-grabbing antics as his knockout blows. As UFC's head PR man Dave Lockett tells me, "Conor always brings the circus." It's not just the caravan of media members who follow the fighter halfway around the globe, in search of a headline. It's also the rabid if carnivalesque allegiance he inspires in his supporters, a band of merry pranksters who follow him like he's a one-man music festival and revel in a kind of in-crowd fun that comes, inevitably, at someone else's expense. In the lead-up to McGregor's UFC debut, his opponent, Marcus Brimage, was stunned by the hostility he received not just from the relatively unknown and as-of-yet unproven Irish fighter, but also from his fans, as they harassed him on social media. "They're all over my Facebook, talking about how he's going to whip my ass," Brimage said at the time, adding, in disbelief: "Dude, you liked my page just to tell me that shit? That's a lot of trouble to do that."

(McGregor won that fight in one minute and seven seconds.)

Which isn't to say McGregor couldn't torment opponents on his own. Against Dennis Siver, who is maybe three inches shorter than McGregor, Conor taunted him as "too small" and "a weird looking, deformed looking guy." He said, "I like to bully these little people," and told the Russian-born German fighter to "kiss them feet," while labeling him a "Nazi."

(McGregor won that fight via knockout.)

Before a 2015 featherweight title fight against José Aldo, McGregor relentlessly taunted his Brazilian opponent. More than once, he stole Aldo's title belt and dared him to "come get it." At a press conference in Rio de Janeiro, McGregor made things even more personal, putting his feet on the conference table and proclaiming, "I own this town. . . . If this was a different time, I would invade his favela on horseback and kill anyone that was not fit to work." When the men went face-to-face at the end of that event, McGregor said, inches from Aldo, "Look into my eyes, little man. Little Brazilian." Then, with an exaggerated, wide-eyed pronunciation, and in the Portuguese he seemed to have learned for the occasion: "You're going to die."

(McGregor won that fight in a record thirteen seconds.)

There is a cruelty (and casual racism) to the way McGregor toys with his adversaries. He belittles, he baits, he boasts—it's a potent and incendiary cocktail. He's being mean, sure. But when McGregor is at his best, he's also being funny and incorrigible, and he exudes a seductive if sharp charisma. He casts a kind of spell. As a fan, it feels like he's bringing you in cahoots with him. Like he's letting you in on the joke, even if it's a twisted generosity. Because, of course, not everyone is being included.

These isolating tactics worked well ahead of his first fight against Poirier in UFC 178, which was considered a test of McGregor's legitimacy as a contender and as a headlining act. (That would be the last time a McGregor bout would not serve as a main event.) In hindsight, Poirier admits McGregor got into his head. "Trash talking, it does affect you," he says. But even at the time, it was obvious McGregor's campaign of disrespect was pushing Poirier into the red. In addition to predicting a first-round knockout win—a guarantee on which he would deliver and then declare himself "Mystic Mac"—McGregor demeaned his opponent as "a quiet little hillbilly from the back-arse of nowhere." He dismissed him as a forgettable competitor, saying, "He's afraid. He's a scared little boy. So I will go out and I'll put him stiff, and carry on my journey." He so thoroughly dictated the terms of rhetorical engagement at their press events that Poirier would concede shortcomings in his game based on McGregor's prodding about his weak chin and getting "wobbled in every fight." Said an exasperated Poirier, "I'll be honest, yeah, I was being overaggressive. But this fight, I'll be cool, calm, and collected."

But the damage was done. Poirier called the fight "personal" and said, "I've never disliked somebody that much." Even in private moments, Poirier would remain clenched, ruminating and fuming, as he obsessed over his smack-talking opponent. "All that talk and everything, over the months, just sat in my head. When the bell rang, I was like a deer in headlights," says Poirier, who was pounded by McGregor for one minute and forty-six seconds before the ref stopped the fight.

As McGregor has done so often, he had put on a master class in how to tilt an opponent by using his emotions against him. And yet the McGregor who would show up six years later, when the two were scheduled to fight a rematch in Abu Dhabi, was nearly unrecognizable. Both men were thicker, about ten pounds heavier, and both had more cauliflower in their ears from the punches they'd absorbed in the intervening years. McGregor was also far wealthier. The young Irish punk who famously cashed a welfare check in the days before his UFC debut had long since parlayed his blooming fame into a growing business empire, which he has predicted will soon reach $1 billion in value. But more than any of that, the biggest change in McGregor was his demeanor. It wasn't just that he was cordial and complimentary in his interactions with Poirier. He was, dare I say, affable. He even asked for a bottle of Poirier's hot sauce—"I'd love to taste the hot sauce," he said—which Poirier provided. The pair then posed for press photos, with their arms slung over each other's shoulders, like a couple of old pals.

It was still McGregor who set the tone. But this all felt less like the preamble to a violent sporting event than a reunion show. According to Owen Roddy, McGregor's striking coach, the reason for the change in McGregor was simple. "He doesn't need to prove anything to anybody anymore," he said.

Or maybe he grew lonely from all the months of social distancing. Who knows?

Whatever the reason, this warmer, more huggable version of McGregor would find himself pinned against the fighting cage, about halfway through the second round, with a badly hurt right leg (after a metronome of calf kicks), as Poirier unloaded a series of punches that eventually found McGregor with his guard down. Taking a clean shot to the face, McGregor collapsed to the mat, defenseless, forcing veteran referee Herb Dean to call the fight. In the immediate aftermath of this defeat, McGregor remained upbeat, heaping praise on his opponent. "Dustin is some fighter," he said.

But the good vibes wouldn't last.

Perhaps McGregor caught wind of Poirier's honest postfight assessment that he "felt [McGregor's] presence less, his aura less," without the trash talk and histrionics, and took that to heart. Said Poirier, "I just saw another fighter tonight . . . another man who bleeds just like me." Poirier would also tell Joe Rogan it was better for McGregor to "be an asshole." Months later, the men shared a tense social media exchange, when Poirier accused McGregor and his team of reneging on the half-million-dollar charitable contribution he had pledged to Poirier's The Good Fight Foundation. Tweeted McGregor, "You will pay with your brain for this attempt at smearing my name." The sniping would continue in the lead-up to UFC 264, with McGregor spin-doctoring his loss to Poirier as a fluke, disparaging his opponent's calf-kicking strategy as cowardly, and alleging that his wife was trying to get into his DMs on Instagram (after the presser, he'd tweet at Poirier: "Your wife wants to see the hair around my dick and balls bro"), and with Poirier giving as good as he got. "We put you on airplane mode in front of the world," Poirier shot back through the media.

But the million-dollar question hanging over this fight and all of its extracurricular acrimony—and what would make trash talk, specifically, such a fascinating subplot of the trilogy—is how, if at all, Conor McGregor, the man frequently referred to as the "king of trash talk" by fellow UFC fighters, could regain his mental edge, after having not only made things easier for Poirier the last time around by dropping the shit-talk routine in favor of respectful dialogue, but also by losing the damn fight. Once you lose that intimidation factor, is it not gone forever? Or were the seeds of psychological warfare planted so deep in Poirier's mind they could survive a season of dormancy? It's a question I would put to McGregor myself.

His response: "I don't give a *bollocks* about all that!"

But his actions would suggest otherwise.

MEDIA OBSERVERS ARE split on what exactly we're witnessing at the UFC 264 press conference. Some welcome back the "Conor McGregor of old" and praise his "return to form," while others feel the fighter is presenting a kind of facsimile of himself—that he may be playing the same notes, but they are somehow off-key. Throughout the Q&A session, McGregor threatens, insults, and interrupts. He calls Poirier a "little bitch" and "a silly little hillbilly" and, my personal favorite, "a stupid tosspot." At times, the attacks seem more precise and purposeful. Other times, he wields a blunter instrument, like when he predicts that Poirier is "going out in a stretcher." He says, "I see a dead body," and refers to Poirier as "a corpse." By the end, when McGregor and Poirier are positioned at centerstage for a nose-to-nose promotional pose known as a stare-down—or face-off, as the UFC calls it—he seems to be almost flailing, if not entirely unhinged. Even as Dana White strains to maintain a safe distance between the two fighters, McGregor rears back and kicks at Poirier's midsection. Though his foot misses its target, the arena fans explode.

(Give the man credit: he knows how to put on a show.)

One theory is that McGregor is acting out not just to make his opponent mad, as he's always done, but also to once again feel the pressures of competition himself: that he is manufacturing emotional stakes—and, in turn, motivation—that might not exist otherwise. There are legitimate reasons to question whether McGregor is hungry for this fight, after all. When he first came to the UFC, he competed with an intensity that reflected a single-minded desire to improve his station in life. Now that he claims to be on a billionaire's path, it's not unfair to wonder how badly he wants to punch another person's face in—or get his own face punched in—and how much physical discomfort he's willing to endure along the way.

Or maybe the explanation is simpler than that. Maybe McGregor is the emotional one.

UFC commentator Jon Anik suggests the image-conscious fighter is genuinely upset about the way Poirier publicly accused him of reneging on his charitable donation and wants to punish him for that reputational assault. McGregor certainly gives off a bloodthirsty vibe the next day, when he and Poirier return to the stage for the ceremonial weigh-in. During the face-off that closes that event—their second such encounter in barely twenty-four hours—White keeps the feuding men comically far apart. (McGregor, shirtless in seersucker shorts, repeatedly tries—but fails—to assume his usual fighting stance, while White slaps down his advancing fists, like a cat batting a ball of yarn.) After, McGregor dials up the heat via an onstage interview with Joe Rogan when he says, "Tomorrow night, I'm going to make this man pay with his *life*"—pronounced *loife*—"and I mean it." And then, addressing Poirier directly: "You're *dead* in that octagon tomorrow night."

Dead.

The interview ends.

Joe Rogan says, "Conor McGregor, ladies and gentlemen."

To my mind, if there's a change in McGregor, it's not just that he's so edgy; it's that he's so charmless, too. He doesn't seem to be having very much fun.

To be fair, I don't think Poirier is having much fun either. Unlike their last match, which was staged during the height of the COVID-19 pandemic and hosted in a sterilized environment on an island in Abu Dhabi, this trilogy bout is being held in front of a packed house—the first time the UFC has performed before a capacity Vegas crowd in more than sixteen months. All around, the Strip is buzzing, flashing. Folks are guzzling hurricane-style drinks, giddy to be rid of their masks. The excitement is as palpable as the 115-degree desert heat, and Poirier knows everyone here wants him to lose. As he waits backstage on the night of the fight, in the final minutes before making his walk to the cage, Poirier can feel his pulse pounding: the stress of the event becoming real. It's a familiar rush of anxiety, these prefight nerves. He tells himself, almost like a mantra, "Here we go again."

He needs to stay calm and block out the noise. Find a measure of peace amid the storm.

As for the fight itself, the first round is filled with exciting action, as Conor comes out kicking. Against McGregor, these opening salvos are often the most critical moments, as we discover whether his campaigns of abuse will bear competitive fruit and possibly draw an opponent outside his game plan in pursuit of hell-bent retaliation. But Poirier remains careful, calculated, restrained. He knows what he's gotten himself into. The crowd sings its *olé*-ing soccer song, as both men bounce in fighting stance and exchange exploratory blows. The attacks slowly escalate. Calf kicks followed by chin-seeking punches. At about the round's midway point, a more brutal phase takes hold, as the fighters go to the mat. Poirier mashes his fists into McGregor's face. When able, Conor responds with a series of stinging elbow strikes to the top of Dustin's skull.

It's painful to watch.

"Herb Dean better not stop this," a reporter sitting next to me says, when it briefly seems Poirier has gained the upper hand. The referee watches closely but does not intercede.

I wonder if this moment of almost intimate violence will ever end. And then: it's over.

With about fifteen seconds left in the five-minute round, Poirier stands up. McGregor greets him on his feet, unleashes two kicks and a lurching right hand. Poirier responds with a left. But as McGregor steps back, he crumples to the mat. It's an unnatural fall, and he quickly scoots back on his ass to brace himself against the cage. Poirier pounces, with his fists firing like pistons, and McGregor turtles in place until the end-of-round bell sounds, signaling a short interlude of peace. But Herb Dean has no choice but to call the fight. As becomes evident from video-board close-ups, and from the simple fact that he remains on the mat, there is no way McGregor can go on: when he took that step back, his lower leg snapped in half, a break of the tibia and fibula.

"Oooooh," the arena crowd cringes in unison, as the replay shows on the big screen.

For a mixed martial arts (MMA) newcomer like me, the whole thing has been a fascinating and heart-pounding display. Each violent collision charged by the sky-high stakes that mounted ahead of the competition. But the most interesting exchange of this main-event fight comes after the actual combat is over. As Dean raises Poirier's hand, in an announced TKO victory that McGregor has already taken great screaming pains to ensure they caveat as "a doctor's stoppage," the winning fighter can't seem to take his eyes off his fallen opponent. He even taunts the injured man, swaggering toward him in a mock rendition of McGregor's signature walk: the leaned-back, arm-swinging billionaire strut. In this moment, it becomes suddenly clear how much each fighter has, in his own way, gotten under the other's skin: despite the many bodies that now crowd the octagon, an emotional rope remains taut between them.

All week, Poirier has demonstrated an outward calm, repressing his instinct for anger, for payback, for indulging McGregor's endless provocations. He understood the competitive consequences of allowing emotion to cloud his preparation—as he puts it, "fighting is chaotic" and any distraction, no matter how small, can lead to a fast and bloody end—and thus dismissed his opponent's verbal tempests as just "noise." But now he's done staying above the fray. In truth, he was deeply offended by McGregor's promise at the ceremonial weigh-in to not just beat him but to leave him lifeless. ("You don't say that type of shit to people," Poirier would later say.) Of course, McGregor has made death threats before—in fact, he used similarly morbid language only a day earlier at the press conference—but there was something about his tone that felt different to Poirier. Heavier. Like an escalation. Like he meant it.

No longer holding his tongue, Poirier says, "This guy is a dirtbag."

But it'll take more than that to chasten McGregor. From the floor of the octagon, Conor offers his analysis in a postfight interview: "I was boxing the bleeding head off him. Kicking the bleeding leg off of him. . . . This is not over!" He even sneaks in a few more personal attacks, as Poirier is somewhat reluctantly being escorted out of the cage. He says, "Your wife is in me DMs. Hey, baby. Hit me back up, I'll chat to you later on. I'll be at the after-party at the Wynn nightclub, baby."

It's remarkable in its way, these outbursts from McGregor (which would continue into the next day on social media). Even with his leg in pieces, the fighter is hyping his next bout, finding a way to spin his loss in this one, fulfilling his paid obligation to promote an after-party at a nearby hotel, and trying to renew his rent-free lease inside the mind of Dustin Poirier. It's a lot to take in. But what it isn't is surprising. Over the past decade, there may be no more widely recognized, openly offensive, or prolific trash-talker than Conor McGregor— and despite the broken-bones outcome at UFC 264, there may be no better recent example or more comprehensive showcase of what trash talk has to offer than this trilogy bout. From the first barb on Twitter to the final moments of verbal chaos in the cage, nearly all of trash talk's various permutations and potential functionalities were on prominent display.

What makes McGregor's fights fascinating from a trash-talk perspective is not just that he never misses the chance to turn routine press events into Kabuki theater, or that his self-promoting bravado and penchant for manufacturing drama—for transforming even small disagreements into epic and battle-worthy affairs—hook the rooting public like a well-produced soap opera. Nor is it just that he leverages this unusual skill as a showman to simultaneously seek a competitive edge by testing his opponents' ability to focus and digest stress via relentless and insulting provocations. Nor is it just that the Irish fighter refuses to show any restraint whatsoever: that he pushes the boundaries of antagonism to their ethical limits—well beyond the borders of good taste—and has proven, time and again, willing to say practically anything in service of his competitive ends, while leaving others to worry about any moral ramifications or why exactly he seems to get away with it.

It's not just any of these things. It's all of them, and more.

In the pages to come, that's what we're about to explore.

QUITE LITERALLY, TRASH talk is the language of competition. It's a specific form of incivility—"competitive incivility," as some sociologists put it—which allows people to communicate when they're going head-to-head. But the nature of that communication is always up for negotiation. Both tactically and tonally, trash talk runs the gamut: it can be used to self-motivate, distract, build hype, or even construct bonds of personal intimacy; it can likewise be funny and playful, strategic and needling, or insulting, edgy, and aggressive. There are times when some folks insist trash talk crosses the line—that it goes too far. (Poirier felt that way.) But those lines are often ill-defined.

At its most basic level, when someone talks trash, that person is offering up a challenge that both acknowledges the fact of competition and seeks to further define its contours: it raises the stakes of the confrontation and asks whether one's competitors can metabolize that added pressure without losing focus—or if they'll instead become emotional, or distracted, or question their abilities to succeed. Talking trash makes the outcome of a contest matter more than it otherwise would.

Nobody wants to eat their words.

Our public awareness of trash talk has spiked over the last three decades, which is when, some have argued, the practice sprouted across the sporting landscape like an untreated weed, like a scourge. But it'd be wrong to think about trash talk as a purely athletic—or even purely modern—phenomenon because that misunderstands this ancient mode of communication, which exists across cultures, has gone by many names, and may well be encoded in our DNA, passed down from our earliest ancestors. In a 2018 paper published in the academic journal *Human Nature*, two Cornell researchers consider the possibility that trash talk has been "selected across evolutionary time because its benefits outweigh the potential costs." But even if you put science aside, it's easy to see that trash talk is here to stay. It's the juicy stuff of Twitter beefs and diss tracks, of guilty-pleasure headlines and the mudslinging of never-ending political campaigns. It's on the lips of CEOs, comedians, gamers, online commenters. Even your mom.

(Just kidding. I'm sure she's a nice lady.)

And yet, despite this ubiquity—and despite trash talk's possible primeval origins—there has never been any serious (or even nonserious) exploration of the topic. *Where did trash talk come from? Why are we so drawn to it? Does it even work? What are the rules of engagement? The best ways to respond? What happens when trash talk goes wrong?* Instead, trash talk has regularly been dismissed as frivolous and unserious, even as marketers leverage its cultural signification for commercial gain. Mostly, and especially in the United States, trash talk is treated as little more than verbal static, or worse, it's stigmatized and racialized and used as an excuse to punish and control other people's behavior.

It's time for trash talk to get its due.

Not everyone with whom I spoke for this project was convinced my efforts were worthwhile. A number of people told me I was reading too much into the topic, that I was wasting my time. "You're overthinking it," said former NFL cornerback Orlando Scandrick. Meanwhile, former NBA guard and Larry Bird mentor Quinn Buckner told me he'd be surprised if we could talk about the subject for even fifteen minutes, and then politely declined to try.

But many others saw the potential—or were at least willing to humor me.

In reporting this book, I interviewed more than two hundred people, including academics, professional athletes, wrestlers, boxers, mixed martial artists, referees, sports reporters, performance psychologists, debate coaches, comedians, neurobiologists, social scientists, cultural critics, historians, marketing gurus, content-moderation experts, linguists, moral philosophers, political strategists, and high-ranking military officers, among others.

Occasionally, these conversations led me to some unlikely locations, like a professional-wrestling academy in South Jersey, where I learned about the art of promotion, and the famed Comedy Store in LA, birthplace of the ultratransgressive insult show *Roast Battle*. At one point, I found myself at the Camp Mackall military training facility outside Fort Bragg, North Carolina, where the army runs a high-stress survival course called SERE. About a month after that, I was down in Key West, at the Special Forces combat-diving school, where soldiers must solve panic-inducing problems while confronting their most primal fears.

(Call it a lesson in mental toughness.)

I always knew this book was going to be about more than trash talk. As I see it, it's also about civility and moral dilemmas and the kinds of people we want to be. It's about risk tolerance and stress hardiness and anxiety and the ways in which we as humans have always sought to endow our lives with deeper meaning. It's about mindfulness, personal insecurities, and the importance of being brutally honest in our self-assessments, even as we push ourselves to the absolute limits of our abilities. Perhaps most of all, though, it's a book about learning to perform under pressure, like those military divers, because that's what trash talk does, fundamentally: it ups the competitive ante.

It puts more on the line.

It demands to know: *Can you handle this?*

Throughout my two-plus-year journey into the depths of trash talk, my goal has been to strip away the sensationalism and stigma and to provide instead some shape and precision to what has otherwise been a flattened conversation. I wanted to uncover not only the art and science of talking smack but also some of its definitional properties: what it is, what it isn't, and how we can otherwise make sense of humanity's enduring impulse to boast, to antagonize, to play mind games with our rivals. Ultimately, it's my hope that, by getting at these truths of trash talk—by understanding *why* we talk so much crap and to what end—we might also better understand ourselves as social and competitive creatures because, if I've learned nothing else, it's that talking trash is inescapably part of who we are as human beings. It's part of who we've always been.

Fucking with another man's hot sauce, however—that might be a McGregor original.

Section I

IN THE BEGINNING, THERE WAS SMACK

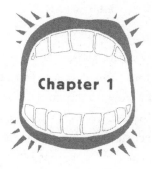

Chapter 1

LOOK WHO'S TALKING

LET'S GET SOMETHING out of the way up top: trash-talkers like Conor McGregor may have the capacity to be first-class assholes, but talking shit is hardly anything new or aberrant, or the sign of civilizational decline; if anything, it might be the mark of intelligent life. As Sigmund Freud once put it, paraphrasing the English writer and neurologist John Hughlings Jackson, "The man who first flung a word of abuse at his enemy instead of a spear was the founder of civilisation."

Really, you'd have to flip pretty far back through the pages of human history to find the first example of trash talk. It dates to biblical times, at least, when David said to Goliath, "I will strike you down and cut off your head," enraging the big man and baiting him to come within range of his shepherd's sling. And to the age of Homer, whose epic poems are drenched with smack-talking deities, leaders of men trying to spur on their troops (Agamemnon: "You pansy archers, you're a disgrace to Greece!"), and braggadocious warriors, who don't go into battle without first trying to big-time each

3

other with tear-you-down taunts and stature-building boasts. As Tlepolemus said to Sarpedon, "You have a coward's heart, and your race is dying. . . . I don't care how strong you are, / You're going through Hades' gates, beaten by me." Certainly, any fan of contemporary combat sports would feel right at home hearing the swaggering challenge of Epeius during the funeral games in the *Iliad*, when he grabs the first-place mule and says, "Anybody want the [second-place] cup as his prize? / Because no Greek alive is going to beat me / In boxing." Meanwhile, if Odysseus had managed to just keep his mouth shut, instead of mocking the blinded Cyclops as he made his escape, there wouldn't even be a damn *Odyssey*.

Point is: Trash talk is as deeply ingrained—if occasionally ill-advised—a feature of human behavior as religious faith or going to war. It is part of who we are and part of how we communicate, especially when in competition—whether we're vying for pride, social status, or scarce resources, like a first-place mule. "It's almost one of the primal forms of communication," says Jonah F. Radding, an assistant instructional professor of classics at the University of Chicago, whose interest in our ancestral propensity for talking smack led him to develop a course on invective poetry through the ages. "Almost as soon as you develop literature, you have trash-talking literature. I don't know if it's necessarily our finest aspect, but it's one that I enjoy."

And what's not to enjoy?

There's Archilochus, a Greek lyric poet writing around 650 BCE, who, as Radding tells me, "does get really personal. I'm thinking especially about sexual exploits with this person's daughter, basically." There's Aristophanes, who was active a couple of hundred years later and would savage fellow poets and contemporary politicians to the point that he claimed to have been sued for slander. And there's Catullus, a Roman poet and truly petty vulgarian. In one poem, which was long deemed unpublishable in modern English (or at least a fully uncensored version), he calls out two men by name, to whom he threatens to "dick you in the face." In yet another, he accuses someone of being "softer than a baby bunny's fur" and the owner of "a dusty, cobwebbed dick"—insults he levels because, as best I can tell, this person stole his good napkins. "As far as I know, that is not a euphemism for anything," laughs Radding, when I ask about the missing linens. "That seems to just be the reason he wrote this poem."

Of course, personal put-downs and quippy one-upmanship don't have to be captured in verse.

By the time Catullus was threatening to turn people "pecker-faced," invective had spilled off the page and suffused Roman society. This time "was rougher than in other periods," according to Martin Jehne, a professor of ancient history at Technische Universität Dresden in Germany. He says, "The quota of personal insults was very high." It was high in the political sphere, where senators disparaged opponents in an effort to rally their supporters. It was high in the judicial system, which contained no fact-based investigations but trials by character assassination. ("They insult each other, especially the defendant, in a terrible way," says Jehne.) And it was high in the private gatherings known as *convivium*, where men would attack one another, in escalating verbal combat, in an attempt to show off their erudition and wit, knowing that highlights of the affair would leak to the wider Roman public. "If you got insulted, you cannot defend yourself by trying to prove that this is wrong. You can only insult the others even more. That is the rule," says Jehne.

That moment in Rome may have represented a high point for vituperation—or low point, depending on your perspective—but it's important to recognize this instinct to talk shit has existed not just throughout time, but also across cultures, from the joking relationships known as *sinankunya* in West Africa to the derisive bickering of Jewish sages in the Talmud, a compilation of rabbinic arguments.* Sometimes this trash talk presents as a tactic or feature of competition

---

* A particularly delightful trash-talk exchange in the Talmud comes in Bava Metzia 84a, when a woman insults a couple of overweight rabbis by telling them their children can't be their own because they're too fat to have sex, and they respond by boasting about the size of their dicks, saying: "For as the man is, so is his strength."

and sometimes as a kind of in-group code. At times, it serves key social functions, as is the case with the Ju/'hoansi people, an ancient population of hunter-gatherers who live in the deserts of southern Africa and have a tradition of insulting a hunter's meat when he returns with a kill (which is done as a kind of social leveler, to both avoid feelings of jealousy and to prevent establishing "unnecessary" hierarchies, per anthropologist James Suzman). Surprisingly often, trash talk transforms into the arena of competition itself. Dating back to pre-Islamic times, there were ritualized and widespread verbal duels, dressed up as poetic contests, throughout the Arabic world, which became a hallmark of social and cultural gatherings and of intertribal relations. Among the genres the poets employed were *fakhr* (boasting about oneself or one's tribe) and *hijā'* (defaming one's opponent). And while either bragging or disparagement could be the name of a particular game, it's easy to recognize these strategies as two sides of the same coin. As Dutch historian Johan Huizinga puts it in his 1938 book, *Homo Ludens*, which explores the importance of play in human society, "boosting of one's own virtue as a form of contest slips over quite naturally into contumely of one's adversary."

Similar traditions of "slanging-matches," in Huizinga's words, can be found in Old Norse literature in contests known as mannjafnaðr (translated as "the comparing of men"); in the practice of Scottish flyting, which were poetic insult battles popular in the fifteenth and sixteenth centuries and which emerged, in the words of scholar Kenneth Simpson, "as both social phenomenon and literary genre"; and in the drumming matches of the Greenlandic Inuit, which would be initiated in lieu of judicial proceedings when one member of a tribe had beef with another (not unlike the trials in Roman times). To the beat of the drum, combatants would heap abuse upon their opponent—offensive words that ranged from silly to slanderous—and the audience determined a winner.

"It is remarkable how large a place these bragging and scoffing matches occupy in the most diverse civilizations," writes Huizinga. That was one of Radding's big takeaways from developing his curriculum, too. "There really are kind of infinite traditions you could choose from," he says, citing *zajal,* a Lebanese pastime of improvised poetic dueling—duels that have attracted north of thirty thousand spectators—as a standout example. "This desire to engage in trash talking in a competitive format seems to practically be a universal human desire." Michael Adams, a linguist and provost professor of English at Indiana University, agrees. "It's typological," he says. "It may be shaped in these particular cultures, but it's somehow grounded in human nature so that it erupts, it manifests itself differently in different and completely unconnected cultures."

In that sense, there should be nothing remarkable about this seemingly innate urge to boast, to razz, to challenge—to build oneself up and, if necessary, tear another down, or at least hurt their feelings. In theory, we should be able to recognize trash talk for what it is, wherever and whenever it appears: the language of competition. And yet, when it comes to situating the eruptions of this deep-seated impulse within a modern context specifically, many of us fail to find the through line from past to present or from one culture to the next. Instead, when folks start talking mess, we just about lose our minds.

———————

THE FIRST TIME the phrase *trash talk* appeared in an American print publication, it received a casual mention in a 1981 *Washington Post* story. It wouldn't reappear anywhere for three years. The *Miami Herald* would trot out the term a couple of times in 1984, while the *Los Angeles Times* and the *Washington Post* would each use it once two years later. But it wasn't until the early 1990s that things really took off.

In the three-year period beginning in 1990 and ending on December 31, 1992, there were 311 newspaper articles that mentioned trash talk. In 1993 alone, there were 734, and then close to 8,000 over the rest of the decade. As the *New York Times Magazine* put it when it gave trash talk the long-form feature treatment, "1993 seems destined to be remembered as the year of Trash Talk," which it defined as "the various gratuitous ways by which players distract, intimidate and infuriate their opponents." Indeed, America's (mostly white) sports editors had picked up on this momentum and were further shaping popular conception by assigning a rash of trend stories, presenting readers with what they overwhelmingly framed as a wholly new and exotic behavioral phenomenon—sometimes with a hey-look-at-this tone of pulling back the curtain and other times with alarmist warnings about the end of sportsmanship. "'Sounds different,' you could hear sports editors across America saying in their Monday morning meetings," Mitch Albom writes in *The Fab Five: Basketball, Trash Talk, the American Dream*, his 1993 book about the University of Michigan's men's basketball team, which scandalized large swaths of the nation with their brash manner, baggy shorts, and black socks.

Phil Taylor was maybe America's first journalist on the trash-talk beat. In 1992, as a staffer for *Sports Illustrated*, he penned what was likely the earliest piece in a national magazine on trash talk as a modern phenomenon—a nice byline for a young writer—even if he knew perfectly well the behavior wasn't exactly new. "I really could have written that story almost out of my head," says Taylor, who grew up hearing trash talk on New York's basketball courts. "It was talking shit or cracking on somebody. I always thought that label, trash talk, was just a euphemism or a way of sanitizing talking shit. This is the PG-rated version." But when he tossed out the idea during a pitch meeting, dubious it would gain much traction, his editors' eyes lit up. "It seemed to a lot of my editors to be this unbelievably new phenomenon, and [they wanted to] get out there on the cutting edge." Equally surprising to him was the reader response. Mail poured in from subscribers across the country, who "found that to be an eye-opening piece," in Taylor's words, and were in disbelief about some of the things said in the course of competition. "Why aren't there more fights?" they wondered.

Some athletes were bemused by the attention being paid to their verbal sparring. "Everybody was like, 'That's a *thing*?'" remembers

B.J. Armstrong, who was playing for the Chicago Bulls at the time. Even his boys back in his hometown of Detroit gave him shit. "They would say, 'If all you got to do is talk trash, *I* should be in the NBA.'" He laughs. "I was perplexed by it at first, but I guess it was new to a lot of people."

From that perspective, there was something noteworthy about trash talk—at least to those (again, mostly white) segments of the population who were unfamiliar with this specific form of competitive hostility. How else to explain the bewildered reaction from so many readers or the bug-eyed excitement of so many of America's editors? "I felt like I was introducing it to the world," says Taylor. "And in a way, I was." But in another way, he was merely the most recent interpreter of an age-old phenomenon.

BEFORE THE 1880S, baseball was considered a gentleman's game. There were governing sets of ethics, and umpires were held in high esteem. Arlie Latham must have missed that particular memo.

A decent hitter and burner on the bases, Latham starred on a St. Louis Browns team that won four consecutive pennants starting in 1885. But it was his badgering antics—a cutthroat brand of gamesmanship that completely upended the previously genteel sport—on which his reputation would be built. At the time, players served as base coaches, and Latham, whom baseball writer and historian Bill James calls "a natural antagonist," would do whatever he could to annoy and distract the opposition. Beyond relentlessly yelling loud and insulting things, he would race up and down the third-base line just as the opposing pitcher was delivering his pitch. (This led to the adoption of the coach's box.) Out-of-town newspapers remarked on his "insane whooping," "incessant howling," and "disgusting mouthings," while labeling him a "clown." But the public shaming failed to have an effect. Latham's teammates would join in on the verbal abuse, as the Browns won 75 percent of their home games from 1883 through 1889. Before long, other teams followed suit.

This essentially was the start of the great baseball tradition known as "bench jockeying"—the practice of heaping abuse on your opponents in hopes of interfering with their concentration or otherwise diminishing their performance. Sportswriter J. Roy Stockton once called it "probably the greatest cruelty in the American sports picture." John McGraw was among those to pick up the mantle from Latham. As a player in the 1890s, he helped pioneer the strategy known as "inside baseball," which was all about finding and exploiting microadvantages of any sort, from tripping base runners to violently intimidating the umps. This knack for nastiness would continue when McGraw—who was said to have "a genius for making enemies" and to have "broke[n] the spirits of some fine men"—became a manager, allegedly going so far as to hire private detectives to dig up dirt on opponents for in-game fodder. "I don't even know if I would call it bench jockeying; there's probably a stronger word for it," says baseball historian and McGraw expert Steve Steinberg. "It was almost unbelievable, the kinds of things he would say." Even Babe Ruth admitted McGraw got under his skin. During the 1922 World Series, with McGraw relentlessly riding him, Babe delivered an embarrassing two-for-seventeen performance at the plate, as the Giants humiliated the Yankees.* As Baseball Hall of Famer Frankie Frisch explained, "If you spot a weakness in the other guy's temperament, you're a fool not to go after it. If he shows he resents it, pour it on."

Known as "holler guys," bench jockeys became standardized across baseball. Those who were most successful at harassing the opposition—whether due to a sharp wit, a piercing voice, or a capacity

---

* Bench jockeying also led to one of the iconic moments of Babe Ruth's career: the called shot. While there remains debate as to what exactly Ruth did with his hands—and whether he was in fact predicting the spot where he would hit a home run—the at-bat came during a crescendo of verbal abuse, which had been building across the 1932 World Series. "Ruth comes up, and the place is going crazy. Guys are out on the field, literally out on the field, taunting him. Can you imagine?" says Ed Sherman, author of *Babe Ruth's Called Shot*. "He definitely was being taunted, probably unlike any ballplayer before or since, and he responded. It's an incredible moment."

for creative slurs—could even maintain a roster spot after their actual baseball skills had outlived their usefulness. Ray Kolp, who played twelve seasons in the big leagues, was one such hanger-on. He was at his best against the squat slugger Hack Wilson, a favorite target, who once got so fumed he charged Kolp in the dugout after safely reaching base on a single—and without even calling for time. Satchel Paige was another master of the craft, though the legendary pitcher did his talking from the mound. Paige would jaw at batters and base runners and brought a measure of self-assured swagger that other jockeys— who relied instead on needling tactics—often lacked. His mind games went beyond the typical insulting fare. Paige named his pitches—like the bow-tie, the trouble ball, and the midnight creeper—and unsettled hitters by telling them exactly which one was coming or by calling in his fielders, confident in his ability to strike out the side. "I'm going to throw smoke at yo' yolk," he would yell. According to Paige biographer Larry Tye, the pitcher possessed "a special kind of courage," not just for what he said, but also to whom he said it. Even in the time of Jim Crow, Paige openly challenged "the fiercest white opponents." Says Tye, "He simply loved to talk, and to taunt."

Bench jockeying wasn't exactly a well-kept secret. As would happen with the advent of the term *trash talk* decades later, magazine editors assigned breathless feature stories about what *Esquire* would call "the verbal needle." That piece, which ran under the headline "The Brutal Art of Bench Jockeying," was published in 1959, thirteen years after *Baseball Magazine* ran an item that seemingly captured the attitude of the era, entitled "You Have to Learn to Take It." In 1965, *Sports Illustrated* ran a piece on Gene Mauch, then manager of the Philadelphia Phillies, which hinted at shifting tides. Opposing players claimed Mauch "gets very personal" and "says things you just shouldn't say." His matter-of-fact response: "It makes some of them less effective, and the idea is to win."

The brutal art did seem to be losing steam in the second half of the twentieth century, though, as evidenced by a string of stories published by *Baseball Digest*—"What Happened to the Art of Bench Jockeying?"

(1975); "Bench Jockeys Are a Dying Breed" (1976); "Where Have All the Bench Jockeys Gone?" (1983)—and even one in the *New York Times*, under the headline "Lost Art in Baseball" (1983).

In hindsight, the relation between bench jockeying and what we now call trash talk seems obvious—they are variations on a theme, like so many of the slanging matches of distant history. Which is why, on the one hand, it's hard to believe that collective memories could be so short, or imaginations so limited, that only ten years would pass between the purported death of bench jockeying and the rise of trash talk as a new phenomenon and hardly anyone would make the connection.* On the other hand, this seeming blind spot is less surprising when considered within the wider cultural context of America—specifically, its racial context. Take Satchel Paige, for instance. His verbal style—which, perhaps tellingly, was left out of so many of those midcentury trend stories on bench jockeying—mixed boastful mind games with playful repartee with a kind of put-it-on-the-line showmanship. It was also meant, at least in part, for public consumption.

Paige's career spanned four decades—five, if you include his one-game stint with the Kansas City Athletics at the age of fifty-nine, in which he threw three shutout innings. He spent most of that time pitching in the Negro Leagues. There, he picked up on a custom of "showboating and clowning" that grew out of Black baseball's "itinerancy, inconsistent competition, and the need to attract crowds," as Jules Tygiel writes in *Baseball's Great Experiment: Jackie Robinson and His Legacy*, and that dated back as far as Arlie Latham's first antics. Black ballplayers were also known for putting a premium on aggressive base running and developing a style of play known as "tricky baseball," which accentuated guile and gamesmanship. But even as Black players increasingly filled out major-league rosters, white

---

* Credit where credit is due: some did. In a 1994 column about trash talk for the *New York Times*, Robert Lipsyte recognized the term as "the latest label for a line of hostile chatter that goes back at least to Cain putting down Abel." He wrote: "Call it Homeric boasting, bench jockeying, psyching out."

crowds would have seen this style—to the extent they recognized it at all—as foreign, lacking the necessary reference points. Equally alien to white crowds would have been oral traditions like the dozens, a ritualized insult game endemic to Black communities that deeply informed not only the language of competition for so many Black athletes, but also, ultimately, what we now broadly conceive to be modern American trash talk.

———

IN THE EARLY moments of a 1998 playoff game between the Green Bay Packers and Tampa Bay Buccaneers, there was a brief stoppage in play as the referees untangled a special-teams skirmish. Somewhere off camera, reigning NFL MVP and future welfare fraudster* Brett Favre was idling near Bucs defensive lineman Warren Sapp. He turned to Sapp and asked offhandedly, "How much do you weigh?"

A disruptive force on defense, Sapp wasn't used to quarterbacks engaging him in conversation, much less questioning his girth. And so, while he answered Favre—"Three-oh-seven Friday"—it wasn't until the next whistle that he really responded.

"It dawned on me," Sapp says. "I said, 'What? You think you can outrun me?'"

Favre: "Oh, I'll outrun your big ass."

Sapp liked what he was hearing. He shouted back, "Don't worry. I'll give you a chance to prove it."

Favre and Sapp continued barking at each other the rest of that day and pretty much every other time they played. After a Sapp sack on Favre—which he would do eleven times over the course of his career—the quarterback turned to see who had dragged him to the turf. "Who you think it is?" Sapp asked. The two jawed so much that Favre's teammates would literally forbid him from talking to Sapp. "As good as he was as a player, he was equally as good as a talker, and if you were not careful, you would get caught up in that," per Favre.

---

* Allegedly.

Favre wasn't the only one to hold that opinion. In a 2006 *Sports Illustrated* piece about trash talk in football, multiple players singled out Sapp as best in class, while the *New York Times* dubbed him "one of the great blabbermouths in the game." But if you ask Sapp about this reputation—and I did—he'll tell you it's off the mark. "I really wasn't that big of a trash-talker," he says. "I just got into conversations with certain dudes." It's not that he denies talking; he just doesn't think of it as *trash*. Todd Boyd would agree with this sentiment. As the University of Southern California professor and chair for the study of race and popular culture explains, "I mean, talking trash—it sounds disposable. The metaphor is disposable."

Says Sapp, "Call it the dozens. Or call it shit talking. That's all it is."

As a kid, Sapp learned to engage in verbal combat both at home, where he was the youngest of six siblings, and in the neighborhood, where he would pedal the bike he asked his mom for every December—as either a birthday or Christmas gift—to wherever his friends were hanging out, where he knew they'd be talking shit. "That was our entertainment. That was our fun," he says. "When we got together, we talked about each other." According to the activist H. Rap Brown, who changed his name to Jamil Abdullah Al-Amin, the dozens served as linguistic training for many Black youth, too. As he writes in his 1969 memoir: "Hell, we exercised our minds by playing the Dozens." And: "We played the Dozens for recreation, like white folks played Scrabble."

If you didn't grow up with it, perhaps the easiest way to understand the dozens is to think about the game as the exchange of your-mama jokes—combatants trying to one-up (and even upset) each other, while vying for verbal and creative supremacy via any vulgar means necessary. Usually, this would transpire before an inciting crowd of observers who served to heighten the accolades of success and deepen the humiliation of defeat. But the dozens isn't so easily defined—neither in format nor content. According to some accounts, the dozens can be traced to the early days of the United

States, when it was played by enslaved people, while Elijah Wald, in his deeply academic book on the subject, *Talking 'Bout Your Mama: The Dozens, Snaps, and the Deep Roots of Rap*, makes the case that the game has African roots. As an informal pastime played in schoolyards, on front stoops, and in barrooms, the dozens can claim no unifying theory. It's always evolving, defined by its participants, informed by context, and infused with local flavor. For many, the dozens is known by other names—like joning, slipping, capping, bagging, or snapping—and individual experiences with the game can be equally varied.

For some, like Sapp, the dozens is an activity undergirded by affection and bonhomie. It is a prosocial endeavor—a bonding ritual—even if there are a few sharp edges. As Steve Jones Jr., the basketball coach and son of ABA star Steve Jones, describes it to me, talking shit was his dad's "love language." Todd Boyd can relate. "My parents talked shit, like regularly. Like every day. It doesn't get any closer than that," he says. "After a while, that's the normal mode of discourse. That's how Black people talk. Black people I grew up around, anyway." This dynamic would speak to what are known as "joking relationships," which were defined by the pioneering social anthropologist Alfred R. Radcliffe-Brown as consisting of "a peculiar combination of friendliness and antagonism," in which intimacy can masquerade as hostility. In which, in other words, insults aren't to be taken personally.

But just as play fighting can become the real thing, the dozens can be a dangerous game: sometimes people get hurt. "It is a risky pleasure," as Zora Neale Hurston put it. In 1939, the white American psychologist and sociologist John Dollard was the first person to give the dozens serious academic attention in his paper "The Dozens: Dialect of Insult." He noted that "the themes about which joking is allowed seem to be those most condemned by our social order in other contexts." Dollard saw the game not just as idle entertainment, but also as serving a utilitarian function for Black folks living in an openly racist society, specifically as "a valve for aggression" that would have otherwise and rightly been directed at white people, which would also have likely led to violent consequence.

Various other ideas and theories about the functionality of the dozens have emerged over the years, though Wald asserts that "all are interesting as much for what they reveal about the explainers as what they tell us about the game." But while there may be no authoritative account—and while the meaning of the game to one person can be in direct contradiction with what it means to another—the explanations are instructive. Some, for example, have cast the game as a means of negotiating social status, a puberty or initiation ritual, an in-group signifier, or a mechanism of survival. These all speak to a kind of testing—a challenge being presented.

This last functionality, in particular, has gained traction with many. In 1970, the psychologist Joseph White writes in *Ebony* "that the brothers and sisters use the dozens as a game to teach them how to keep cool and think fast under pressure." The following year, in their book *The Jesus Bag*, psychiatrists William H. Grier and Price M. Cobbs describe the dozens as "a highly evolved instrument of survival" that introduces Black youth "to the humiliations which will become so intimate a part of their life." They write, "In the deepest sense, the essence of the dozens lies not in the insults but in the response of the victim." Nigerian poet, scholar, and journalist Onwuchekwa Jemie—who links the dozens to similar West African traditions—describes this learned stoicism as a kind of immunization process: "It is as if the system is inoculated with virtual (verbally imagined) strains of the virus."

But to gain true inoculation, one's immune response has to be put to the test. And in that sense, the goal of the game is to not just best an opponent, but to get them to lose their cool. It's why H. Rap Brown described the dozens as "a mean game," wherein "what you try to do is totally destroy somebody else with words." He continued: "The real aim of the Dozens was to get a dude so mad that he'd cry or get mad enough to fight." As Dollard writes in 1939, "it is good technique to attack the other fellow at his weak point, if that be found" and that "the one who fights first tends to be viewed as the 'weaker kidder.'" Warren Sapp can barely imagine his childhood duels devolving into fisticuffs: "No, you throw a punch and nobody is going to hang out with you. You soft-skinned bastard."

And yet violence was always a possible outcome with the dozens. Any insult contains an implicit and necessary threat, a violation—it's what gives the insult its power—and if you're going to disparage someone, especially by "getting close to dangerous truths in comical ways," as Wald puts it, that invites retaliation, verbal or otherwise. But even more than that, the dozens could be deployed at times with the explicit intention to hurt or to escalate an encounter to physical conflict. That distinction may not always be clear. As Jemie writes, the dozens is "always ambiguous and double edged. Always, it could be used either to amuse or abuse." Many who understood the dozens for its bloody potential felt it was best avoided altogether, per Wald. At least one Mississippi establishment even hung a sign to that effect in the late 1920s: *If you want to play the dozens, go home.* Others opted out simply because they didn't want to get their feelings hurt.

Soft-skinned bastards.

———

THE DOZENS EXISTS within a constellation of similar insult-dueling traditions in the African diaspora. Others can be found in Colombia, Ecuador, Barbados, Jamaica, and elsewhere. In Trinidad and Tobago, for instance, there is *picong*, sometimes known as *extempo*, which emerged in relation to calypso music, where it featured improvised insults and heated battles between performers using stage names like the Mighty Sparrow and Lord Executor. In the introduction to his biography of the Trinidad-born writer V.S. Naipaul, Patrick French describes picong as a "style of conversation . . . where the boundary between good and bad taste is deliberately blurred, and the listener sent reeling." Dozens-style corollaries exist across other cultures, too, like razzing in Native American communities and *albures* in Mexico. On the Faroe Islands, there is a Viking tradition of taunts known as *duga at taka* or "knowing how to take it."

Still, to properly understand the connection of the dozens to modern trash talk, it must be situated not just within a broader landscape of insult games and rituals, but also within the wider oral traditions of Black Americans, like the epic poems known as toasts, which relate sensational tales of boastful badmen and cunning folk figures, and the speech events known as signifying. *Signifying* is a term with a somewhat slippery definition, but it can be used both as a synonym for verbal duels like the dozens and in reference to a rhetorical manner of speaking that conceals a person's true intention by saying one thing while meaning another. Each of these traditions places a premium on improvisation, cleverness, and verbal skill and contributes to a generalized conception of talking shit, which Boyd defines as "a way of speaking in which you consciously violate the rules of modesty, humility, and perhaps decorum."

But while Black culture has always been steeped in oral traditions—and has always helped shape what is conceived of as American culture more broadly—it really wasn't until Black figures started moving into the mainstream that large white audiences had to swallow their first, unadulterated dose of dozens-inflected shit talk. In that progression, there is no more important figure than Muhammad Ali, the veritable godfather of modern trash talk. Even though that term was still decades away from being coined, no one would deny the brash young boxer who burst onto the scene in the early 1960s—known as the Louisville Lip and Gaseous Cassius (in reference to his name at the time, Cassius Clay)—was doing anything but talking trash. It wasn't that he was the first Black athlete to offer boastful challenges or dabble in competitive mind games, but as a headline-grabbing athlete in an individual sport, he was the most prominent person to bring that Black style of talking shit to an enthralled national—and even global—television audience, even if many often clucked in disapproval. "A lot of people called him a loudmouth. Even many Black people didn't like the way he carried himself," says Boyd.

There was no denying the man had a hell of a mouthpiece, though, from his pompous predictions (which he usually backed up) to his promotion-minded antics to his strategic disparagement of opponents. And the boxer's success—both within and beyond the ring—rippled throughout Black communities and American culture at large. In the 1970s, Black baseball players started to make Ali-like statements—"When the leaves turn brown, I'll be wearing the batting crown," bragged Dave Parker—while Black basketballers increasingly unleashed what was considered a showy style on the court. "All of a sudden, they're playing in-your-face, trash-talking, acrobatic, aerial basketball," says Theresa Runstedtler, an associate professor of history at American University and the author of 2023's *Black Ball*, which is about the impact of Black basketball players in that era. That expressive and improvisational manner was an outgrowth of the street game, which was incubated on city playgrounds like Harlem's Rucker Park and indoor gyms like Detroit's St. Cecilia's—venues that naturally accommodated dozens-style verbal duels as part of their put-up-or-shut-up character of competition, where glory and humiliation were always on the line, where a dunk was the pinnacle of dominance, and where the crowds could be as vicious as any opponent. George Gervin, the Hall of Fame basketball player known as the Iceman, still remembers performing before those Detroit crowds. "I played in front of the hood, who was very critical," he tells me. "If you come down, and you can't play, they gonna dog you." Plenty of competitors couldn't handle the added pressure, he says, "and a lot of them caved in."

Len Elmore, a college standout at the University of Maryland who played ten years in the pros, credits the street game for teaching him necessary lessons in competition. In his first experience with organized basketball, as a sophomore in high school, Elmore played a scrimmage against the powerhouse Boys High School in Brooklyn.

At the opening tip, he was greeted by an elbow to the face. "My mouth is bleeding, and up and down the court, guys are pushing me, telling me I can't play, *you ain't nothing but a punk*, you know, all of that stuff," he says. "And I'm thinking, well, I didn't sign up for this!" Even though he had grown up playing a gentle version of the dozens, this was a more visceral and physical form of taunting. "That was kind of my first taste of real smack talk." But after a summer playing at Rucker Park, Elmore returned for his junior year with a different mentality, which he showed off in a rematch against Boys High. "They toss the ball up, and honestly, I knocked the shit out of the guy," he says. "Now I am the one blocking shots, pinning them against the backboard, staring guys down." He had learned not only the importance of playing with physicality and attitude, he says, but also "how important it was not to be embarrassed."

"That's what the game was about," per Richard "Pee Wee" Kirkland, a streetball legend, who went toe-to-toe against pros like Julius Erving and Tiny Archibald but abandoned his career in favor of a more lucrative life of crime. "It was about living up to what you said," or facing the public shame of coming up short. James "Fly" Williams was another playground icon whose breathtaking talent led to frustrating fizzles—but his foundering had nothing to do with off-court opportunities. According to Vincent M. Mallozzi's *Asphalt Gods*, which chronicles the history of the Rucker Park summer tournament, Fly was one of the brittle-minded. He couldn't handle the aggressive jabbering from players like Kirkland. "I'd let guys get into my head," Fly says. Still, as he explains in *Doin' It in the Park*, a documentary about pickup basketball in New York City, "This is the place where all that garbage come from."

AROUND THE SAME time as the influence of the dozens was trickling up from streetball courts to the pros, there was another emergent cultural force that came to shape what we now think of as trash talk, a new music category bubbling up from the same cultural cauldron: hip-hop. "This is a whole genre of music built around shit talking. That's what hip-hop is," says Boyd, who brings up "Rapper's Delight" by the Sugarhill Gang, which was released in 1979 and is widely credited as the first hip-hop track. "That whole song is talking shit." As were the back-and-forth diss tracks that broadcasted individual beefs (like the invective poetry of old) and the freestyle rap battles—clear extensions of both the dozens and other dueling traditions, like cutting contests in jazz—that took off after tapes of an onstage confrontation between Kool Moe Dee and Busy Bee Starski went 1981's version of viral, passed from palm to palm. According to the Brooklyn-raised rapper Talib Kweli, freestyle battling soon grew from an obscure hobby that only existed in the shadows of places like New York's Washington Square Park to a "supercompetitive, fierce art form" that could be found on street corners and in schoolyards everywhere. For both basketball and hip-hop, "the playground became a new locus for the convergence of black expressive culture," Onaje X. O. Woodbine, an American University assistant professor of philosophy and religion, writes in his book *Black Gods of the Asphalt: Religion, Hip-Hop, and Street Basketball*.

But what happened on the playground didn't stay on the playground.

Throughout the 1980s and into the 1990s, as hip-hop gained pop-cultural purchase and the sports world increasingly adopted changing styles, "the culture becomes more visibly Black," per Boyd. He says, "The mainstreaming of hip-hop, the mainstreaming of Black athletes in various sports—that's the mainstreaming of shit talking." And the mainstreaming of the dozens along with it. As a result, America's predominantly white sports editors and its similarly hued chattering class suddenly found themselves in need of a way to talk about what was happening on the courts and ball fields—what felt to many in the country as new and uncharted: not just because of what was being said, but also because of who was saying it. Specifically, *trash talk* as a term was created primarily by white people to describe the behavior of Black athletes in this time. It was an attempt to allow the uninitiated to understand all that sneering bravado and fearless raising of the stakes—all that dang *noise*.

But *trash talk* was always an imperfect term because, aware of it or not (usually not), it also spoke to these wider trends, outside of sports, and the deeper linguistic traditions from which they came. Even as a high schooler, David J. Leonard, now a professor in the School of Languages, Cultures, and Race at Washington State University, Pullman, was struck by the reductive thinking. "Trash talk was attributed to the influence of [college basketball programs like] Michigan or UNLV or the NBA," he says, "and not like, hey, this ain't that much different than those chants we did in Little League." Omitting that connective thread from the media coverage had consequences. It allowed the conversation to focus—sometimes explicitly, sometimes implicitly—on race, with the behavior framed as exceptional, deviant, and worthy of punishment. Often the coverage was inflected with notes of moral panic, which comes as no surprise to someone like Warren Sapp. He says, "So white boys didn't have it? And when it got introduced and they were the ones getting the shit talked to them, the finger pointed in their face, they felt inferior so they stigmatized it, like they stigmatize every fucking thing else the Black man does? It's America. Welcome to America."

For all the brouhaha, though—and for all those folks who clutched their pearls or otherwise misunderstood the nature of this ancient behavior of competition—there have been others who recognized something important amid the moralizing discourse. It's a trash-talk truism that performers like Muhammad Ali have expertly leveraged time and again by twisting public attention forever in their direction: talking shit can be good for business.

THE BUSINESS OF TRASH TALK

WHEN RONDA ROUSEY stepped off the scale in November 2015, during the ceremonial weigh-in before UFC 193 at Etihad Stadium in Melbourne, the confrontational women's bantamweight champion and burgeoning media darling charged straight at her challenger, Holly Holm. As of yet undefeated, Rousey had built a reputation of seeming invincibility by dispatching her opponents with blink-and-you-miss-it speed (each of her last three fights had ended in thirty-four seconds or less), while employing an all-up-in-your-grill mix of shit talk and physical intimidation tactics. At the time, though, Holm had only one thing on her mind: *I can't spill my drink.*

This was Holm's first fight since the United States Anti-Doping Agency banned UFC fighters from using IVs, even for rehydration purposes after making weight, when they wring themselves dry, and Holm and her team had spent all week scouring Australia for the necessary ingredients to concoct an FDA-approved rehydration drink from powdered greens, table salt, caffeine, aminos, and other tasty things. "It was disgusting. The most disgusting drink ever," she says. "But this is gold, and there's no way I can replace it."

Holm, who has always been a rule follower (her father is a preacher), was taking her first sips when she registered the intensity of her fast-approaching opponent. "I'm like, 'Oh! It's going to be one of *those* weigh-ins,'" she says. If you watch video of the event closely, you can see as Holm quickly—and carefully—places her beverage on the floor, which is instantly scooped up for safekeeping, while Rousey comes crowding in, raising her fists. What followed was a memorable—if brief—physical altercation (also reported as a "scuffle" and a "skirmish"), as Rousey pressed her face toward Holm's, and Holm pressed her fist through Rousey's chin. The contact was a kind of logistical accident, according to Holm. Rousey had watched Holm at previous weigh-ins and noticed her challenger liked to have her right arm flanked to the outside during the stare-down, when fighters square off for a final press photo and one last chance at face-to-face intimidation. Per Rousey, "I just wanted to place my hand on the outside. That was it." A little mind fuck to cramp her style. As Holm explains it, "She didn't like where my fist was, so she goes over mine and hits my arm with her arm, which then puts my fist against her face."

And, well, what do you expect a fighter to do in such a situation?

"I can't say I punched her in the face," Holm tells me. "But I did push her face off with my fist."

"Preacher's daughter, my ass!" Rousey screamed, as Dana White pulled the fighters apart.

In some ways, the whole of these prefight events is designed around the stare-down. All of the promotional apparatus builds to this point, when the microphones are stripped away and the fighters are invited to share a final moment of aggressive intimacy—to look into each other's eyes from a distance of mere inches. It's a kind of spiritual confrontation that throbs with a violent compact: the promise to meet each other again soon. This prefight ritual has become standardized across many combat sports, but it would be wrong to reduce the custom to a simple formality—to think of it as nothing more than a photo op.

A stare-down can reveal a fighter's intensity or expose his or her uncertainty.

Boxing-ring announcer David Diamante pays close attention when fighters square off in this way. "A stare-down is like nonverbal shit talk," he says. "You're looking at the other dude like, 'Yeah, motherfucker, this is what you're gonna get. You're about to taste the fucking pain.'"

In the case of Rousey and Holm, the altercation lasted maybe five seconds. And while it's doubtful that taking a fist to the face was the outcome Rousey had intended when she marched off the scale, there was no denying the thrill that pulsed through the room when the women's bodies collided, which led to all those scuffle-skirmish headlines. It's exactly the sort of drama that gets people talking, that gets them to tune in.

———————

IT HASN'T ALWAYS been like this.

The idea of promotional press conferences and prefight weigh-ins as major media events—with personal antagonisms and physical fireworks—is one we take for granted nowadays, but these used to be more perfunctory affairs, a way for reporters to squeeze a few quotes into their copy, for the boxing authorities to make sure no man tipped the scales above his appointed weight class. That all changed on the morning of February 25, 1964, when—who else—a twenty-two-year-old named Cassius Clay rolled up to the Miami Beach Convention Center and made just a hell of a spectacle. Later that day, Clay was to take on Sonny Liston for the heavyweight championship. It was a confrontation seven months in the making. Clay had been tormenting his supposedly unbeatable opponent since the previous summer, when Liston was in Las Vegas for a rematch with Floyd Patterson. There Clay showed up at a casino and mocked Liston as "a big, ugly bear" from across a craps table, while the big man gambled.

Then, in the moments after Liston dispatched Patterson, Clay snuck into the ring, found the TV cameras, and called for a fight that plenty of folks didn't believe he deserved. "Liston is a tramp! I'm the champ!" he hollered. "I want that big, ugly bear."

When a deal for the bout was struck, critics griped that Clay was skipping the line and had simply taunted his way into a title fight. But Clay's crusades of public harassment were a feature of his appeal, not a bug. Against Liston, the abuse wouldn't climax until the morning of their fight, when he arrived for the weigh-in wearing a denim jacket with "Bear Huntin'" inscribed on the back and flanked by an entourage that included legendary fighter (and Clay's idol) Sugar Ray Robinson and personal motivator Drew Bundini Brown.* After changing into his trunks and robe, Clay burst into a room choked with cigarette smoke and made more claustrophobic by the tangle of reporters, and where he immediately cranked up the volume. "Float like a butterfly, sting like a bee," he screamed, along with Bundini, the author of that famous line. "Rumble, young man, rumble!"

During the actual weigh-in, Clay focused only on Liston, who stood about three feet away. "You ain't got a chance!" he boomed, amid a stream of frenetic put-downs and angry gesticulations aimed at his stoic opponent. The performance would continue off the scale, too, as Clay kept up his wide-eyed abuse. "I can beat you anytime, chump. You ain't no giant! I'm going to eat you alive!" Clay refused to stay still, was practically bursting through his skin. Bundini and Sugar Ray did all they could to hold him back, to keep him from charging at Liston, while he screamed his madness. "I predict that tonight somebody will die at ringside from shock!"

Where the boundary between good and bad taste is deliberately blurred . . .

---

* While some music critics credit Ali as a progenitor of hip-hop for his brazenness, his bravado, and his rhymes, we can likewise see Bundini's fingerprints on the genre—specifically, in his trailblazing role as what we'd now call a "hype man," which is someone whose job is to keep the energy and excitement at a fever pitch.

The media didn't know what to make of him. Those in the room thought he was "an absolute lunatic" or maybe "was having a seizure." Clay was seen as so out of control—and his behavior so transgressive—that the Miami Boxing Commission announced it would fine him $2,500, while a commission doctor threatened to call off the fight. "The reporters are genuinely flabbergasted," says Jonathan Eig, author of *Ali: A Life*. "I think they genuinely thought that he had gone crazy, that he was having a panic attack."

. . . and the listener sent reeling.

There wasn't a soul outside of Clay's camp who didn't think he was suffering some sort of breakdown. But as Clay would later claim, he knew exactly what he was doing. For months, he had been waging a campaign of disrespect not just to raise his profile and earn a shot at the title, but also because he believed it would enrage the image-conscious Liston—and an enraged Liston would likely be less careful and overly aggressive in the ring, Eig writes. According to Todd D. Snyder, author of *Bundini: Don't Believe the Hype*, there was even more to it than that. Behind the scenes, Bundini advised Clay that, to gain the psychological edge, he needed to make Liston believe he was nuts. Like, cuckoo for Cocoa Puffs nuts. "The only thing that scares a tough guy is a crazy guy," he told him. Says Snyder, "That was their technique with Liston. They would convince him that they were insane." The whole routine was essentially choreographed, per Snyder. He says, "They would practice in the gym with Ali getting up and Bundini holding him back, and then Ali would break free. They actually practiced that stuff in the gym, almost like professional wrestlers would, getting ready for a show."

Eig has his doubts about the level of premeditation that went into Clay's performance. "I don't think Ali planned it. He was cutting loose and being himself, and he had a lot of nervous energy," he says, noting how the boxer showed up for the weigh-in about an hour earlier than he needed to. "He had to sit in a dressing room, waiting. He was probably all cooped up and needed to explode." Still, Eig sees the outburst, which the boxer would eventually describe as "my finest piece of acting," as fitting cleanly into the pattern of disrespect that provided the drumbeat of publicity in the lead-up to the fight. Some would call this selling woof tickets. (*Woofing* is another word for playing the dozens.) But in truth, whatever Clay intended is almost beside the point. Whether he was trying to psych out Liston, letting off nervous steam, stirring up interest in a fight that was seen by many as a one-sided affair, or simply mugging for the cameras as he'd done so often, the man who would soon be known as Ali showed the world what was possible if you wanted to insert a little drama into a typically mundane prefight event. He provided a model for all future braggarts, shit-stirrers, and showmen—all the Rouseys and McGregors of the world—and laid the groundwork for pretty much every memorable weigh-in and presser in combat-sports history, from the all-out brawl that ensued after Mike Tyson's failed attempt to intimidate Lennox Lewis by walking up on him in 2002 to Tyson Fury arriving at a 2015 press conference dressed as Batman, where he tackled a Joker who appeared in the crowd and promised his opponent, Wladimir Klitschko, "to rid boxing of a boring person like you."

"Muhammad Ali reinvented the rituals of boxing, and after the show he put on in Miami Beach, weigh-ins would never be the same," Thomas Hauser writes in *Muhammad Ali: His Life and Times*. Or as Eig puts it to me, "I think that's the Rosetta stone. That's the one that starts it all."

THERE'S A WHITE hangar-like building tucked into the recesses of Mantua Avenue in the township of Paulsboro, New Jersey, just over the Delaware River from Philadelphia. You wouldn't think much of the structure from the outside. By day, the building is home to the Paulsboro Wrestling Club, amateur gymnasium. (It says so on the plain red awning that umbrellas two windowless metal doors.) But by night, it converts into the Monster Factory, a pro-wrestling training center, where grown-ups of various ages, sizes, and athletic abilities engage in choreographed physical combat—or, alternatively, in performances of impromptu verbal violence. When I visit the Monster Factory, for instance, class instructor Missy Sampson has her students climb, one at a time, onto a blue box-jump platform—about three feet high and with almost no room to fidget—and then gives each of them sixty seconds to start some shit.

One student points at a peer and says, "You know what I see over there? I see a weak body."

Another calls the group a bunch of "idiots and fools."

And: "That slap that you gave me? That was nothing! Please bring it a little harder."

And: "I'm not asking for your respect. I'm demanding it!"

There's a reason everyone is talking so much crap. Tonight, the Monster Factory is teaching a class on how to cut a promo. For those who don't make a habit of watching adults in spandex bounce around a ring, the best way to think about promos are those moments when a wrestling character gets the chance to talk on a microphone—either via media interview or in-arena monologue—and uses that time to deepen a feud, hype a match, call for a fight, explain a plot twist, or otherwise juice public interest by advancing the tensions of a particular storyline, with the promise of an impending resolution by way of physical altercation. At its most basic level, a promo sets the stage and establishes the stakes. It leverages shit talking to invest the audience in the outcome of a match—in a particular performer's success or failure—and to motivate them to tune in or to buy a ticket. (It's also exactly what Muhammad Ali used to do, when the cameras were rolling: *I predict that tonight somebody will die at ringside from shock!*) The top stars develop a kind of shorthand for these antagonisms and dramatic escalations by way of catchphrase: it's The Rock telling an opponent to "know your role and shut your mouth" or Macho Man Randy Savage chanting "oooooh, yeah." The ability to cut a compelling promo is essential for any aspiring professional wrestler and a skill that goes back to the time when wrestling shows rolled from one town to the next as part of traveling carnivals. The viability of pro wrestling as a business was built on shit talk—on the ability to snooker someone into your tent instead of spending money to see the bearded lady.

"We call that talking people into the arena," says Gerald Brisco, a World Wrestling Entertainment (WWE) Hall of Famer, who spent fifty-plus years in the business, doing everything from performing to backstage producing to talent development. Brisco may be best known for his role as one of Vince McMahon's henchmen, referred to as "the Stooges," who served as foils to Stone Cold Steve Austin during his heyday in the late 1990s, but he cut his teeth thirty years earlier, when the pro-wrestling landscape was balkanized, divided into regional territories, and small-time promotions put on live shows staged anywhere from marquee arenas to local auditoriums to even more intimate venues, and everywhere from New York City to Raleigh to Amarillo. "What we gauged by," he says, "was the number of tickets sold and the reaction when you went in the ring."

When you get a big reaction, that's called getting heat.

According to author and wrestling historian Greg Oliver, careers could be made or submarined by a person's ability (or inability) to speak—to generate heat. "The wrestlers were encouraged to be creative and colorful," he says. "They knew that, basically, their paycheck depended on how many people were at those shows." As Jason Bryant, who has been inducted into the National Wrestling Hall of Fame as a broadcaster, announcer, and journalist, puts it, "If you can't cut a promo, you're not going to last."

A muscled barrel of a woman, Missy Sampson managed to last. Now forty-two and eighteen months into her pro-wrestling retirement, she spent most of her twenty-five-year career working the local independent circuit—where she started as one of the only female wrestlers in the tri-state area—and during that time, she never stopped thinking about the art of the promo. It became a kind of obsession, really, something she felt she could always improve on. "It's not normal to get up [in front of a room of people] and talk shit about someone," she says. But with enough practice, she found, it could become second nature. Sampson worked hard to perfect her craft. She practiced her promos in the mirror before a match and again when the match was over. She practiced when she was taking a shower or when she was in the car—always and everywhere, basically. "I was probably better at talking shit than I was at wrestling," she says with a laugh.

Sampson, who speaks in a ball-busting Philly accent, which is cut by a genuine affection for those around her, hasn't lost that command of a room. It's perhaps why Danny Cage, who has owned and operated the Monster Factory since 2011, asked her to help him coach this next crop of talent when he heard she was retiring. Though Sampson was ready to leave wrestling behind and settle into her life as an insurance adjustor, she agreed.

On the one hand, it seems highly implausible that any of the students from this Monster Factory training class—several of whom struggle to fill their sixty-second promo allotments without suffering panic attacks—will one day be climbing the top rope for WWE, AEW (All Elite Wrestling), or any of the other national wrestling promotions. Just as it seems unlikely that anyone from a local improv troupe will ever make it to *Saturday Night Live*. But long odds are the nature of the business, and the Monster Factory track record speaks for itself. Alums include Steve Cutler, Damian Priest, Matt Riddle, Nick Ogarelli, Cody Vance, Q.T. Marshall, and more. When I ask Gerald Brisco where I should go to learn about promos, he says, "There are very few schools that I recommend."

Then he points me to the Monster Factory.

There's a reason Sampson asks her students to climb atop the box-jump platform. In addition to heightening the sense of spotlight—with everyone else sitting in a semicircle of folding chairs—the limited real estate of the platform forces students to acclimate to the needs of television. "If you're on TV, the camera's not going to follow you all over," she explains. "You have to be able to convey what you're saying in that camera frame shot." After sixty seconds pass on top of the box, Sampson cuts each student off—midsentence, if necessary—and gives her review.

To more than one student, she says to dial up the "oomph."

To others, she issues warnings about telling fat jokes, which she calls "cheap heat," and about cutting what she calls a "*Pulp Fiction* promo," which is a promo that "didn't make any fucking sense."

Her most common response is tilting her head back and rubbing her eyes—in disbelief? In consternation? It's hard to say. ("Maybe don't do that," she advises one student who took a dramatic pause after saying his opponent wanted to "touch a boy." "You lost me after that.") All in all, though, she seems pleased with the class's effort, even with those students who are participating in this exercise for the first time and do all they can to not puke as they attempt one minute of extemporaneous public speaking. To a certain extent, she knows this is an unteachable skill because what constitutes a compelling promo for one person will almost surely fall flat for another. It's as much art as science. But there are some rules of the road.

For starters, you have what Rick Bassman, who founded Ultimate Pro Wrestling in the late 1990s and suspects himself to be one of the first people to teach promo classes, calls "the classic ingredients." That's the who, the when, and the where of a match. "It's got to have all those aspects in there," Brisco agrees, "but without being a blatant shill." When done well—when a promo is truly affecting—the audience may not even realize they're being sold to because they're also being told a story. A story about winning and losing, about pride and humiliation, about redemption or revenge.

Promos are riddled with smack talk, too, of course. But unlike in other competitive spaces (even other combat sports), the hostility must walk a fine line, defined by wrestling's unique promotional imperatives. Specifically, the idea is to antagonize, but not disparage. Says Brisco, "The number one rule during my time was blast your opponent but don't belittle him."

This is what is known in the business as "putting your opponent over."

Brisco continues, "You got to sell the guy you're wrestling. Make him worthwhile." If you talk a bunch of shit about how terrible your opponent is and how easily you're going to defeat him, then why would anyone tune in? The key is to build him up while you're tearing him down. In this way, selling the fight requires cooperation between two rivals. "You are playing a much more complicated game than just swearing at," Indiana University professor Michael Adams says of these trash-talking partnerships. "The collaboration is at its very essence, just as the violence is at its very essence."

Believability is also key. At Bassman's wrestling school, Ultimate University, he wanted his students to fully embody their characters, "to get to the point where they can make it real, and it's not just words," he says. One of his early pupils, who billed himself as a half-man, half-machine named The Prototype, stood out as a natural. Even his body movements came off as convincingly yet menacingly robotic. "How dare you . . . mock an engineered genius like The Prototype," the student scowls in a clip of the class that was captured on a 2000 Discovery Channel documentary. That student's name: John Cena. But it didn't come so easily to everyone. Bassman took an almost method-acting approach in his curriculum. He had students run exercises in which they wrote and recited in-depth bios of their characters before answering questions designed to poke holes in those backstories. "They had to do it all in the first person," he says. The students would also sit for Larry King–style interviews. "It wouldn't be wrestling-style. It'd be like, 'OK, Prototype, I understand that you came from a different planet. What was that like?'"

When Danny Cage listens to student promos, he pretends he's in the kitchen, two rooms over from whoever is speaking. "Is it going to make me want to stop what I'm doing and go and check this person out?" he says. "I just put my head down. And when I lift my head up, that is when they have got my attention." The worst promos, per Cage, are when he can feel someone being inauthentic, when he gets what he calls the "douche chills." A famous example of this, Brisco tells me, is when a young wrestler who went by the name Rocky Maivia was booed out of Madison Square Garden and serenaded with chants of "Die, Rocky, die!" That wrestler was played by Dwayne Johnson, who went on to become The Rock, a WWE superstar. In time, Johnson changed his fortunes in the ring by adopting a cooler, cockier, and more preening persona: he stopped chasing the audiences' affections. (That pivot was so successful that Johnson eventually parlayed his wrestling fame into becoming what he is now, in many people's minds: Hollywood's most-muscled, yet aggressively inoffensive movie star.) But on that night, the MSG crowd could sense Johnson's desperation to be liked and lustily rejected his performance. "This guy was as talented as you could be, and Rocky nearly cried that night, if he didn't cry," says Brisco. "They booed him out of Madison Square Garden, the Taj Mahal of professional wrestling."

IN OCTOBER 1985, a tall, rotund man dressed in blue jeans and the top half of a three-piece suit, sporting a bleached-blond Brillo pad of a mullet, walked onto a television set and started talking shit. That man was Dusty Rhodes, known to wrestling fans as The American Dream, and what came out of his mouth would soon go down in wrestling history as perhaps the most masterful promo work of all time. On the heels of a beating delivered by nemesis Ric Flair and his entourage, Rhodes began by recapping that particular indignity and the ensuing "hard times" that Flair had put on him and his family. But in short order, in his trademark Texas accent and with the escalating passion of a tent-revival preacher, Rhodes connected his own troubles to those of ordinary Americans—to the hard times of unemployed textile and auto workers, to those being unceremoniously kicked to the curb after decades of labor, only to be replaced by computers. "That's hard times!" he said. "That's hard times! And, Ric Flair, you put hard times on this country by taking Dusty Rhodes out—that's hard times!"

Just like that, in the span of a few words, Dusty Rhodes, a man who looked like nobody's idea of an athlete—he said as much himself—pulled a remarkable rhetorical trick. He took the specifics of his storyline and made them universal. And in so doing, he endowed his own fate—his comeback pursuit of the heavyweight title—with far greater significance than a simple wrestling match. Now he was fighting for the common man. And he was asking for folks to fight along with him because "the world's heavyweight title belongs to these people!"

To be sure, Rhodes was one of the best to ever do it. According to wrestling historian Greg Oliver, guys like Rhodes and Superstar Billy Graham and Blackjack Mulligan just "talked this magic" when they were given a microphone and a few minutes to fill. "You were captivated," he says. And in casting their spells, they demonstrated one of the necessary ingredients of generating heat: They gave folks a reason to care. They made their battles *mean* something.

———

IT FEELS INTUITIVE that talking trash would up the ante in a competitive encounter. If you're talking a big game, you don't want to look like a fool by not backing it up. On the flip side, if an opponent is talking smack, you want to shut that mother up. Former NBA great Ben Wallace was describing the clarifying effect of a trash-talking opponent when he said, "Now you're both in that spotlight."

And science agrees.

Jeremy Yip is an assistant professor of management at Georgetown University's McDonough School of Business, a research scholar at the University of Pennsylvania's Wharton School, and kind of obsessed with trash talk. "I grew up in Canada, which is a place that is known for civility and politeness," says Yip. "But then you went to a hockey rink, and it just got thrown out the window."

A few years back, Yip conducted a series of studies, in partnership with two Wharton professors, that explored trash talk in the workplace—or what they termed *competitive incivility*. As Yip explains, "There is a lot of evidence suggesting that incivility is harmful and should be avoided, but there really wasn't any understanding about the function of incivility or the different consequences of incivility when it is expressed in a competitive setting." Their research, which focused on employees of Fortune 500 companies and was published in a 2018 issue of the academic journal *Organizational Behavior and Human Decision Processes*, aimed to rectify that. What they found goes a long way to explain why trash talk can be such a potent tool. Namely, it "raises the psychological stakes" of competition.

It was this relational component of trash talk that was of particular interest to Yip. "This type of communication, it shifts how we view the relationship with our opponent," he says. "We no longer just see that person as a mere opponent, but we see that person as a rival."

This is important because rivalry relationships are defined by their increased stakes. It's why rivals try harder, take more risks, and are more prone to unethical behavior. Against a rival, it's not just about winning and losing; we are also competing for our sense of identity, status, and self-worth. "Rivalry is all about comparing," says Cody T. Havard, a professor of sport commerce at the University of Memphis, whose research focuses on rivalry in sport. "We all want to feel good about ourselves, and one way to do that is through comparison and competition." Or as Yip and his coauthors put it in their research paper, "rivalry increases the subjective significance of competitive outcomes."

In the presence of trash talk, competitors feel they have more on the line—both more to gain and more to lose. Fans, too.

After all, there's nothing inherently meaningful about an athletic event, despite what supporters of teams like the Yankees and Red Sox might insist. We inject those contests with significance, based on the stories we tell ourselves about what those organizations and their players represent with regard to things like regional pride, cultural identity, or personal legacy. What Yip discovered is that trash talk is effectively a cheat code for imbuing a competition with that kind of drama, for endowing it with meaning. It is, in the words of the *New York Times Magazine*, in 1993, "a permanent doubling of the stakes." Really, it's borderline existential. As Steven Kotler writes, in reference to Nietzsche, in *The Art of Impossible: A Peak Performance Primer*, "If God is dead, and there's no divine meaning to life, then we need to make our own meaning." Trash talk does exactly that. It contributes to the stakes of a narrative we're all constructing together from whole cloth, and it gives people a reason to care, like a teary-eyed Dusty Rhodes.

It also happens to be terrific for marketing purposes.

Put a couple of guys in a wrestling ring, and . . . meh, what else is on?

But have them start talking smack to each other, and suddenly it has the potential to become Achilles versus Hector. A battle of epic proportions.

Havard sees this promotional instinct throughout the sports world, from hometown radio programs that introduce opposing teams to local fans via "reasons to hate" segments to newly minted rivalry games in college football, like the Battle Line Rivalry between the Arkansas Razorbacks and Missouri Tigers, which was only introduced in 2014 after Missouri switched into a new athletic conference. In the 1980s, a decade of immense growth for the NBA, the league largely staked its marketing efforts on the perceived rivalry between Magic Johnson and Larry Bird. "Rivalry is an important part of promoting the product," says Havard. "And if you can have that kind of tension, that makes those particular games more interesting."

Kosha Irby has plenty of experience adding "that kind of tension" to matchups. Now the chief marketing officer for Clemson University's athletic department, Irby served previously as CMO for Professional Bull Riders and spent the better part of a decade earlier in his career running live WWE shows. But his most challenging assignment was as team president for the Memphis Express of the then upstart (and now defunct) Alliance of American Football, where he had no built-in fan base and spent week after week conjuring up potential new rivalries. "Your goal is to try to create a choice, to create some dichotomous situation, where people now have a vested interest in seeing an outcome," Irby explains. "This is the art of rivalry creation. You have to find the stitch that makes that rivalry matter." It could be good versus evil, or big versus small, or offense versus defense, or anything else, really. The specifics are almost irrelevant, as long as you offer folks a choice. "Whatever it may be, you just pull at that stitch until you unravel a story that people can wrap themselves into."

Until people pick a side.

Today, that truism is the basis for entire genres of popular entertainment, from reality television to talking-head debate shows, in which sports and political pundits scream from either side of an issue, ensuring the constant production of conflict with small matters blown up to grand proportion. (Of Stephen A. Smith and Skip Bayless, who used to yell at each other on ESPN's *First Take*, Gerald Brisco says, "Those guys. That's a wrestling promo. That's a wrestling show.") You can find the same tendencies online, where corporate social-media accounts try to gain followers by serving up snark and starting Twitter wars and where everyone else scrolls to catch up on the latest celebrity feuds and rap beefs. Multiple hip-hop artists have alleged they were offered large sums of money and record deals if they were willing to write diss tracks about Nicki Minaj as a way to gain notoriety.

The idea of starting a feud for marketing purposes—that is, using trash talk not just as a tool of *psychological* manipulation, but also as a tool of *public* manipulation—is not new, according to actor, author, and comedy historian Wayne Federman. He tells me about the on-air hostilities between Edgar Bergen's ventriloquist dummy Charlie McCarthy and W. C. Fields, which began on Bergen's radio show in the summer of 1937, by way of example. "It was wild. They would hurl insults back and forth," he says. "Audiences ate it up." Another famous (and fake) feud kicked off between radio comedians Jack Benny and Fred Allen around that same time, in December 1936, and lasted for years, as listeners continually tuned back in to see how one would respond to the other's latest gibe, per Federman. "Benny and Allen sort of stumbled into their feud, and it became an extraordinary promotion for both of their shows," he says. "It was a big thing."

Such promotional tricks work for athletes, too—and not just for those in combat sports.

Take Shaquille O'Neal. The seven-foot center wasn't much of a shit-talker on the basketball court, by most accounts, but he was never afraid to talk mess when reporters put a microphone in his face. In the early 2000s, for instance, Shaq maintained a running feud with Mark Cuban, the outspoken new owner of the Dallas Mavericks. Through the media, the two men aimed constant barbs at each other, with Cuban attacking Shaq's poor free-throw shooting and Shaq dismissing Cuban as unworthy, dubbing him "Little Mark" and "the little guy that won the lottery."

Shaq and Cuban were rewarded for their efforts with headlines that found the previously bland Lakers-Mavericks matchup to be suddenly "full of intrigue." Shaq made little secret of his intent. Sportswriter Jeff Pearlman tells me "there was always a wink" with Shaq's smack talk, while Howard Beck, who covered the team during that time for the *Los Angeles Daily News*, says the big man would go so far as to tell him outright, "It's all marketing, brother."

"We call it 'marketing-sparring,'" Shaq has confessed. "You have to do certain things like that to bring the excitement up, keep people watching, keep people buying tickets." In other words, he was creating hype around an event—no different than Muhammad Ali or Conor McGregor or any other athlete who wants to up the drama or emotional quotient before a competitive confrontation. It's what legendary boxing promoter Tex Rickard might call a little bit of "ballyhoo."

―――――――

IN THE BEGINNING, it was a kind of side hustle. A lark. It was 1906, and Tex Rickard decided he wanted to stage a prizefight. To that point, Rickard had already tried his luck as a Texas rancher and lawman, and he'd chased gold to Alaska, where he became a professional gambler and saloonkeeper (well, until he lost the saloon in a card game). His latest endeavor was running a casino in Goldfield, Nevada, and the idea behind putting on this boxing match—what would turn out to be a lightweight title fight between Joe Gans and Oscar "Battling" Nelson—was to gin up interest in his new hometown.

It wouldn't be long before Rickard was recognized as boxing's first big-time promoter.

Rickard had a natural gift for the sensational and dramatic. To attract attention to that first bout, for instance, he stacked the entirety of the $30,000 fight purse in gold coins in the window of a local bank. Other times, he'd stage bidding wars or seed fake rumors (to which he'd respond with a strategic "no comment"). Rickard didn't say much himself, but he knew how to get people talking—how to stir up some ballyhoo.

What is ballyhoo, you ask?

"That is the conversation around the fight," says Colleen Aycock, boxing writer and coauthor of *Tex Rickard: Boxing's Greatest Promoter*. "Rickard came in, and he changed the notion of ballyhoo." The thing he understood was that he was always selling more than just a boxing match. A fight had to be more than a fight. It had to be an event, a spectacle. And he had to "put it over," as he would say. Rickard, whose fights would feature champions like Jack Dempsey and Jack Johnson and draw boxing's first $1 million (and $2 million) gates, would boast via the press of gaudy presale figures and big-name attendees to expect in the front rows. At a time when boxing matches were magnets for criminals and prostitutes, Rickard welcomed women and children and eventually turned his events into black-tie affairs.

"He made the people a part of the drama," says Aycock. "If you had presales of eighteen thousand, were you going to miss that event? No, you were not." Fans didn't show up to see the fight, she adds. "They came to be *a part* of the fight. That is a huge difference. Rickard knew that, and that is what he was trying to create."

In the lead-up to a 1927 rematch between Gene Tunney and Jack Dempsey, the *New York Times* observed that "there is almost as much ballyhoo about the ballyhoo than there is actual ballyhoo."* But Rickard did more than eat up newspaper column inches. He changed the requirements of being a contender. It was no longer enough to be talented in the ring. A fighter also had to be a draw; he had to incite the passions of a crowd. In fact, as the *North American Review* literary journal put it, shortly after Rickard's death in 1929, "If the fighters were sufficiently colorful it did not matter particularly if they were well matched."

It was the draw that mattered. For Rickard, the draw was often based on the pairing of opposites—on finding that stitch, as Irby would put it—because he recognized the power of exploiting conflict (or even the perception of conflict) for the sake of narrative.

Black man versus white man (Jack Johnson v. James J. Jeffries).

War hero versus draft dodger (Georges Carpentier v. Jack Dempsey).

American versus foreigner (Jack Dempsey v. Luis Ángel Firpo).

High hat versus ruffian (Gene Tunney v. Jack Dempsey).

"He understood the drama," says Aycock, "because the drama makes it more than just talk."

LIKE TEX RICKARD, Muhammad Ali was calculated in the way he manipulated the press for promotional purposes. The media was not an adversary to be conquered, as he saw it, but a tool to be leveraged against less-savvy opponents. He knew what the press

---

* The quote reminds me of the promotional blitz and attendant media coverage that preceded the 2017 exhibition boxing match between Conor McGregor and Floyd Mayweather Jr., when the two men set off on an international prefight press tour that filled arenas and had scalpers working the doors, hawking tickets that were free to the public for forty dollars apiece. Tens of thousands of people, in multiple countries, turning out just to see two dudes talk shit.

wanted—some conflict, some drama—and he was happy to be the one to give it to them because, in so doing, he got to steer the public narrative. Rickard may have pioneered ballyhoo, but Ali learned to control the whole conversation.

In a press conference before his 1971 fight against Joe Frazier, for instance—in which Ali would attempt to reclaim the championship belt that was stripped from him in 1967—the boxer boasts in no uncertain terms about his impending victory. (In reality, Frazier would win via decision.) Ali scrunches his forehead with a kind of indignant certitude and projects his voice as if he's in the center of a large lecture hall. With Frazier in almost comically close quarters— the men are close enough to kiss—Ali compares the upcoming matchup to an amateur taking on a professional. He dismisses Frazier as "easier to hit" than past opponents. "I predict the fans will be angry," he says. "They'll be mad at the experts for misleading them so much."

When Frazier tries to get a word in—to tell the gathered media that Ali is spouting "nothing but a bunch of noise" and that he (Frazier) is going to end the fight before it goes the distance—Ali slips a banana peel in his path.

"He's agitated, he's agitated," he says.

And the press goes wild with laughter. Just as he knew they would.

While Ali always recognized the importance of how he was perceived—and that he could wield language in order to help shape that perception—there's something more sophisticated about this version of the boxer and the way he handles this press event compared to his raw and raging outbursts against Liston. From the very first camera shot, it seems clear Ali is in control against Frazier, whom he has been disparaging as a coward and an Uncle Tom for years. Ali barks, he needles, he jumps out of his seat when a particularly noisy exchange is in need of punctuation. At one point, he even baits Frazier into accepting a side bet that the losing boxer will crawl across the ring in submission to the victor. "Write it!" Ali then screams to the reporters. "He says he's going to crawl."

Ali never thought of himself as a bully. In his mind, the verbal abuse and conflict creation were functions of competition—they were part of the deal, an act, nothing personal. His opponents didn't always see it that way. There's something inherently violent about forcing another person to play a game—even a rhetorical one—without the other's consent. Before his fight against Chuck Wepner, Ali tried to convince his white opponent to use the N-word to flame interest in the bout. When he refused, Ali claimed Wepner had used the word anyway. Frazier, in particular, was deeply hurt by the way Ali treated him and nursed a grudge for the rest of his life. What opponents like Frazier never seemed to realize, though, is that, by engaging with Ali in this way—by trying to reason with him in any way, really—they fall into the man's rhetorical traps, which wind like a maze through a fun-house logic of his own creation. Even when Frazier was unanimously declared the winner of that first bout, he couldn't escape Ali's exasperating logic system. After the bruising match, both men were sent to the hospital. But while Frazier spent the better part of a month convalescing, Ali discharged himself almost immediately, refusing to even stay the night, and used that fact—and the insinuation that he had done the most damage—to claim he was the real winner.

An even more perfect metaphor for Ali's promotional and rhetorical mastery—for his ability to direct the extracurricular discourse and force opponents to accept his terms of engagement—would come four years later at the end of a press conference before Ali and Frazier's third and final bout, the Thrilla in Manilla. With the electrified promoter Don King looming just over their shoulders, the two fighters pose together for press photos. There's something meta about the scene. "Look mean," Ali says, contorting his face into an exaggerated scowl. At his side, Bundini chants, "He don't have the look. He don't have the look." Frazier seems to chuckle. But then, as if suddenly levitating, Ali rises a few inches off the ground.

It's no magic trick. Ali is up on his tiptoes.

The flashbulbs pop.

"Come on down. You ain't that big," says Frazier.

"That's the way I'm going to look the night you meet me," Ali replies.

Meta or not, the moment is no joke for Frazier, and it seems to stretch in his mind, as he surely hears the camera shutters click. Once again, Ali is forcing Frazier to play his game—or to look for all the world like the much shorter man. Frazier repeats himself, "Come on down." But his pleas are futile. There's no choice but to participate.

Frazier goes up on his tiptoes, too.

WRESTLING IS SIMILAR to boxing in that it has long relied on the perception of simple conflict to fuel its foundational dramas— or angles, as they're known. At first, it was mostly out of necessity. "A traveling carnival doesn't really have time to develop storylines," explains Jason Bryant. "It's just like, OK, here is a guy in red, white, and blue, and he is kissing babies. And the other guy is sneering and wearing black and eye gouging." In wrestling terminology, that was your "baby face" and "heel," the good guy and the bad guy. The baby face fought with honor and was the people's champion, while the heel would bite, claw, pull hair, and engage in any other cheap, cheating trick designed to enrage the crowd and intensify their sense of injustice and their hunger to see him lose. "So much of professional wrestling is based around that primal animosity," says Bryant.

Over the years, there have been many variations on this basic conflict structure, but the fundamentals of heat generation are largely the same now as they were in wrestling's earliest days. As a performer, you want fans to be rooting either for you or against you. That's essentially the lesson Missy Sampson drills into her Monster Factory class, as they practice their promos. From her folding chair, she implores her students to keep in mind whether they're "going face or heel," good or bad, and then to stick to a simple script that ruthlessly advances that narrative. "You kinda do want to spoon-feed people as if they're idiots," she says.

Talking to me after class, Sampson compares a good promo to a car that's driving down a one-lane road. Those who overcomplicate their promotional efforts with nuanced beefs and convoluted plot twists are effectively swerving from one street to the next, she says. "Chances are, once you jump to two or three separate points, the fans stop following you. They give up. The success comes when you just grab on to something—you pick one topic, no matter what it is—and take that person on a journey with you."

It would be easy enough to dismiss wrestling's largely straightforward feuds as trivial or childish. But in their simplicity, they tap into something universal, too. There's a reason folks would loiter outside appliance store windows in the early days of television and watch the action through the plate glass. "It was almost a pantomime," says Greg Oliver. The viewers understood they were being given a choice, and the most compelling wrestlers could generate heat without saying a word because they embodied one side of that choice so completely.

The promotional pushes of professional wrestlers can sometimes seem over the top, to be sure. Campy even. But ultimately, the squared circle of a wrestling ring is no place for subtlety. Inside the ropes, it's all about extravagance, embellishment, and bravado. It's a space where everything is personal and matters deeply—where small issues will always be blown up to grand proportion. Forget false modesty. "Hype up the match! Make me want to watch it," Sampson tells one student who downplays an upcoming contest. Because what happens in the ring needs to be of almost cartoonish importance, and the fans need to feel that, and to either love you or hate you as a result, nothing in between—that's the key. As the best performers have all come to understand, hate is just love by another name. And a paying customer's money is always green.

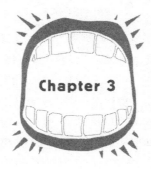

Chapter 3

A GOOD HEEL IS HARD TO FIND

GEORGE WAGNER WAS never going to make it big. For nearly a decade, throughout the 1930s, he competed on the wrestling circuit as a baby face. A handsome man of medium height with short dark hair, he looked the part, too. Maybe that was the problem: the young grappler had always been a natural in the ring and possessed a dramatic physicality that thrilled the paying crowds. But even so, this good guy from Harrisburg, Texas, came off as largely unexceptional. Among the other wrestlers, he fit right in.

To many, that may have been a good thing. It was a time of conformity in America, when the footsteps of global warfare crept ever closer to our shores, and when men were supposed to be men—reliable, sturdy, predictable. But by the early 1940s, a newly married Wagner knew something needed to change. As things were going, he was just barely scraping by, and the last thing he wanted was to wash out of the wrestling world and back to his family home. Of his lowest days on the circuit, Wagner has said, "The only thing that kept me from hitchhiking back was what my father said to me, that I wouldn't make it as a wrestler."

On the one hand, his dad was right: George Wagner's career had plateaued; he'd reached the end of the road. But on the other hand, the old man couldn't have been more wrong because the landscape-altering career of Gorgeous George—a transcendent sports-entertainment figure who would remake what it means to be a heel—was just about to begin.

———————

IN THE YEARS since Gorgeous George first stepped into the spotlight, there have been any number of effective wrestling heels. Some famous ones, like Buddy Rogers, aka Nature Boy, inspired personal animus with their smug and self-aggrandizing manners, while others, like the Iron Sheik and Nikolai Volkoff, appealed to American audiences' jingoism and xenophobia by leveraging larger societal tensions, like the Iran hostage crisis and the Cold War. In the days before the WWE, the first thing Gene Kiniski would do upon arriving in a new town was pick up a local newspaper, Greg Oliver tells me. That way, when he did promotional interviews, "he knew what buttons to push to get those fans riled up." For many heels, the real heat came when you tapped into what Gerald Brisco calls "personal issues," those things that people are most sensitive about. And perhaps nobody did that better than the man known as Gorgeous.

According to Oliver, it's always been "the villains that drive the business."* But before Gorgeous George rose to fame in the 1940s, wrestling heels were mostly one-dimensional characters. They may have been haughty or cowardly or devious, "but [they] essentially existed to be conquered. They weren't leading men," John Capouya

---

* And not just the wrestling business. In 2004, for instance, when the Lakers were set to take on the San Antonio Spurs in the NBA playoffs, Jeff Miller of the *Orange County Register* griped that the Spurs were too damn boring to hate. He writes, "It was a lot easier to dislike the opposition when the opposition was owned by Mark Cuban or employed Rasheed Wallace. . . . But these Spurs present so few such opportunities it can be maddening."

writes in his biography of the wrestler, in which he makes the case
that Gorgeous George all but invented the pop-cultural category
of the antihero. With George, who insisted on being introduced
before matches as "the Toast of the Coast" and "the Sensation of the
Nation" and referred to himself as "the Human Orchid" and "the
Beautiful Bicep," he was the main attraction. He made sure of that.
Even his entrances, which could take fifteen or twenty minutes to
unfold, antagonized the audience. With platinum-blond hair that
he styled in marcel waves and kept in place with gold-plated bobby
pins—which he dubbed "Georgie pins"—George would appear
before arena crowds wearing satin robes and bespoke gowns, with
sequins and frills. Slowly, with his skirts swishing around his legs and
an upturned nose, he would make his way to the ring to the sounds
of "Pomp and Circumstance." (He was a pioneer of arena entrance
music.) Fans would yell and throw things at him, debris and whatnot, as he peacocked along. George would meet these abuses, when
he acknowledged them at all, with looks of bemusement or derision
or with dismissive remarks. "Peasants," he'd say.

In the ring, after wiping his feet on a patch of rich red carpet and
curtseying to all corners of the arena, he would make a show of pointing out the spots of canvas where his valet, his manservant, had not
sufficiently perfumed—a prefight requirement. When it was finally
time for the referee to check each of the wrestlers for foreign objects,
George would recoil and shriek, "Take your filthy hands off me!"

Everything about Gorgeous George was designed to antagonize, and he was a master of teasing the crowd's desires. In a world of
macho men, he sashayed with a self-assured femininity. During wartime scarcity, he flaunted his means and indulged in every manner
of luxury. He was as immodest as he was unapologetic. Though he
likely took inspiration from the boastful boxer Max Baer—who traveled to fights with ten trunks filled with custom suits, disrespected
opponents in the press ("they aren't fit to lick my boots," he'd say),
and proclaimed himself to be "the world's greatest fighter and the
world's greatest lover"—George was an original. The man behind the

character, Wagner, and his first wife, Betty, who was equally instrumental in the creation of Gorgeous George, were sensitive to the boos—and when they were rewarded with jeers that were extra loud or extra lusty, they knew they were onto something.

They recognized that, as Capouya points out, the *real* competition was for attention. And no wrestling heel had ever attracted attention like Gorgeous George. From the moment he stepped foot in a new town, where he would schedule press interviews in hair salons, George had all eyes on him. This was meant to be Harry Truman and Dwight Eisenhower's America, not a land of vainglorious beauty queens. Responding to these provocations, fans called him "queer" and "sissy," per Capouya, but George didn't mind: "In his business any strong reaction was a good one; homophobia was just another form of heat."

SOMETIMES THINGS COULD get a little *too* hot.

In the ring, Gorgeous George had to contend not only with opponents, but also, on occasion, with the violence of the fans, whom the wrestler had just worked into a righteous fury. They threw glass bottles, charged the ropes, and even, one time, beat him over the head with a prosthetic limb. The greats knew how to play with people's emotions, per Gerald Brisco, how to take them for a ride. But just because a wrestler could manipulate how a person felt didn't mean those emotions were any less real—or any less dangerous. Brisco tells me about the time Italian American wrestler Angelo Savoldi showed up in Oklahoma City to take on local hero Danny Hodge in 1960, for example, and teased the crowd with themes of urban condescension. "This Savoldi guy comes in from the Northeast, 'Hey, I'm from New York. We're superior to you yokies out here,' and blah, blah, blah," says Brisco. "Well, this old guy jumped in the ring with a damn knife and started to stab him." As it happened, that old guy was Hodge's father. "I just stood it as long as I could," Mr. Hodge told the police. That's just how things were, sighs Brisco. Wrestlers had to deal with slashed tires, flipped cars, and more. In terms of security, forget it. "We had no security," he says. Instead of barricades, they had bicycle rope. "Of course, that didn't stop anybody. We had more in-ring riots just because it was so personal." On nights when things were liable to get extra hot, the wrestlers would stick around to watch each other's backs. (One night, Brisco and his brother Jack had to escape a raging horde of drunken cowboys beneath the helicoptering chain of Killer Karl Kox, after opening a bloody gash in the head of Texas legend Dory Funk Sr.) Back then, wrestling was a risky pleasure, and violence was always possible. It was the cost of doing business.

Still, there were some wrestlers for whom that violence presented a clearer and more present danger. WWE executive Bruce Prichard has called the Iron Sheik "a perfect bad guy" for the way he inflamed wrestling crowds, exploiting the fears and insecurities of American audiences as a perceived "foreign menace." Irate and ill-intentioned fans would wait for him outside venues. Once, a gun-wielding father-and-son duo marched on a television station, where the Sheik was cutting a live promo, with assassination on the brain. At Madison Square Garden, arena officials would help the Sheik escape by bringing his car inside the venue, or by loading him into the back of an ambulance. There were times he genuinely feared for his life. Reflecting on those years, the Sheik has said, "I was worried maybe somebody shoot me."

Black wrestlers dealt with similar hostilities. Brisco remembers being in the ring with tag-team partner Thunderbolt Patterson— after whom Dusty Rhodes basically modeled his promo style—when fans would start throwing whiskey bottles at them. He says, "I used to wonder—I don't know how to say this; *you're* the word man—but how is this Black man going to get out of here alive?"

"It's kind of the dark side of trash talk," says wrestling journalist Jason Bryant, in regard to those who leverage things like bigotry and ultranationalism in service of generating heat—because there's no telling what may be unleashed. For his part, Tex Rickard stopped playing into the racial biases of his time after the Great White Hope fight between Jack Johnson and Jim Jeffries, per Colleen Aycock, when he saw the prefight animus explode into deadly violence, as white people across the country rioted on the heels of Johnson's easy victory. "He wasn't going to go there [again]," she says.

But there's a case to be made that the villains of any given era are simply a response to that particular cultural moment: they reflect society's biases, insecurities, and fears back to us. In that sense, someone like Jack Johnson would have been a lightning rod with or without the promotional efforts of Tex Rickard. As the first-ever Black heavyweight champion, the simple fact of his existence was enough to earn the contempt of boxing crowds, who jeered him with the passion of a lynch mob. His ostentatious lifestyle and dalliances with white women, though nothing to do with the sport, only added to those audiences feeling like they were being needled by the boxer. It wasn't just that he beat white men in the ring, according to Theresa Runstedtler, the American University professor and author of *Jack Johnson, Rebel Sojourner*, it was "how he did it." During the time of Jim Crow, when Black folks who challenged the status quo were often met with violent retribution, Jack Johnson put on a show. He toyed with opponents and fought with taunting intentions. He played to the crowds and flashed his gold-toothed smile while throwing his punches, aiming not just to beat but to embarrass his rivals. Before his 1908 title fight against Tommy Burns, Johnson responded to the booing crowd by bowing and blowing kisses. When the opening bell rang, he talked to Burns directly. Per Runstedtler, "He would say, 'Poor little Tommy. Don't you know how to fight, Tommy? They said you were a champion.' So yeah, he was literally trash-talking."

Johnson wasn't necessarily trying to be a heel, but he didn't shy from the role, either. His heat was born of genuine (and malicious) hatred—hatred for who he was and for what he represented. But in that hatred, future Black boxers, like Muhammad Ali, would also see opportunity. Ali studied films of Johnson's old fights and even went to see *The Great White Hope*, a play based on Johnson's life, during its Broadway run. He recognized a lot of himself in Johnson.

As a young fighter, Ali similarly antagonized white America—with his brash confidence, his outspoken views, and his gall to live life on his own terms. But rather than silence himself in an effort to appease the masses, Ali appreciated the heat-generating potential of playing a societal heel—and of joining "that longer lineage of Black fighters who build their brand and sell tickets by being the guy that white people hate," as Runstedtler puts it.

Johnson wasn't the only "bad guy" from whom Ali would draw inspiration, either. In Gorgeous George, he'd similarly see a kindred spirit.

It was 1961 when their paths crossed during a joint promotional appearance. Ali was just nineteen—and still known as Cassius Clay—when he first heard George proclaim himself to be "the most beautiful wrestler who ever lived" and insist "that the fans only want to gaze upon my manly beauty." He was intrigued by the on-air performance and accepted an invitation to come watch George in the ring. He would not be disappointed. As the boos poured down on the Gorgeous One, Clay felt himself swept up in the passions of the arena crowd. He would later tell his camp, "Everybody was mad. I was mad! I saw fifteen thousand people coming to see this man get beat, and his talking did it. And I said, 'This is a *goooood* idea.'" After the show, Clay went backstage. Years later, Ali told an AP reporter, "I made up my mind after seeing Gorgeous George to make people angry at me."

Because the real competition is for attention.

The thing Ali most appreciated about Gorgeous George was that fans didn't just hate him. They *loved* to hate him. They "hated him with affection," as one writer noted in *Boxing Illustrated*. They paid good money and traveled from great distances because they wanted to see him lose. They thirsted for it—for that delicious moment early in every match when George's opponent got his mitts on that platinum blond hair and mussed it up something awful. The crowd would explode, while George threw a fit. (Wrestling has always had little ways like this to raise the stakes and emotional payoffs of a given contest, like fighting a loser-leaves-town match or battling over a briefcase that holds a title shot. George took advantage of this trope by risking what he valued most: his hair. In those "hair matches," he'd agree to put his beloved locks on the line, promising to shave his head should he lose. Which he eventually did.)

Like Jack Johnson (but for very different reasons), George tormented audiences by his very presence—not just in his deeds, but also in his being. And the more heat he got—the bigger crowds he drew—the further he expanded America's imagination about the possibilities of being a villain. Says Capouya, "Everybody saw that this became the currency, the coin of the realm. This is the way to become more of a star."

For Ali, who would soon deem himself "the greatest" and "as pretty as a girl," none of this was a put-on. As an amateur, he would knock on neighborhood doors to stir up interest in his Friday-night fights. He'd boast about tussling with the toughest kids in town and even prophesize about one day becoming the world's heavyweight champion. Jonathan Eig sees Ali's encounter with Gorgeous George being akin to Bob Dylan "recognizing something of himself in Woody Guthrie, and then adding to it." He says, "When you combine [Ali's understanding of Jack Johnson] with his conversation with Gorgeous George, it suddenly clicks. This Gorgeous George thing is kind of an act. It's kind of a stunt. But it taps into the same thing that Jack Johnson was generating without trying. I can put those two together, and I've got gold. It's a moneymaker."

After all, the louder you are, the more everyone wants to shut you up.

———————

SURPRISING AS IT may seem now, when the UFC's weekly press conferences are reliable fiestas of trash talk that spill onto social media and beyond, the MMA scene was fairly sedate in its early days, dominated by values like honor and respect, which grew out of the individual martial arts on which the sport was built. The idea of kicking up some ballyhoo or selling a fight via trash talk was pretty much unheard of. But when a fighter named Chael Sonnen started to antagonize stars like middleweight champion Anderson Silva around 2010, he was rewarded almost instantly, receiving not only outsized media coverage, but also a title shot—and others took notice. Sonnen is rightly credited as the first person to meaningfully introduce heel tactics to the UFC. But as veteran referee Herb Dean tells me, there was at least one man who was talking aggressive mess years before Sonnen wormed his way to the top of a fight card—and he may be the wildest heel that no one has ever heard of. His name is Josh Dempsey.

Or actually, his name is Josh Gormley. That's his given name, at least.

"I'm a Dempsey, bro," he tells me, when we speak on the phone. "Jack Dempsey was my grandpa."*

According to Gormley/Dempsey—whom I will refer to as Dempsey from this point forward—his parents hid this fact from their son because they were practicing Jehovah's Witnesses and didn't want him to become a fighter. But boxing bloodlines or not, there was no stopping him: he was built for this. While still in high school, Dempsey would stand six-foot-five and weigh in at 230 pounds. As a junior, in the spring of 1990, he won the California state heavyweight wrestling title for West Torrance High School. And as a senior, the *LA Times* would write of him, "Forget about winning. At this point, surviving a wrestling match against Josh Gormley is worth high-fives and hugs."

Soon thereafter, he started punching people for a living.

Dempsey spent most of the '90s as a professional boxer, fighting twenty-three times and earning nineteen wins, nearly all of them by knockout, before deciding to hang up his gloves. He says, "I was talking funny; I was shaking. I retired from boxing because I was taking too many head shots, you know?" Whether or not ditching the boxing ring in favor of life as a pro-wrestling and MMA aspirant lessened his risk of head trauma may be debatable, but that's what

---

* As best I can tell, this is not true.

he did. Dempsey was one of the earliest pupils at Rick Bassman's Ultimate University wrestling school, where he competed under the name J.D. Dempsey and was a classmate of John Cena's. Says Bassman, "His catchphrase was, 'Who's your daddy?' so he was kind of known as Who's Your Daddy Dempsey. I think we even made a T-shirt for him." In 2001, Dempsey debuted at King of the Cage, an early mixed martial arts promotion. That's where Herb Dean crossed paths with him—and, well, he obviously made an impression.

Twenty years later, Dean still remembers the smack-talking brawler as being a disruptive force. "It was strange," he says. "In our MMA scene, the California scene that was developing in the late '90s and early 2000s, guys were not talking much trash. Then this one guy showed up and started talking trash to everybody. 'Yeah, I'm going to knock him out, and I'm going to knock you out, and then I'm going to do this.' It was kind of a shock."

There was a method to his madness. As a boxer, he let his fists do the talking. But now, as he started a new career in a fledgling sport, he felt like his dreams of being a fighter were slipping away. He needed to find a way to stick out—and to stick around. "In MMA, I changed the whole thing up. I went like, 'I'm here to make a statement. I'm here to knock every motherfucker out,'" he says. "I didn't want to not be a fighter. I wanted to make my name known, so I started talking shit."

But that was just a warm-up.

Only months after first appearing at King of the Cage (a fight he lost in a split decision), Dempsey, who bears a passing resemblance to Ethan Hawke, if the actor were to mainline creatine and get punched in the face for a few years, found himself with a chance to compete in an upstart Japanese promotion known as Pro Wrestling Zero-One. The way professional wrestling works in Japan, Dempsey tells me, is that some of the matches are real (what are known as "shoots," in wrestling lingo) and some are not (which are known as "works"), and the crowd is not supposed to know the difference. "They bet on that shit, so it's got to look fucking real," he says. "You're fighting a work, but you're still getting your ass kicked." For his first match, Dempsey was to take on Naoya Ogawa, a Judo world champion who had earned a silver medal at the 1992 Summer Olympics. And he was supposed to lose.

He was no patsy, though.

"I beat his ass," says Dempsey. "I beat his ass the whole fight, and then I let him armbar me at the end." So he lost, like a good soldier. But Dempsey wasn't done making his statement. After the fight, he attacked Ogawa in his own corner. "I just went crazy. I was swinging on everybody. I was talking shit, spitting." He didn't know how the Japanese crowd was going to react, how this would go over. "I took a chance," he says. "I went crazy because I was trying to stay in Japan, trying to get seen, so they'd want me back."

It worked.

"They loved it," he says. "Next thing you know, I was fucking killing it in Japan."

Dempsey was booked on bus tours to fight across the country. Wherever he went, he continued to push the envelope of abuse. He broke cameras, spit on fans, screamed in people's faces. "I just took it to the next level," he says. His biggest opportunity would come in July 2002, when he was asked to fight Musashi, a Japanese kick-boxing star, in a K-1 match at the Fukuoka Dome, which held about fifty thousand people. "To this day, it was the craziest experience of my life. We'd walk through crowds. The girls would throw their bras and underwear at me. It was nuts." It was also the biggest platform he'd yet received to showcase his newfound shit talk. At the press conference before the fight, Dempsey showed up in a suit, designer sunglasses, and a Musashi collector's doll dangling from his zipper— "like a dick hanging out," he laughs—and made a beeline for his opponent, pushing him, trying to fight right then and there. "I made a big spectacle. They couldn't believe it. I just was really going over the top."

Part of his appeal to Japanese crowds, Dempsey speculates, was how countercultural he was in the country at that time. He brought a brash fuck-you attitude to a culture defined by politeness and respect: he was transgressive, a natural heel. "They really weren't down with that shit," he says. "They don't like disrespect. I came with the disrespect, bro." But he also suggests a strain of anti-Americanism could have been at play. "They treat us really good, and they host us really well, but they fucking hate us," he says. "They want to beat an American's ass."

Whatever the reason, Dempsey's antics seemed to be accepted, by and large. He tells me how he would get the crowds to chant with him, "Fuck Japan, fuck Japan!"

Bassman, the founder of Ultimate Pro Wrestling and Dempsey's former teacher, spent time in Japan, as well, where he was working with Zero-One. "One thing I remember about Josh is he didn't have much of a filter, that's for sure," he says. The other thing he remembers are Dempsey's arena entrances. They weren't planned. He wouldn't be on the microphone, just shouting at the top of his lungs to the Japanese crowds as he made his way to the ring. He'd yell, "I'm here to drop the bomb!"

As in, the nuclear bomb.

(Talk about personal issues.)

"It was pretty awesome," says Bassman. "I mean, I know Josh. He has no desire to bomb millions of people, but when he came out and did it, man, it's like, 'Oh my God, this guy is in full-on psycho believable mode.'" And the fans took offense. "It wasn't the kind of thing where the fans were laughing." But that was the point—to find a sensitive spot, and then blow right through it. "Here's the thing," adds Bassman. "If you're a bad guy or a heel, and they don't boo you, you're doing a really bad job. If you're going to be a heel, you *want* to be hated. That means you're getting over."

Or as Sonnen says, "Boos are a heel's cheer."

EVERYBODY HATES DUKE University—especially its men's basketball team. Ever since Christian Laettner laced up his stomping shoes for the legendarily pucker-faced Coach K, the Blue Devils have somehow mastered the art of recruiting an endlessly replenishing stream of players who give off an effortless air of pretension with extremely punchable faces.

In the public imagination, they are villains, perfectly cast.

Still, Shane Battier and his Blue Devil brethren didn't hear a lot of trash talk from opposing players during games, he tells me; it was only when they were surrounded by crowds in rival arenas that things got nasty.* "Fans loved, loooved, *looooooved* to talk," he says. "And that was part of the fun. We used to love going into Cole Field House and going into the Dean Dome because we knew we would get it from everybody." Battier recalls playing one year against the Maryland Terrapins, a bitter rival, and noticing the fans had gone so far as to print a bunch of T-shirts that read *Fuck Duke.* "You saw grandmas wearing it and little kids wearing it, and we were like, 'Aw, this is great!'"

The intensity of competing on the road, as the object of the fans' ire, was part of the appeal of playing for Duke, Battier assures me. "That was one of the selling points," he says. "That's something I still miss, going into an opposing arena and knowing these people hated me. You learn to embrace it." Battier recognized the boos for what they were—heat—and understood the alternative to be far worse. He explains, "The opposite of love isn't hate. It's apathy. If you're not evoking an emotion, you're not making an impact. That's scarier than being hated."

Because it means you don't matter.

Warren Sapp has a similar perspective. The athletes that want to make a real dent in their sports have no choice but to step into the brightest and harshest lights, he says. To accept every manner of challenge, regardless of how high the stakes might be raised, or how tense an environment. "If they don't recognize you as one of the

---

* While out in Las Vegas for the 2019 NBA Summer League—an off-season tournament with relatively little at stake—I was genuinely surprised at the full-throated vitriol and lusty boos that met former Duke star Grayson Allen, then on the Memphis Grizzlies, every time he touched the ball.

motherfuckers that they want to see go down," he says, "you ain't that guy."

When LeBron James left his hometown Cleveland Cavaliers to form a superteam in Miami, he found himself cast in the unfamiliar role of sports villain, and he did his best to embrace being "that guy." He sneered; he played angry; he egged on the booing crowds and gestured for more. According to basketball journalist Howard Beck, it's not unusual for athletes to put on these kinds of character performances. "I learned early on that who you are on the court does not represent who you are in real life, for most guys," he says, citing longtime Lakers forward Rick Fox, who'd undergo a seismic transformation when stepping between the lines, as an example. "Rick Fox was one of the nicest guys in the locker room, and he was the ultimate Jekyll and Hyde." Former basketball pro Marc Jackson, who was never afraid to run his mouth* and whose career spanned more than a decade and most of the globe, tells me he specifically thought of himself as stepping into the character of a heel before games, especially when he played overseas, and would use the opportunity of pregame introductions to turn his back on the opposing team. In those moments, he imagined himself to be not on a basketball court but in a fighting cage, and he'd bounce on his legs and shake out his arms in a warm-up routine he copped directly from UFC champion Tito Ortiz. When fans screamed for him to turn around and show some respect, he'd just stare them down. "I was absolutely being a character," he says.

And yet, not everyone is meant to be a heel.

During his second season in Miami, LeBron James went out of his way to say he was hanging up his black hat—was done embracing the role of the bad guy, regardless of how other people may continue to feel about him and his decision to take his talents to South Beach. "It basically turned me into somebody I wasn't," he said.

---

* As a first-year player in the NBA, Jackson talked so much crap that Dirk Nowitzki marveled during a game, "You sure do talk a lot of trash for a rookie."

Of course, for many folks, that's the whole point: they adopt a competitive persona to become somebody else, somebody they wouldn't normally be, in the same way certain players cultivate dislike (if not actual hate) for their opponents because it will be easier to feel justified doing the occasionally vicious things required in service of winning, like sliding with your spikes up to disrupt a double play, delivering a hard hit or foul, or saying something that might tear at another person's soul. "I mean, why do you see dehumanization processes in wartime? Why do people do that? Because you want people to do things that people normally wouldn't do," says University of Rochester psychologist Jeremy Jamieson.

But here's where we get into questions of self—of where a person ends and where his or her persona begins—and that's where things can get really slippery. It was exactly this kind of blurring of identity that plagued Gorgeous George in his later years. As the wrestler's fame and fortune grew—and he further insinuated himself into the pop-cultural fabric of America—the man behind the act, George Wagner, seemed to almost recede from existence. Increasingly, Wagner would stay in character even when he wasn't in the ring. At one point, he even told his children, "Don't call me Daddy anymore. Call me Gorgeous." Which is not only creepy, but also deeply sad. Those who knew the man best gave up hope that Wagner—who would legally change his name to Gorgeous George—would ever return. When his first wife, Betty, informed him that their marriage was over, he swore he'd change—he'd cut out the drinking and become a more present father. To which she responded, "You've changed enough."

It's a cautionary tale. George Wagner became Gorgeous George. But in time, Gorgeous George became George Wagner, too. We become who we allow ourselves to be.

———

THE WAY JOSH Dempsey talks about his time in Japan, it sounds like a movie. Like one of those hallucinogenic montage scenes, in which his face stays in sharp focus in the foreground, as the rest of the picture softens and swirls with a frenzy of sounds and flashing images. The ding of an opening bell. A screaming crowd. The neon lights of nightlife. The detritus of hotel rooms. Of tiny booze bottles. Of pills and women, of men he thinks are women. More booze. Partying with pro wrestlers. Manic and muscled. Men who like to fight. To shoot up. The crash of knuckle on bone, on bone, on bone. The pace quickening like a bullet train. The noise becoming oppressive. Everything blurring together. His eyelids drooping. But no time for sleep. Time for another show. To party. More pills. To do it again.

I'm here to drop the bomb!

That's how it eventually felt for him, too, Dempsey says. Like a movie. Like he was there, but not really. Like he was watching himself instead from a psychic remove. He was a far cry from the guy who used to step into the boxing ring stone-cold sober. Who was up to train every morning at 4:30 a.m. Who was married, had a family. Coached youth soccer and baseball. But when he hung up the boxing gloves, Dempsey started running with a new crowd. He picked up new habits. Started talking shit. That was a gateway to Japan; the weed was a gateway to everything else. "Next thing you know," he says, "fucking, I lost control."

At first, Dempsey's bad-guy act—which included all manner of "really fucking aggro shit," as he puts it, like breaking cameras, spitting in people's faces, and attacking fellow fighters and fans—was just for show. It was to secure his place on future fight cards. It was a character. But the longer he spent on the road and the more drugs he fed into his system, the more the line between movie and real life began to fade. At some point, he suspected it wasn't actually an act at all—or he was losing his grip on which part was which. Dempsey barely recognized the man he'd see looking back at him in hotel mirrors and in the reflection of bus windows, as he rode to his next gigs. "I wasn't proud of myself," he says.

As a lapsed Jehovah's Witness, Dempsey had abandoned his faith but still believed in a higher power—but that was part of the problem.

The religious lessons of his youth were permanently seared inside his head, and he was now convinced the God of his parents was going to strike him down for his rapidly expanding list of sins. "When I got on drugs, bro, I was so scared. I felt like God was going to kill me. I thought I was going to die," he says. "I'm going to die because of the drugs I'm doing. I'm going to die because I'm partying. I'm going to die because I'm cheating on my wife. I'm going to die." Dempsey was so scared of God, in fact, that fear itself became almost meaningless. He knew he was a dead man, and he figured, what the fuck? Might as well speed things along. "I was trapped in hell," he says of the cycle of drugs and shame that came to define his time in Japan. "I just tried to die partying. I didn't want to feel no more. I didn't want to be scared no more."

In a way, he got his wish.

Talking shit didn't cause Dempsey's downward spiral, but it gave him an easy outlet for his negative intentions, his hatefulness, his self-loathing. "I hated the world, and I wanted the world to know I hated them," he says. It allowed him to continuously spin the wheels of chance like a Russian roulette chamber, to see if he'd ever reach his limits—or instead just meet his end. The "aggro shit" was decidedly not for show anymore, and the boundary between movie and real life evaporated completely. The cameras kept rolling. The bad guy took over. Willing and even wanting to die, Dempsey was freed from mortal fears and, in some ways, from the concept of consequence altogether. As a result, he was always down to throw. Not that he got into many actual fights, he tells me. "Everyone is punks, bro. Nobody wants to fight me."

It wasn't that he was fearless; he simply had an absence of fear. "I was more scared of God than anybody else, and I really felt like I was dead," he says. "I would look you in the eyes and I said, 'Listen, I don't give a fuck, bro.' For real." Those who found themselves physically challenged by Dempsey could see he was serious. As a fighter, that had to be respected. But even among his colleagues and party companions, there was only ever an uneasy peace. As he says, "They liked me, but they didn't like me. They were nervous to be around me. I was a time bomb."

That time bomb finally went off when Dempsey returned to the US.

As a teenager, Dempsey had run with a crew of dudes, whom he describes as "crooks." But those crooks had also been the ones to help him get on his feet as a fighter when he was first starting out. They managed his affairs and gave him a place to stay when he escaped from his parents' home. It shouldn't be surprising, then, that Dempsey had dabbled in some unsavory activity over the years—selling dope here and there, mostly. But this was different. When Dempsey got back from Japan, he was confronted by the unwelcome realities of a broken marriage, a dimming combat-sports career—which no amount of shit talk was likely to revive—and no real job prospects. The lifelong brawler wasn't done swinging, though. He entered what he calls "gangster mode."

He says, "I started robbing and cheating and stealing. I fucking went to the streets."

It's not entirely clear what happened in the days and months that followed Dempsey's arrival on American soil—but it's safe to say: nothing good. According to the California Department of Corrections and Rehabilitation, Dempsey—known to them as Gormley—was in and out of prison four times (for a total of almost four years) from August of 2004 to February of 2011. As he tells it, the legal trouble started when his ex-wife emptied his bank account. In need of money, he went to see about collecting an old debt. "This guy owed me five thousand bucks for a long time, and so I went to his house. I broke his door down, beat him up, and took his shit," he says. Which, as it turns out, was behavior that didn't go over as well with the local police as it did with Japanese fight fans. "I went to prison, bro," he says. "They charged me with home invasion, robbery, mayhem, all kinds of shit."*

Only once he was behind bars did Dempsey reach his limits.

---

* A public records search shows he was charged with burglary in June 2004.

"I'm going to tell you the truth. I didn't talk shit," he says of his time in prison. "Because I'm not a killer, bro. Those guys are straight killers. They don't play. They are into drama. They like it when someone . . ." Dempsey trails off. His silence implies, *you know*. He says, "It gives them something to do. They don't give a fuck about killing nobody."

Now that he had no choice but to be sober, he didn't want to die. "Once you are sober, you think completely different," he says. During his time inside, Dempsey kept his mouth shut and his head down. He followed the rules. He did calisthenics. Read books, wrote letters. "I really, really stayed focused on trying to be a better person," he says. Today, Dempsey is living in Florida, working as a trainer. When he and I first speak, he tells me he's two years sober and almost ten years out of prison. Despite a slew of traffic violations in that time, things are going well: he's remarried and has taken up meditation. He's even coaching Little League again. "I do shit right," he says. "I don't lie. I don't cheat. I don't steal. I don't do drugs. I say my prayers. I'm all positivity, bro. All light. I'm trying to be the best person I can be."

MATTERS OF SELF are never easy to untangle. For example, Christy Martin is actually Christy Salters—that's the former women's boxing phenom's real name—and Christy Salters is quite shy, she tells me. "I promise you, I'm very shy." Anyone who followed Martin's career in the mid-1990s would be excused for thinking otherwise. For a time, it seemed like she was everywhere—morning shows, Leno, the cover of *Sports Illustrated*, a guest appearance on *Roseanne*. Known as much for her thumping punches as her verbal provocations, she would sit at press conferences alongside guys like Mike Tyson, Héctor Camacho, and Ricardo Mayorga and tell her opponents exactly what was coming: they were going to get knocked the fuck out.

For Martin, trash talk has always been performative. It was part of who she was as a fighter, who she believed she needed to be—someone who was more assertive, more self-assured. "That's the competitive athlete in me," she says. "I've been talking shit since I was probably in junior high."

And she loved doing it—most of the time, at least.

At some point, after Martin signed with Don King and was earning higher-profile fights, she started to wonder if the words coming out of her mouth were still her own. Looking back on it now, she can say with certainty: they were not.

For two decades, Jim Martin was not only Christy Martin's husband, but also her coach, and more so than anyone else on the planet, including Christy herself, the mastermind behind the abrasive boxing persona the world came to know. "Martin was Martin," she says. "Martin was Jim Martin." As a trash-talker, Jim wanted Christy to traffic in insults and put-downs. The worst of it, from Christy's perspective, was when he'd instruct her to disparage opponents by questioning their sexuality. Christy would push back. She'd tell him, "Jim, you want me to say this negative stuff about these women that are clearly homosexual. I'm telling you what it's going to do. It's going to open up the door and somebody from my past is going to pop up." He knew she was gay* but didn't care; he insisted. "In Jim's mind, I needed to say that," she says. "My mouth moved, but his words came out."

She hated herself for it.

That dynamic was indicative of a deeper rot within their relationship. Nearly a quarter-century older than his wife, Jim was as controlling outside the ring as he was within it—and abusive, too. He'd constantly tell Christy the world was against her, fight fans were against her, her family was against her, and he was the only one she could trust. Mostly, the abuse was emotional (and financial), but it could get physical, too. The worst of it came in November 2010, when Christy finally had enough: she was done pretending to be someone she was not and told Jim she was leaving him for a former girlfriend.

---

* Martin is now married to former boxer Lisa Holewyne, whom she first encountered in the ring in November 2001.

Jim responded by stabbing Christy repeatedly in the chest, beating her, and slicing off a section of her leg before eventually shooting her point-blank with her own gun.

Incredibly, she survived.* But she still bears the scars from that time. All of them.

"Even though it's been ten years, those mental scars are hard," she tells me, and her voice seems to shrink through the phone line as we speak. She hears it, too. "I'm afraid," she says. "I can hear it in my own voice. This is really who I am. Kind of sucks."

Christy Salters does not like Christy Martin. She describes her as "an arrogant ass" and "pretty much an asshole." And yet, the former boxer can't help but admire her alter ego, too—her brashness, her confidence. At times, she even wishes she could be more like her. "If I could be a little more confident, truly, it would be better. I would be better," she says. "But is that the kind of person I want to be? Nah, nah, nah."

Don't get the wrong idea: this coal miner's daughter is still no pushover. But Christy Salters *knows* she's not Christy Martin.

That's a good thing.

---

* Jim Martin was sentenced to twenty-five years in prison in 2012.

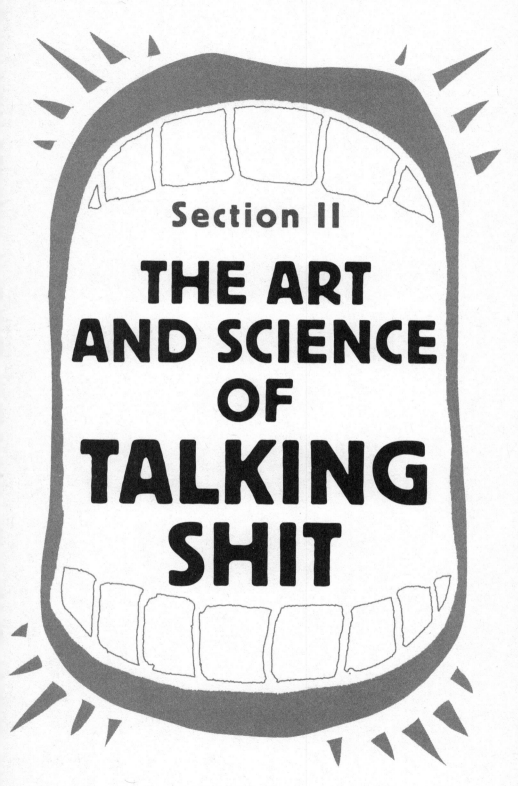

Section II

THE ART
AND SCIENCE
OF
TALKING
SHIT

Chapter 4

ARE YOU A KANGAROO?

THE FIRST TIME Phil Taylor saw Gary Payton play basketball, the NBA legend—a college senior at the time—was literally trash-talking the air. It was the end of practice, and Taylor, on assignment for the *National* sports newspaper, waited as Payton went through his final shooting drills, talking a whole lot of noise . . . to nobody, in particular.

Put your hand down. You can't stop this.

Too late. Take the early bus and get here quicker next time.

Don't even turn around. You know it went in.

Ooh, another one. How'd that feel?

Despite Payton's already growing reputation for in-game chatter, the sportswriter didn't know what to make of the young point guard and still marvels about it decades later: "I was just like, 'He is talking to nobody!'"

For many trash-talkers, the goal behind their verbal assaults is to put psychological pressure on an opponent—to turn the rhetorical screws on that person and make him more acutely feel the stresses of competition; to add mental stress to what are already serious physical demands. When Payton entered the NBA, no one in the league was as relentless with his in-game antagonism—as committed to the loudmouthed craft—as the man who once taunted air. Taylor would hardly be the last person stunned by Payton's volubility. In the middle of his second game as a professional—he was drafted in 1990 by the Seattle SuperSonics—Detroit Pistons superstar Isiah Thomas picked up the ball in the middle of the court and gawked at the gabbing rookie in disbelief. "He was talking so much trash," says Thomas. According to longtime Portland Trailblazer Damon Stoudamire, Payton's talk knew no bounds. Per Stoudamire: "This dude would follow you to the parking lot if he could." Cheryl Miller, the Hall of Fame hooper and former NBA sideline reporter, tells me Payton is "the most intrusive human being on this planet," while former Sonics teammate Michael Cage perfectly captured the mental and emotional fatigue of competing against him when he said, "When you're done, you just want to go find a library or something, someplace totally silent."

It wasn't just the nonstop nature of Payton's chatter. It was his hounding, hands-on defense and the infuriating way he'd manage to disparage your game even when you were succeeding against him. "If a guy scored on him, he would talk trash," says Taylor. *I hope somebody got footage of that shit, man, because you* know *you ain't going to do that again.* It was the way he'd chew his gum and bare his teeth, the way he'd cock his head and stick out his jaw—what veteran NBA reporter J.A. Adande calls his "presentation"—and then spit out some truly dismissive provocation or just some nonsensical shit, like threatening to hoist a jumper from the wrong side of the court. *Dude, I will pull up from seventy-five feet!* "He was just so cocky," says Taylor. "He was so sure of himself at such a young age."

Payton had a way with words, too. In contorting the English language to his competitive purposes, he somehow transformed the simple act of speaking into a kind of performance art. Everything just sounded different coming out of his mouth. "He would make up phrases and terms or change something with the pronunciation," remembers Adande. Payton also had a nickname for everyone—players, coaches, executives, trainers, whomever—which revealed what George Karl, who coached Payton for seven years in Seattle and had a courtside seat for countless games and practice sessions, calls his "ways of seeing things." Karl explains, "Instead of calling the referee a referee, he'd call them *mayor* or *governor*. 'Who made *you* boss?'" In his book *Black Planet: Facing Race During an NBA Season*—a season-long meditation on race, the NBA, and Gary Payton, in particular—David Shields muses that "sometimes I think he is a machine meant solely for the production of language." And while that language may not have made complete sense on occasion—"I could not understand what he was saying," Sam Perkins, who spent six seasons as Payton's teammate, has admitted—Payton always got his message across: he was coming for you, ready or not.

———

IN MANY WAYS, talking trash was Gary Payton's inheritance. The son of Al Payton, a man known as Mr. Mean throughout Oakland, California—it even said so on his license plate—Gary was an apt pupil of his father's many lessons, which often centered on toughness and respect. Per Payton, "I got good at talking trash for one reason and one reason only. Because I saw my father do it so often in the streets." Mr. Payton would also talk from the sidelines, as a youth coach in the Oakland Neighborhood Basketball League. It was the same attitude he wanted to instill in his kids. He'd tell Gary in particular: "If they talk shit to you, talk back to them."

Al Payton was hard on his son. He never gave Gary the satisfaction of a compliment, while the threat of punishment always hung overhead. When Gary started acting up in school, his dad showed up to class to set him straight. Early magazine profiles of Payton refer to a turning point in his sophomore year, when his dad embarrassed him in front of his classmates. According to Mr. Payton, "I kind of spanked him in front of everyone"; according to Gary, "Wasn't spank-ing. That's a beating." The previous year, a former classmate tells me, Mr. Payton did almost the same thing: "He came up to the school for the whole week. He sat in classes, came to practices. I've never seen nothing like that in my life." Gary had to endure his teammates clowning him—*Man, you got your daddy coming up here?!*—but no one messed with Mr. Mean, who made clear to his son there could be a cost to flapping his gums, whether in school or on the court. He told Gary, "If you trash-talk and you can't back it up, and you come home and you whooped, I'm gonna whoop you, too."

On the one hand, he was instilling ideas about courage and accountability. But growing up in Oakland in the 1970s and '80s, where drugs and violence brutalized the neighborhood and where perceptions mattered, he was also offering seminars in survival. "One of the things I always noticed, because I was good in every sport—it was rough and it wasn't nothing but trash talk, everybody wanted to be hard," says Bernard Ward, a onetime athletic standout, who played for Mr. Payton and shared a backcourt with Gary in the ninth grade. "I think it's a defense mechanism. You had to be like that out here just to survive. If people see you on the street, and you're weak, they're going to take advantage of that. Know what I'm saying? Even if you ain't tough, you got to act like you tough." And talking trash was a way to act tough—to signal you were no pushover, couldn't be intimidated, were a threat to be taken seriously.

No one ever doubted the Paytons' toughness. "When I played, I liked to hurt people," the elder Payton once said. As a kid, Gary would travel to different neighborhoods around the city and chal-lenge players on their local courts. Even there, on alien asphalt, he would bring his swaggering verbal game, which broadcast a mes-sage of unblinking toughness. "You knew you had to do it or you'd be punked all the time," Payton has said. At times, Gary's mouth would get him into trouble, even as a preteen. Guys at the park would conspire to jump the young player—to rough him up and exact a physical toll for his big talk. To see how tough he really was. But Mr.

Payton wouldn't allow that. He'd intervene and tell them to take it up with him instead. And then, as Payton puts it, "my dad's suddenly in the middle of a brawl on the playground."

Official games weren't much better.

In high school, as a star guard for Skyline High, Payton competed in the Oakland Athletic League (OAL), which infamously played in the afternoon instead of the evening and typically under the surveillance of armed guards. "How crazy is that? We had to play our high school games, varsity games, at 3:30 p.m. because of the violence and the stuff that was going on. A part of that was trash talk," says Ward, who played for a rival school. "I remember one year they banned the fans." Fred Noel, who coached Payton at Skyline, described the verbal battles in the OAL as being "as important as the game itself." He said, "There is a lot of taunting back and forth, a lot of putting my reputation against your reputation." It wasn't just the players that would talk. As Payton told *Sports Illustrated* in 1990, "The players were on you. The refs were on you. The stands were on you. You had to talk back or you were a sissy; you'd get run out of the league."

For Payton, trash talk was in the air and in his gene pool. It was an environmental and cultural imperative. But it was never perfunctory. As a child of only ten or eleven, he recognized his brash talk was already eliciting emotional responses from opponents on the playground—his father's sideline scuffles testified to that—and understood his words were doing more than communicating the neighborhood language of necessary machismo; they also held utilitarian value. If Payton could use his mouth to mess up another player's performance—to disturb or anger that player—that meant trash talk was a legitimate tool of competition. As Payton says of those early observations, "They started getting mad and they started changing their game. I was like, 'You're mad at me, but I am killing you.' I just said, 'This is what I'm going to do.' And I kept doing it." He did it in the playgrounds, where he built his name. He did it at Skyline, where he induced boneheaded fouls and sent rival players to the bench.

And he did it in college at Oregon State University, where he grew even more self-assured, more aggressive. Payton barked at opposing coaches (*Get somebody out here who can guard me! I'm going to tear his ass up!*) and terrorized their guards with that Oakland-grown bravado (*Man, why are you out here?!*). "That's how we grew up," says Ward, who attended some of his friend's college games. At times, Payton's collegiate opponents could seem to be almost panicking on the court. It was like they were under genuine attack and didn't know how to respond. Says Ward, "He had the other point guards so scared, man. He did the mental game on them."

———

TRASH TALK WASN'T always in Kevin Garnett's game the way it was with Payton's. NBA insiders describe a transformation in Garnett, the seven-foot forward who came into the league straight out of high school in 1995 and would go on to intimidate a generation of professional basketball players with his quick-tempered intensity. Two-time NBA All-Star and current San Antonio Spurs broadcaster Sean Elliott remembers his earliest impressions of Garnett, then a wide-eyed rookie. "The first time we played against KG, I'll never forget, he walked on the court, and he was this really skinny, this young kid. He was looking around like, 'Wow.' He was like, 'Oh, man.' Almost like he was enamored," says Elliott. Other teams tried to exploit that innocence, testing the rookie physically and mentally. Veteran players used their size and strength to bully Garnett, to push him around and bark dismissive things like, "He's not ready." Cheryl Miller has always found Garnett to be a curious case. "Kevin fascinated me," she says. "His first couple of years, he was a sweet guy. Quiet and everything else."

And then, per Miller: "Something snapped."

Garnett had formative experiences with smack talk that preceded his entry to the NBA, of course. There were the playground courts around his hometown of Greenville, South Carolina, and the kitchen of a local bar, where he took a job as a dishwasher and the back-of-house banter exploded each night like a busted pipe. More recently, there was his time at Farragut Career Academy in Chicago, where a high school assistant coach taught him to spot fear and hesitation in his opponents. "Nervous man," Garnett would say, when one such player entered the game.

Still, at his competitive peak, Garnett was sui generis in his on-court belligerence. "Kevin brought it to a different level. He was more aggressive in his taunting," says Bennett Salvatore, who started officiating NBA games in the 1980s and retired in 2015. Whereas Payton is often described as a mess of contradiction for his in-game demeanor—Phil Taylor says, "he was part intense competitor, trying to rattle you, and part comedian, class clown," while David Shields has noted Payton's "weird mix of threat and warmth"—Garnett was unflinchingly hostile and took an almost *Art of War* approach to upsetting his opponents. The epigraph to his autobiography reads, "He who angers you, owns you," a quote he attributes to himself. Garnett's disruptive efforts extended beyond the verbal realm: he'd tap opponents' legs, blow in their ears, and make other forms of annoying body contact, especially if attention was elsewhere, like when the ball was being brought up by the point guard. "He would kind of lean into them with his head. Not really fouling them, per se. But just making the slightest contact, and he'd be mumbling stuff," says former NBA referee Eli Roe, who spent eleven years working games in the league. "He would do that on throw-ins a lot, too."

His tactics weren't all designed to be under the radar. At times, Garnett aimed to deliver public humiliations. Steve Jones Jr. recalls a defensive sequence when he was a coach with the Brooklyn Nets in which Garnett was guarding the Orlando Magic's Channing Frye and he loudly yelled "I'm good" over and over and over, for about ten seconds straight. "'I'm good' means I don't need any help. I'm fine. He's not going to score," says Jones. It was a direct challenge to Frye, who pivoted, dribbled to his left, spun, pump-faked once, twice, three times, and then threw up an air ball. "He was yelling for what felt like forever. That was probably one of the greatest moments I've ever experienced."

Garnett, who had a tendency to talk shit in the third person ("This is what you're going to do, Kev")—or by talking *about* a person instead of directly to him—also availed himself of the captive audience inherent to free-throw situations, when players line up to battle for potential rebounds. Garnett would use these silent moments to monologue. "He would be going on about the player next to him, about how he's getting dominated, or whatever," says Roe. "But he's not looking at the guy, and the guy is obviously getting embarrassed. And he's exposing that to everyone." Blake Griffin, a six-time All-Star, has admitted the indirect nature of Garnett's trash talk was perhaps the most unsettling aspect. Per Griffin, "You knew he was talking to you, but he would never look at you, so it was like a weird—like, you couldn't look back at him, and you couldn't look away. It was just like a very intimidating thing." For many players, competing against Garnett presented an unusually stressful experience.

He could be outright mean, too.

That's what Brian Scalabrine remembers from his days playing alongside Garnett (and Paul Pierce, for that matter) with the Boston Celtics. "Those two were so demeaning to people," he tells me. They were constantly denigrating opponents. Saying things like: *How is this guy on the court? We won a championship last year, and now we're playing* this *guy? Isn't he in the G League?* It was Scalabrine's job to cosign whatever his teammates were saying, with peanut-gallery-style affirmations. "Garnett would be like, 'Why is this guy talking to me?'" he says. "I go, 'I know! I took like two months before I talked to you, and this guy is doing it in the middle of the game.'"

Sometimes Scal would take friendly fire, like when Garnett told an opponent, "I have a feeling you can't even guard Scalabrine. How are you on me?"

But he didn't take offense.

Even now, he chuckles at the memory. Says, "He was cold-blooded."

THE KEY FOR Gary Payton was this: his trash talk was never personal, even when it was personal.

And it was always personal.

More than anything, Payton wanted his opponents to feel the pressure of competing against him—to be anxious about it, even. He wanted their pulse to quicken or just to feel plain-old mad. To achieve that, he would talk about your game and what you could or couldn't accomplish against him. He would talk about your career prospects, and how you likely weren't going to make it, like he did with journeyman Jamie Feick when he said, "Man, you won't even be in the league next year." (According to Feick's teammates, that really hurt his feelings.) Hell, he would talk about absolutely anything—your mama, your daddy, whatever. "Gary didn't have a filter, and Gary certainly didn't have any boundaries," says Cheryl Miller. Payton cut close to the bone because he wanted opponents to stew on the aggressive nonsense with which he impugned and challenged them. He *wanted* to hurt their feelings. "It's not fun if you let a person get to you," Payton tells me when we sit down for an interview inside a locker room at Milwaukee's Fiserv Forum. He is here as a coach for the BIG3, the three-on-three summer basketball league backed by Ice Cube, which features rosters mixed with NBA graybeards and hoopers who didn't quite make it on the biggest stage but can still electrify the crowd in a streetball-style environment. Now in his fifties, Payton is a little thicker around the midsection and saltier in the stubble of his goatee, but the essence of the man who tormented so many players on the basketball court—who could find reason to shit-talk the air—remains surprisingly intact. The years have done little to smooth the gravel in his voice or to tame the curl of his upper lip that contorts even smiles into snarls.

He says, "A lot of players, they just took it personal, and then they wanted to take it against you."

In his verbal degradations, Payton was effectively daring opponents to come at him—to shut him up—and many couldn't resist the temptation. The noisy guard was infuriating, and opponents often responded impulsively, emotionally, because they were so eager to prove him wrong. They would start playing one-on-one basketball or take low-percentage shots. Or they'd swipe at Payton's dribble and pick up a careless foul. Or on the other end, they'd gather a head of steam and barrel into Payton, the defensive wizard, who would draw the charge. Part of the temptation for opponents was the relentlessness of Payton's jabbering—his mouth was like the eighth wonder of the world: he never stopped talking—and it would only increase "if he thought he was getting you off your game," according to George Karl. "He would just kill you with, 'You can't score on me. That shit doesn't work. You got to go home,'" says Karl, who adds that Payton's stifling, in-your-jock defense made his talk all the more potent—and aggravating. Sean Elliott remembers how desperate some players would become to make Payton eat his words: "I *got* to do something to shut this guy up."

But before long, the coach would be yelling at them, compounding their anger and frustration, or they'd find themselves on the bench and out of the game. That's when Payton would rub it in, when "he really made you feel bad," per Karl. He'd say, "Yeah, yeah. I'm in his head," Elliott tells me. Or he'd just walk over to where his victim was resting on the sideline and calmly ask: *How's it feel to sit over here?*

"They'll be mad, cussing. It just is what it is," Payton says with a shrug. "That's what I did a lot."

Mahmoud Abdul-Rauf, the former NBA player whose career was cut short after his national anthem protests in the mid-1990s and who now plays for Payton's BIG3 team, has been listening to our conversation and cuts in to tell me he quickly realized there was really nothing vicious about Payton's trash talk, regardless of tone or content. "I noticed it the first year we played," he says. "After the fact, I saw him in the hallway and"—he makes a hearty handshake gesture, like a glad-handing politician. "I knew then it was nothing personal." But it's easier for a player to remind himself of that in the afterglow of a game than in the heat of competition, and Payton had a whole bag of badgering tricks to harass, upset, and intimidate his opponents. To make the routine tasks of competition seem more difficult against him than they otherwise would.

Payton entered every game with a plan to "talk crazy," as he puts it, but his antics were almost never premeditated. Instead, he relied on his in-game instincts—honed on the Oakland playgrounds—to identify what line of attack would most disturb the equilibrium of an opponent. "It was coming off the dome," he says. In time, though, Payton accumulated mental files on pretty much all the league's top guards. "If you played against somebody enough, you know how sensitive they are," he says. "You know who you're talking to—what they can take and what they can't take. And then you know you've got him." Against Jason Kidd, for example, with whom he had a preexisting relationship and whom he had mentored as a young player in the Bay Area, Payton would give the cold shoulder. "I wouldn't even shake his hand before the games," he says. "And he'd be like, 'Man, what's wrong with you? What did I do to you?' And I wouldn't say nothing." Against Eddie Jones, who was also a friend, Payton would blow in his ear, "and he'd be like, 'Stop it, stop it!'" Another go-to tactic, per Payton, was to pseudo-encourage an opponent by saying, "Come on, pick your *motherfucking* game up," and then: "POW! Slap him on his ass hella hard."

He assures me, "That will get somebody mad."

ACCORDING TO KEVIN Garnett himself, the transformation in his verbal game—such as it was, since he'd always harbored an instinct to bark back*—wasn't a result of any personality change or the mentorship of older players. It was a function of recognizing the way his on-court behavior could diminish opponents in the course of competition. Per Garnett, "I started getting off on that." It was only then—when he saw his words having an in-game effect—that he fully embraced the signature array of antagonistic gamesmanship for which he'd become known. "Once I started seeing it actually help, *it was over.*"

Which seems both true and not the whole story.

As much as Garnett's smack talk and badgering presence discomforted those he played against, his trash talk might be better understood not as a series of one-off tactics, but as an ever-present manifestation of—and metaphorical fuel source for—the scowling intensity that informed everything he did on the court and some things he did off it, too.** There were the primal screams that followed dunks or defensive blocks, or even came during opposing shot attempts. *Get that shit outta here!* There was his refusal to ever *not* play, like the time he forgot to bring socks to an off-season pickup run and bled through his sneakers. Or the time he was relegated to the sidelines during a Celtics practice for mandatory rest but spent the whole session mimicking the actions of Leon Powe, who had taken his position. And then there was the way he redefined the phrase *leave it all out there*: as a high schooler, Garnett drained himself so completely at a predraft workout that he fell asleep when it was over, right there on the court. "His intensity is NBA famous," says

---

*   This instinct appears as early as his rookie season. In a 1996 profile in *Spin*, magazine writer Charles Aaron catches Garnett in a pseudo-back-and-forth with then head coach Bill Blair, after Garnett warns the writer that some team staffers might be checking out his ass. Blair says to KG, "What you worried about? You haven't got an ass to check out. Somebody give him some suspenders to hold up those shorts." Garnett's response: "Listen to that shit—old Captain No Ass trying to talk." But he only snaps back when the coach is safely out of earshot.

** Garnett once got so worked up while watching an episode of the reality-television program *Making the Band* that he punched a hole into the wall of his home.

Karl, who coached against KG for years. When Marc Jackson was with the Minnesota Timberwolves, he and Garnett used to talk so much trash in practice that some on the coaching staff wanted him to dial it down because his famously intense teammate could get too swept up in the intrasquad competition. Jackson says, "One of the older coaches would come to me like, 'Hey, Marc, don't talk trash to KG during practice, it gets him a little too hype.'" But Garnett wasn't having that. When he caught wind of those marching orders, he told the coach, "Get the fuck out of here, man! What do you mean, don't talk trash? That's what I do. I'm a trash-talker."

Throughout his career, no matter the setting, Garnett played like a loaded weapon. He was a seven-foot ball of raw nerves, a hair trigger of emotion just waiting for the lightest touch. Garnett had no patience for those who didn't match his level of competitive fanaticism. "He never had a funny side," adds Karl. On the court, Garnett was offended by friendliness, and he would give no grace to those who lined up against him. It didn't matter if he was playing an intrasquad scrimmage (former teammates talk about the "boot-camp-like" environment that Garnett cultivated during team practices) or if a younger opponent was confessing fan-boy-like admiration. That happened toward the end of a game against the Chicago Bulls, at the foul line, when Joakim Noah told Garnett he'd grown up idolizing him, and KG responded with an escalating series of verbal attacks and by saying, "Fuck you, Noah."

Meanwhile, Garnett's pregame frenzies were legendary. Before tip-off, he would work himself into a fever state of emotion, screaming to the stands and banging his head against the basket stanchion. "Everyone just stayed away from him," says longtime NBA columnist Jackie MacMullan. "He was just a lunatic who got himself all frothed up." Former players tell stories of Garnett talking shit to himself in the opening minutes of games, like his own personal hype man—*Come on, motherfucker!*—while MacMullan tells me that Garnett's coaches with the Boston Celtics would avoid him on the offensive end in the early going, for fear of what he would do.

"Doc Rivers wouldn't draw plays for him at the beginning of the game because he would just shatter the backboard," she says. "He was just so revved up. You didn't want to give him the ball the first five minutes."

Garnett made no apologies for his in-game ferocities. As he put it, "It's the way I play." All emotion and intensity, all the time. Which is why it's so easy to believe that Garnett didn't talk shit just because it was effective, but also because he needed it.

———

AN ATHLETE LIKE Garnett may be an extreme example, but he's far from alone. Babe Ruth has been described by the writer Rich Cohen as "one of those players who had to whip himself into a righteous fury to reach peak performance," while Maya Tamir, a psychology professor at the Hebrew University of Jerusalem who studies the instrumental benefits of emotional regulation, tells me about Yoel Razvozov, an Israeli politician and former judo champion who has said, "I try to enter fights with tears of fury." Former football player Bryan Cox would invent elaborate and horrible fantasies before he stepped onto the field. He'd imagine his wife being raped by a guy wearing the opposing team's jersey, or his kids being kidnapped with a ransom note left on that team's stationery, or he'd walk through the locker room naked, pretending he was about to step onto an auction block, where he would be sold into slavery. "Fucking racist!" he'd then scream at opposing white players. As Cox has explained, he subjected himself to these fabricated waking nightmares because he wanted to be emotionally charged up. He wanted to play with "madness."

Something you'll hear athletes and coaches say often is that emotions are to be avoided, that they represent a competitive vulnerability. "The more emotional you are, the worse decisions you're probably gonna make," says Jones. "Once that emotion sets in, anything could happen. It's almost like a ticking time bomb." By and large, he's correct—under stress, people lose the ability to think critically and

they act more impulsively; anger in particular can cut both ways[*]—
but it's also more complicated than that. According to John Raglin,
a professor of kinesiology at Indiana University, so-called negative
emotions like anger or fear are "adaptive, evolutionarily." He says,
"They're orienting emotions, and they are emotions that force you to
make decisions or to pay attention to your environment, internal or
external, because you have to act in one way or the other." This evolutionary mechanism can be manipulated for trash-talk purposes—
emotions become detrimental to one's performance when they hijack
a competitor's focus (more on this in the next chapter) or lead to
impulsive, poor, or unnecessarily risky decisions—but there's nothing *inherently* detrimental about playing with emotion. As Payton
tells me, "I was always emotional. People just couldn't handle the way
I was emotional."

Sports psychology has a framework that helps explain why some
athletes want to work themselves into a precompetition tizzy—or
into any specific emotional state, elevated or otherwise. It's known
as the individual zones of optimal functioning, or IZOF. Developed
by Russian psychologist Yuri Hanin, the IZOF model is based on
the idea that athletes will perform at their best when they are experiencing a personally appropriate level of anxiety. For some, that
level may be cartoonishly high, à la Garnett or Cox. For others, it
may be somnolently low, as seemed to be the case for KG's relaxed
and stone-faced rival, Tim Duncan, or for someone like the Turkish
weight lifter Naim Süleymanoğlu, who was known to sleep before
competitions. The key is that it's different for everybody. "There's this
old idea that a certain amount of anxiety is good, but too much or

---

[*]   This was unquestionably the case for Cox, who was frequently fined for his
    on-field behavior—in 1998, he claimed to have already been forced to pay
    more than $200,000; public records showed the figure to be $146,000, per
    the *New York Times*—and was at constant risk of losing control or drawing
    a penalty flag. In a single game against the Green Bay Packers in 1997, he
    got into two fights and earned three unsportsmanlike fouls.

too little is not," says Raglin. In that old conception, which many would recognize as the Yerkes-Dodson law, the effect of anxiety on sport performance was seen as an inverted U-shaped curve—and the prescription was for all athletes to find their way into that sweet spot in the middle, to achieve moderate anxiety. The Goldilocks of anxiety. The IZOF model, on the other hand, "paints a much more complex picture," per Raglin. "It suggests, quite controversially for a lot of sports psychologists, that there are athletes who really need—and do best with—not only high levels of anxiety, but a lot of negative emotion." For those athletes, negative emotion may be not only beneficial for reaching peak performance, but also necessary. "And when they don't experience that, that's when they're in trouble."

In the IZOF model, which offers us a new way to understand the competitive intensities of players like Payton and Garnett, among others, emotions are not considered to be positive or negative. They're deemed either useful or detrimental—optimal or dysfunctional—based on their utility in helping athletes achieve the requisite anxiety level to be in their optimal zone. "Maybe you need to be happy; maybe you need to be a little bit angry," says Edson Filho, associate professor of sport, exercise, and performance psychology at Boston University. "Every athlete has an emotional component that is related to being in the zone."

HERE IS PROBABLY a good time to explore what exactly we mean by anxiety.

"It gets complicated quick," laughs Mark Aoyagi, the codirector of sport and performance psychology at the University of Denver. As he explains it, there are two basic components to anxiety—what's happening in your head (cognitive anxiety) and what's happening in your body (somatic anxiety). Cognitive anxiety includes things like racing thoughts and the fear of future events, while somatic anxiety mostly describes physiological arousals, like fast breathing, increased heart rate, sweaty palms, and the feeling of needing to use the bathroom, among other things. The two components are connected. "It's commonly thought that we have cognitive anxiety and then we have a somatic response to that," says Aoyagi. "What we know now is that it can go either direction." In other words, it's possible for someone to be running on a treadmill and experience a panic attack, based on how that person interprets the physiological arousals that emerge as a result of that physical effort, like a rising heart rate. *Why is my heart racing? Oh, it's because I'm overwhelmed by nervousness! Ahhhh!*

It's also worth noting that optimal zones are not static. They vary not only by individual, but also by sport, and can even shift at different points of a competition or based on the requirements of a given task therein. The optimal activation level for a basketball player who is driving to the hoop, for instance, is very likely different than the optimal level when that person is throwing an in-bounds pass. There can be other factors, too. "I mean, weather, time of day, whether I had a good night sleep or not, whether I'm hungry or not—any condition you can put on a performance that's even tangentially related to the performance is going to impact what your zone of optimal functioning is," says Aoyagi.

Still, taking that nuance into account, it's fairly safe to assume that a player like Kevin Garnett regularly resided on a significantly higher end of the IZOF spectrum—that he needed to be more aroused, more anxious—than someone like Tim Duncan. According to Aoyagi, most people tend to be above their optimal zones and seek ways to lower anxiety levels rather than raise them. As such, Garnett's verbal (and generalized) aggression can be seen as serving a dual competitive purpose: it helped him get into his own zone of optimal functioning,* while potentially angering, intimidating, or otherwise agitating opponents to the point that they were knocked out of their peak-performance states—ideally, by exploding them through their zone's upper threshold, which could have particularly devastating

---

* Garnett has written about how trash talk "zapped me into a zone."

effects. "If a player can use trash talk to push someone beyond that threshold, they're really going to mess them up," says Aoyagi, who describes a relatively smooth curve of performance improvements up until that point. "Once you surpass your threshold, you have this dramatic decline in performance."

JOE ANDRUZZI PLAYED nine years in the NFL, starting more than one hundred games in that time. But Brett Favre tells a story about Warren Sapp effectively paralyzing the offensive lineman during a Monday night game in 1998, when Andruzzi was making his first-ever start. Before the Packers' opening snap, Sapp lined up across from the rookie, dropped to one knee, and said, "Joe, you picked the wrong night to make your first start." As Favre tells it, Andruzzi didn't even leave his stance when the ball was hiked. Sapp just ran right past him.

It's hard to believe that such a thing could happen on a professional football field, but I hear similar stories from other players. A defensive standout in the Canadian Football League, Charleston Hughes tells me he's done this to opponents on at least three occasions. The first time, he could barely believe it, as the ball was snapped and his hulking opponent remained motionless. Like, "doesn't move a muscle," per Hughes. It took half a beat for him to even realize what was happening. "I was watching the ball, but he was listening and watching me," he says. Hughes started laughing. "And I fucking destroyed the quarterback."

That's what can happen when people go above their optimal zone of arousal, per Aoyagi. "That's when you get into the fight-flight-or-freeze response," he says. "It's when you are flooded. It's when you cannot manage what is going on."

An evolutionary survival mechanism, fight, flight, or freeze is a deeply encoded stress response that's characterized by a cascade of hormones and physiological changes, which are designed to prepare the body for instant action. The response is involuntary, and it's triggered by perceived threats or dangers, like an attacking wild animal or, apparently, Warren Sapp. As the name suggests, when individuals enter the fight-flight-freeze response, they will either physically confront the threat if they believe they can overcome it (fight); run away from it if they believe they cannot (flight); or do nothing if they're not sure about their ability to overcome it, or if the threat is novel and they hope either the threat will go away or they can gather more intel about it (freeze). But while such a response has proven terrific for survival over the course of human history—because here we still are!—it's not so terrific in the course of competitive performance.

At its core, trash talk is the presentation of a challenge. It raises the stakes of competition by adding stress to an encounter and increasing the pressure on each player's performance. Gary Payton understood that, which is why he so openly vocalized the idea that his opponents would fail—that they didn't have what it takes. "Trash talk is a direct confrontation to your status," says Ashley Merryman, coauthor of *Top Dog: The Science of Winning and Losing*, about the science of competition in sports, business, and politics. And for some players, that kind of confrontation can create a potentially threatening situation.

As Jeremy Yip and his collaborators put it in their study of trash talk in the workplace, people often signal their intent to either cooperate or compete with one another in social interactions, and talking shit "signals an intention to compete fiercely," which not only highlights—or even increases—the demands of a competition, but also makes the prospect of losing that much less palatable. It should not be surprising, then, that trash talk is likely to cause activation on a biological level: anxiety spikes. "You have now introduced a threat. You have kind of thrown the gauntlet," as one sports psychologist who works with the military puts it to me. Personally, I can confess that, on the very few occasions when I have talked real trash during games of pickup basketball, saying something to the effect of, "He can't guard me, get me the ball," I have regretted it instantly because

I didn't enjoy the added pressure and I questioned my ability to back it up.

It's not my fault, entirely. When any kind of threat is introduced, "it pings our danger center, the amygdala, and the reptilian brain," explains Scott Goldman, a performance psychologist with the Golden State Warriors, who has previously served in similar roles for the Detroit Lions and Miami Dolphins, among other organizations. Trash talk taps into some of humanity's most primal instincts, as our brains are basically programmed to find threats lurking everywhere. "It's in our DNA to overestimate risk. It's this whole ancient function to scan the world and find danger," says Michael Gervais, a podcaster and psychologist who works with elite performers across the worlds of sports, music, business, and more. "This is a survival mechanism." And it can be deeply disruptive to performance.

But not always.

A THREAT DOESN'T have to be threatening. Even more important than whether we detect danger in our environment, and even more important than whether we experience an attendant anxiety spike—even more important than whether we *are* stressed, that is—is what we *tell ourselves* about that stress, about what it means. "The key component within all of this is, how do we interpret these things?" says Aoyagi. "How do we make sense of these things?"

Just imagine being in a locker room before a game, backstage before a performance, or in a classroom before a final exam. Can you imagine feeling nervous? Your heart rate going up, your breathing getting fast, your palms starting to sweat, your stomach panging like you need to poop? That's anxiety—and that's a good thing because this anxiety (or stress) is providing your body with the activation it needs to optimize performance. To respond to a potentially threatening situation. "The stress response, it's a resource," says Jeremy Jamieson, a professor of psychology at the University of Rochester, whose research focuses on the impact of stress on decisions, emotions, and performance. "It's helping you address demanding situations. It's getting blood out to where it needs to go. When you're being challenged, you want to be stressed. If you're not stressed at all, that means you're not sufficiently activating. You are not sufficiently aroused to optimize what you should be performing with."

This anxiety is, in a word, adaptive. Or at least it can be.

Some may balk at the idea that stress is good because we've been taught the opposite: that stress is bad—something to be feared and avoided. "In our culture, stress is seen as a negative," says Jamieson. "But stress and distress get conflated. When people say, 'I'm so stressed,' they don't mean, 'I'm experiencing a lot of sympathetic arousal.' They mean, 'Something bad is happening.'" But we set ourselves up to fail—and especially so in the face of confrontational trash-talkers like Payton and Garnett—when we misunderstand our physiology in this way. When we interpret our heightened anxiety (racing heartbeats, sweaty palms, etc.) as evidence of a threat and reason to be afraid, we compound the problem and risk jolting ourselves into a dysfunctional state, just as someone can experience panic from nothing more than running on a treadmill.

The meaning we make about stress in high-pressure moments is critical. When we experience physiological activation, our brains do a kind of instant assessment: they take an inventory of our perceived resources versus the demands of the situation. "Anything that's increasing the uncertainty or anything that's increasing the demand, that can definitely throw someone off," says Jamieson. Of course, those perceived resources and demands can be different from one person to the next. For example, a trained concert pianist waiting to go onstage would likely feel fewer demands on her impending performance than I would in that person's shoes, since I do not know how to play piano. Or even consider the difference between two basketball players going to the free-throw line: a player like Stephen Curry, who rarely misses, would surely feel confident in his abilities to succeed, while a player like Giannis Antetokounmpo would have more reason for self-doubt, since he's had stretches of poor free-throw shooting throughout his career.*

Regardless of the specific situation, though, a performer will have one of two divergent stress responses as a result of that activation. They will enter either a challenge state, in which they believe they possess the resources to meet the demand, or a threat state, in which they don't. It's the difference between feeling excited to take on a task or dreading it. "Exact same physiological state," says Aoyagi, referring to the underlying arousal (the increased heart rate, the fast breathing, and so on), "but how I interpret it has a huge downstream impact on the experience of that." In fact, in his lab studies, Jamieson has found that people can tip the scales from potential threat states toward challenge by doing nothing more than *telling themselves* that stress can be good—that their elevated physiology is a sign of being excited, not scared. "Changing these cognitive factors upstream, it changes the downstream response we are having in our body," he says. "The body's response is literally coming from that, from our stress appraisals." From simply telling ourselves that we can handle it—that we have the resources to meet the demand. That Kevin Garnett's in-game hostilities are no reason to be afraid.

In a challenge state, a person's heart rate goes up, but so does his heart rate variability, which is a measure of efficiency. His peripheral vasculature dilates, which allows that hard-pumping blood to flow easily to the body's extremities. "Blood rushes to our limbs so we can do something, so we can respond to the challenge," says Aoyagi. According to Jamieson, the challenge response is particularly helpful for "proceduralized movements," by which he means those things that have been practiced again and again, which have effectively

---

* During the 2021 NBA Playoffs, opposing fans latched on to this fact— and the fact that Giannis takes a long time at the line, which can result in a violation—by loudly counting up during his free-throw attempts. What the fans were doing, effectively, was highlighting the demands of the situation and hoping to disrupt his routine.

become automatic, like swinging a baseball bat, putting a golf ball, or throwing a dart. "The more activated we are, the better we do those things," he says. Which explains why many athletes "want to be in these high-arousal stress states."

In a threat state, on the other hand, heart rate still increases, but heart rate variability goes down. The peripheral vasculature constricts, which prevents blood from reaching the body's extremities. "Basically, your body is preparing for some sort of physical threat, so it is rushing blood back to your internal organs," says Aoyagi. "This is where you get that experience of feeling your pulse pounding in your head." Such a response makes sense from an evolutionary perspective: by returning blood to the body's core, we maximize our chances of survival, in the event of a violent attack. We are less likely to bleed out. And this response is hardwired: the brain does not distinguish between physical and social stressors—between the perils of an approaching lion or the vocalizations of an aggressively foulmouthed point guard. A threat is a threat. Per Jamieson, "We are essentially telling our bodies that something bad is going to happen."

And in response, our bodies prepare for damage.

Unsurprisingly, when we feel threatened, our performance craters. In addition to the physiological changes that quickly sap our energy levels, self-doubt creeps in, which is pernicious for multiple reasons. (Self-doubt not only primes a person to be overly sensitive when exposed to disparaging comments—or any other cues that resonate with those doubts—but it can also lead to negative expectations that can dampen performance and make tasks seem more threatening.) In a threat state, we become *even more* sensitive to potential dangers; we see all the ways that things can go wrong, all the mistakes we can make, and we worry about how best to avoid those negative outcomes. Our minds wander to fears of failure, like: *What if I don't succeed?* "Which is a completely inappropriate thought for that moment," says Jon Metzler, a performance psychologist who works with the military and elite athletes across the professional, collegiate, and Olympic ranks. This line of thinking is especially problematic for athletes and other high performers because it "disrupts the grooved motor pattern that they need in that moment," adds Metzler. Which is to say: it makes them self-conscious. They think about specific aspects of what they're doing—about movements that were previously performed automatically, like swinging a bat or putting a ball—instead of just doing it.

As Brian Decker, a former Green Beret who now serves as the vice president of team development for the Carolina Panthers, explains, an athlete who does this is "taking a proceduralized task and applying conscious effort to it." This is also known as reinvestment. And when it happens, Decker adds, the athlete "is going to fuck it up."

———————

IN HIS ROLE as a performance psychologist, Scott Goldman will sometimes have athletes come into his office who have been upset by something an opponent has said on the court or field that stuck in their head for one reason or another. When that happens, Goldman often responds by asking the athlete what is—on its face—a silly question. He says, "What if he called you a kangaroo?"

The athlete will usually laugh.

"Why is that funny to you?"

"Because I know I'm not a kangaroo."

Goldman will nod. The player is helping him make an important point; trash talk is far more likely to work when you let it feed a doubt that's already inside you, when it exposes a perceived weakness or pokes at a genuine insecurity. As the performance director for the England and Wales Cricket Board (ECB), Mo Bobat has witnessed plenty of shit talking at both the developmental and professional levels of sport.* From his experience, the most effective trash talk is indeed when something is said that resonates with a person's internal

———————

* While many folks, especially Americans, think of cricket as a genteel game, for its white-sweatered uniforms and breaks for tea, it's actually riddled with trash talk, or what they call sledging.

dialogue, that feels threatening. "If someone said something to me that I had no insecurity about, it's just like, 'Yeah, whatever, I'll just have a laugh at you,'" says Bobat. "But if they say either something that your inner voice is already whispering at you, or they say something that makes your inner voice shout it at you, then I think they've done their job."

One of B.J. Armstrong's favorite moments to talk trash on the basketball court was at the end of a blowout. Whether his team was winning or losing was immaterial. It was only important that one team was ahead by a lot because that's when the respective coaches would pull most of their starters and rotational players and empty their benches. Armstrong would intentionally foul one of those opposing players who was only in the game because the score wasn't close, and then he'd say, "Now, go get your average." In other words: all you need is one or two free throws to match your scoring average because you play so infrequently and contribute so little. "People would be so upset," he says, with a laugh. And in their anger, they'd betray themselves. "You find out who is who. 'Oh, this guy is sensitive. We can get him.'"

It's a common refrain across sports: calling attention to an opponent's fringe status—both on his own team and in the league, more broadly—because it speaks to a material concern (potentially getting cut and losing one's job) and highlights a likely insecurity. It's effectively what Kevin Garnett was doing when he'd question if an opponent shouldn't be in the G League and what Gary Payton did when he told Jamie Feick he wouldn't be in the NBA the following season. The idea, of course, is to attack someone who is vulnerable, or believes themselves to be vulnerable. That's why Payton went after young point guards as soon as they came into the league. "Chris Paul, Jason Kidd, Jason Williams, all of them," he tells me. "I always would test whoever. I told them, 'You're a rookie. I'm going to come at your head *all day.*'"

For a long time, international players were also regular targets in the NBA because they were viewed as soft. A stigma existed around

European leagues, in particular, for cultivating a more hesitant, less physical brand of basketball—and so the presumed book on those foreign-born players was simple: intimidate them. Spanish great Pau Gasol dealt with it. As did Luis Scola, who was born and raised in Argentina and played professionally for years in Spain before coming to the NBA. Scola still remembers the bull's-eye on his back in his first preseason. As he tells it, the worst of it came against the Memphis Grizzlies and Stromile Swift, as the Grizz kept running plays to isolate Scola on defense. "Five plays in a row through the same guy, toward me. All five times," he says. "And you can hear the bench, they are screaming and laughing and making jokes about it." (To be fair, Scola suggests this dynamic may have been exacerbated by culture shock—that foreign-born players were simply not used to the level of verbal antagonism that greeted them on American shores. He says, "Maybe we talk about it more.")

Muggsy Bogues, who at five-foot-three is the shortest person to ever play in the NBA, has denied an oft-told story about Michael Jordan allegedly talking shit to him by screaming, "Shoot it, you fucking midget!" But the incident, regardless of whether it happened (and I'm happy to take Bogues's word that it didn't), speaks to a larger point: it easily could have. Because on the field of competition, anything that stands out about a person becomes a potential vector for abuse, whether it's your height, your weight, your hairline, your background, your temper, or that weird hitch in your jump shot. Anything that implies: *you're different; you don't belong here; be afraid, be very afraid.*

––––––––––––––

IF YOU'RE LIKE me, you might feel there's a bit of absurdity at play here. On the one hand, it makes tactical sense for trash-talkers to increase the perceived demands on their opponents—or to otherwise try to intimidate and frighten them—in an effort to up the threat quotient. After all, on a basic level, most trash-talkers are functionally saying the same thing, which is: *the demands of competing against me are too high; you cannot win.* As Aoyagi says, "If trash talk quote-unquote works, it's almost always going to be because it pulled somebody into a threat framework." But at the same time, it's patently obvious that an athlete is in no actual mortal danger during the course of normal competition, no matter how aggressively that person may be taunted at the foul line, or how many times someone blows in his ear or insults him. No one is worried about being eaten by a predator on a court or ball field, and it's been decades since the prospect of free-swinging brawls regularly hovered over professional sports leagues.

All of which begs the question: What are people so afraid of?

Most likely, the answer is public shame and the attendant fear of social rejection.

Scott Goldman speculates that it's this vestige of early humanity that powers much trash talk today. "If you go back to this sort of tribal mentality, it's really this mechanism of—if I'm kicked out of my tribe, I have to hunt more, I have to forage more, I have to find more resources. Life would be really, really hard outside of the tribe," he says. Many things have changed since humans first formed tribes, of course: just as we're less concerned with the prospect of being attacked by a wild animal, it's likewise easier to hunt for food (thanks, Trader Joe's!) and secure other essential resources. Even still, Goldman is right that this relic of collective living continues to inform our deepest phobias, like the fear of public speaking, which regularly tops the list of most common human fears. Public speaking is a social phobia, and the associated fear is not just about being evaluated and judged by others, but also of being deemed unworthy—of being ostracized and left to fend for oneself. "If you think about trash talking, at its essence, a lot of it has to do with rejection," says Goldman.

It's making a person feel like an outsider. Like they don't belong.

"It's a public awareness that you might not be good enough," says Michael Gervais. "You are being called out, and if you don't rise to this moment, then there is public shame and rejection taking place."

It was that same specter of rejection that Gary Payton learned to weaponize against his opponents via constant verbal challenge—and as it turned out, that was a highly effective way of flipping on their threat receptors. Per Aoyagi, "I think many evolutionary psychologists would argue that the most profoundly problematic state for a human is isolation because nothing would get you killed quicker in the savannah than being isolated from the pack."

Or as Kevin Garnett might put it, *Get that shit outta here!*

THE MOST CRITICAL DIMENSION

BEFORE THE ATLANTA Thrashers took on the New York Rangers in the 2007 NHL playoffs, the Thrashers players held some unusual meetings. They didn't gather to discuss strategies or line shifts, but to gird themselves against a single member of the opposing team—Sean Avery.

The message was simple: "Stay away from him. Don't let him get to you."

Only in his fifth NHL season and his first with the Rangers, Avery had already earned a reputation across the league for his maddening style of play, which included everything from swinging his stick at opponents (slashing) to showering goalies with sprays of ice from his skates (snowing) to kicking players' legs out from under them (slew-footing), and his piercingly wicked tongue. In hockey they call it chirping—the in-game banter between teams that can range from playfully antagonistic to outright vicious—and I don't need to tell you on which end of that spectrum Avery resided. Everything about him was designed to disrupt and irritate the opposition, to burrow beneath their skin and pluck at their nerves like a concert harpist. On the one hand, there was nothing new about any of this. In his provocations, Avery was merely filling the classic role of hockey agitator or pest. Every team has one—a guy who goes out of his way to annoy the opposition through verbal and physical tactics, which often test the boundaries of what's legal in hopes of throwing off their concentration or even angering them to the point of physical retaliation. "The ultimate goal is for them to take a penalty," according to retired NHL player and renowned pest Matthew Barnaby, another expert chirper.

But in a sea of pests, Avery managed to stand out.* There was almost nothing he wouldn't say—as he put it, "I say whatever I think will disturb them the most." From his mean-spirited digs at the personal lives and professional insecurities of opponents to the exploitation of rule book loopholes, Avery always found ways to irk his opponents. Most famously, he turned to face longtime nemesis Martin Brodeur, the Hall of Fame New Jersey Devils goaltender, aka Fatso, per Avery, during a five-on-three Rangers power play in the 2008 playoffs, and proceeded to wave his arms and stick as a form of visual distraction before eventually putting the puck past Brodeur himself moments later.** As Avery explains it to me now, "I tried to challenge myself to always push the envelope."

There was a kind of twisted creativity to Avery's agitations. In the same way a cryptographer spots patterns amid the chaos of an encryption, he saw opportunities to annoy that would never have occurred to other hockey players. For fucking with people, Avery had a beautiful mind. Of that incident with Brodeur, in particular, he says, "If there was ever a time to *not* do something, that would have been it." His team already had a two-man advantage and therefore a great chance to score. But doing nothing—or even doing less than the absolute maximum—was never an option for Avery, regardless of

---

* Seriously, look up the term on Wikipedia, and (as of this writing) you'll find a picture of Avery.
** The league responded to this the very next day by instituting what's known as the Avery Rule.

the circumstance. "There was never a bad time for me," he says. "It was always that time."

His antics were hard to ignore, and they seemed to genuinely upset opponents. League-wide polls would confirm this, as he would be voted the most-hated player in the NHL by fellow players. After that 2008 playoff series, Brodeur would betray his feelings toward Avery by refusing to shake his hand. A former ref equated Avery to "a case of jock rash," while the late Wade Belak, who played fourteen years in the league, said, "It goes beyond just getting under guys' skin." Avery, he added, "takes it to a personal level and that is what guys hate about him." But that hatred worked in Avery's favor, and he knew it.

The point of his agitating tactics, after all, wasn't just to be a nuisance. Avery aimed to do deeper competitive damage than that: he wanted to be such an undeniable menace on the ice—and make the experience of playing against him so off-putting and so unpleasant— that his opponents would lose focus on the game happening around them. At his pestering best, Avery forced other players to pay attention.

IN A 2008 piece on Sean Avery, the *New Yorker* compared the hockey player's disruptive efforts to that of a terrorist. Specifically, the author writes that the role of a pest "seems to have no analogue in sports—or in any line of work, except maybe terrorism." But that's hardly the case. While enraging, frustrating, or otherwise baiting an opponent to the point of emotional distraction and knuckleheaded retaliation may be a more explicit goal during a hockey game, that particular utility of trash talk—provoking action that leads to a strategic error, penalty, or even ejection—extends well beyond the ice rink.

According to George Karl, every basketball team in the 1970s had an end-of-the-bench player whose main job was to harass the opposing stars. "I have been used as that guy," he says, "where you go in there and you try to rough up their best player, and maybe he'll throw a punch and you get him thrown out of the game." Decades later, Gary Payton was similarly accused of filling a pest-like role in the NBA. In a 1996 profile, *Sports Illustrated* described Payton as a "gnat buzzing around, willing to do anything to annoy an opponent." And he wasn't alone. Reggie Miller was a master at crawling underneath other people's skin, even the sport's best players. "Playing Reggie Miller drives me nuts," said Michael Jordan, who once tried to gouge out Miller's eyes during a 1993 altercation, for which he was suspended.

Infamously, it was on soccer's biggest stage, during the 2006 World Cup final, that French star Zinedine Zidane attacked Italian defenseman Marco Materazzi, who had insulted his sister. Zidane leveled Materazzi with a forehead to the chest and was instantly given a red card and sent off, as France went on to lose the match.* Landon Donovan, who played fourteen years for the US Men's National Team, tells me that baiting tactics are par for the course against certain teams in international competition, especially those from Central America. "It could definitely be verbal, but more often than not, it was nonverbal," he says. "Every time the ball goes out of bounds, they're like punching, hitting you in the gut, stepping on your foot, sometimes to the extent of spitting on you. There would just be a whole host of things to get under your skin and really, ultimately, to provoke you, to get you to do something stupid." Chilean defender Gonzalo Jara has earned a reputation for similar antics. Most notably, in a 2015 Copa America match, he was accused of telling a Uruguayan opponent that his father, who had been arrested the previous day after striking and killing a motorcyclist in a car accident, "will get twenty years [in prison]," and then he stuck his finger up the guy's ass, out of sight of the referees.

Meanwhile, on the American football field, All-Pro cornerback Jalen Ramsey has been tormenting wide receivers since college at

---

* Twelve years before the Zidane incident, former secretary of state Henry Kissinger observed that the Italian soccer team plays "like Machiavelli" and tries to "disconcert their opponents" and "rattle them with operatic performances."

least, when he'd send direct messages to opponents' girlfriends on Instagram before games, and then tell them about it on the field. "I was grimy, like super grimy," he says. On the other side of the ball, former wide receiver Lamar Thomas used to study opposing teams' media guides when he played at the University of Miami. He'd learn the names of opponents' family members and "I'd bring up those persons' names in a degrading way," per Thomas. He'd "apologize after the game," he says. But on the field, opponents often became outwardly upset and would respond by trying to injure him.

That was when they'd make mistakes.

―――――――――

THERE'S A CERTAIN art to annoying other people—maybe not a noble art, but an art nonetheless. For example, those who are most artful and wisest in the ways of the pest understand it's not just a matter of what they can do or say to make another person's blood boil, but also which of those things they can potentially get away with. Because when they get away with it, the offense is that much more biting and difficult to reconcile for the victim. The injustice rubs coarse salt in the wounds.

Reggie Miller has always been this kind of irritant. Long before the beanpole kid from Riverside, California, introduced the NBA to his infuriating game—a style of play comprised of boundary-testing microtransgressions, including push-offs, cheap shots, flops, and the flailing leg kicks that felt like the natural conclusion to the chaos of his unconventional shooting form (which resembled nothing so much as one of those collapsible thumb puppets: the ones with the string that crumple into a pile of limbs with the push of a button)—Miller had a gift for crawling under people's skin. As the second youngest of five kids, it was perhaps inevitable.

Cheryl Miller, the basketball legend who is nineteen months older than her brother Reggie, describes the Miller kids as being close, loving, but highly combative, with relationships forged during heated games of driveway hoops and "the gauntlet of the dinner table." On the court, they muscled one another and sent errant shots into the neighbor's yard.* At dinner, they jockeyed for the best pieces of meat and corners of cornbread, while conducting under-the-table warfare.

She just kicked me!

No, I didn't. I nudged you. I never kicked you.

They learned the nuances of being annoying and explored the crevices of getting on each other's nerves in a way only siblings are able to. For the younger Miller siblings, in particular, it was all about figuring out what they could get away with. Reggie, for example, developed his high-arc jump shot to avoid the outstretched arms of older brothers Darrell and Saul Jr., while Cheryl went so far as to once punch Darrell in the face. But only because he dared her to do it, she swears—and because she knew she could reach the safety of her mother's legs faster than Darrell could get to her. She says, "Man, Rafi. I cracked him in his jaw, and the next thing I know, I got to Mom and I'm yelling, 'He's going to kill me! He's going to kill me!'"

(Don't feel too sorry for Darrell: one of the older brothers' favorite pastimes was tying up Reggie and Cheryl and tossing them in a closet, in a game they dubbed "Houdini.")

The fiercest taunts were usually reserved for the one-on-one battles between Reggie and Cheryl, who would torment her younger brother en route to her usual victories. "It was just stupid comments," says Cheryl. "Like, 'Reggie, if your friends—your boys—knew how much I wear you out on a daily, hourly basis, what do you think they would say?'" He'd respond, "Shut up, DeAnn [her middle name, which is pronounced Dee-Ann but Reggie pronounced as Dean]. I'm not listening to you." Siblings are like truffle pigs for raw nerves. For finding that one button to push—and then push and push and push.

---

* Retrieving these balls could be a daunting task, as the neighbor's dog had a reputation for biting. There was one time, at least, when Reggie, who had resisted the assignment, wouldn't make it back unscathed. "Sure enough, he had bite marks and everything else, and we were laughing. Like, *laughing*," remembers Cheryl. Reggie didn't cry, but he did perseverate. "I'm traumatized. I might be traumatized," he repeated. Even back then, the kid had a flair for the dramatic.

In time, Reggie learned to give as good as he got. What he could say that most got under Cheryl's skin was: "You're a girl and you play like a girl." This bothered her "because most guys don't want to play against a girl," she explains. "That was it. That's all he had to say."* On occasion, he'd talk a little too much for Cheryl's tastes and then she'd be the one doing the chasing. She would race after Reggie with a skateboard overhead, shouting, "You got to say one more thing. Say *something*. Say *something*!"

But Reggie was never one to hold his tongue.

Even before he was old enough to join the driveway games, he'd hype up Cheryl by talking shit to his brothers' friends, saying, "Oh! I'm telling you right now, my sister could beat anybody on this porch." Or, while watching Cheryl's high school games, he'd shout from the stands: "Tell her! Tell her who's boss!"

It was this same younger-brother instinct for needling basically everyone that informed his game as a high schooler and then a student-athlete at UCLA, where he would spit at and elbow opponents and show up referees. Per Reggie, "I was a psycho in college." When he joined the NBA, it didn't take long for the media to anoint Reggie "a high priest of trash talk," or for Indiana fans to embrace him as a kind of smack-talking folk hero.** By his own admission, Reggie was one of those players who imagined himself to be stepping into character when he walked onto a basketball court—and he saw that character as, well, "an asshole." According to Phil Taylor, Reggie genuinely annoyed his opponents. Whereas many players would

---

* Cheryl admits this area of sensitivity grew even more tender as she entered adolescence—not because she didn't *want* to be a girl, because she *was* one. With his put-downs, Reggie was effectively telling his older sister that he rejected that part of her identity: that it was something contemptible and insult-worthy. "Was it hurtful?" she says. "Yeah. Because you're going through all kinds of stuff, as a woman, as a girl. And that was hard. Ooooh." Cheryl practically shudders through the phone line. "I don't think I've ever said that."

** Local radio stations aired a song to this effect. It went: "R-E-G! G-I-E! Reggie! From the top of the key! Shoot the three! Talking trash and playing some D!"

line up to give shit-talkers like Gary Payton dap after games, in spite of the verbal abuse, they would hold grudges against Reggie beyond the final whistle. As Payton tells me, "He was an asshole all the way. Reggie stayed an asshole." Phil Taylor suggests that Reggie is "probably more popular now among the guys he played against than he was at the time." He says, "He was the kind of guy you'd imagine doing stuff behind the ref's back. He was like the kid in class who would throw the spitball when the teacher was turned around. That *nyah-nyah-nyah* kid. He was *that* guy. And I think that's why guys really didn't like him."

DESPITE ALL THE backyard bickering, Cheryl Miller didn't talk much on the basketball court. At least not in game settings, not at first. As a high schooler at Riverside Polytechnic, where she was always the best player on the floor (and it was never particularly close, as evidenced by the night she dropped 105 points, as a senior), Miller let her game do most of the talking.

And, oh, what a game!

A self-described "showboat," Miller competed with a level of above-the-rim confidence and run-and-gun charisma that would have been more at home inside the LA Forum, where the Showtime Lakers raised their championship banners, than in any high school gymnasium. She was demonstrative and self-assured, as fiercely competitive as she was seemingly fearless. She possessed a style of play that was so electrifying—so *undeniable*—that the media was knocking down her door for publicity interviews before she'd even made a college commitment. At a time (the early 1980s) when women's sports were an afterthought, at best, Miller was on a path to pop-cultural stardom—and she was never one to shy away from the spotlight, on or off the court.

Even still, there were some rival players who would, on occasion, muster the courage to talk shit to Miller as a high schooler. When that happened, she'd respond with a simple and silent message of dismissal. "I would always point to the scoreboard," she says. "That's what my mom taught me."

But the six-foot, two-inch sensation picked up some new influences—and new habits—in the fall of 1982. That semester marked Miller's first season with the Women of Troy—as the University of Southern California's women's basketball team is known—and the beginning of her trash-talk transformation. On that USC team, which would go on to win back-to-back national titles, Cynthia Cooper (now Cynthia Cooper-Dyke, a fellow Basketball Hall of Famer) was the most prominent talker, despite coming off the bench. She'd make declarations like, "I'm about to drop thirty!" This in-your-face style was shocking to Miller. At one point she even asked her teammate, "Coop, seriously, why do you talk so much?"

Cooper's response: "Because—I can!"

Elsewhere on the floor, twins Pam and Paula McGee deployed a more nuanced brand of psychological subterfuge. Says Miller, "They would see you struggling with something, or you'd be wide open and somebody wouldn't pass to you," and that's when they'd pounce. They'd say something to the effect of, *I can't believe it. Did she do that on purpose? Because you were wide open.* The idea, of course, was to plant seeds of discord. Pam, in particular, found a ready target in Louisiana Tech's Debra Rodman, whose younger brother, Dennis, would become a world-class agitator in his own right. "She was in her head so bad," says Miller. "She's like, 'Debra, you've been killing me down low. Why aren't they passing you the ball?'" Rodman would agree with McGee's assessment, and it would only be a matter of time before she started cursing out her teammates and coaches.

For Miller, it happened in stages—a series of turning-point moments that revealed a capacity for verbal gamesmanship equal to her teammates, and of which her brothers would be proud. The first was in the waning moments of an early season game against Pepperdine University. Despite winning the contest by more than forty, Miller had a lackluster performance, netting only eleven points. "I remember fouling out, and Annie Meyers's sister [Pepperdine coach Patty Meyers] walked by our bench and goes, 'Oh, so you're the great Miller?'" says Miller, who felt what she describes as "an inferno" rising inside her, in reaction to the sarcastic comment. It wasn't anger exactly; it was a yearning to respond. "That's when I realized I had a voice," says Miller. "I go, 'You haven't seen the last of me, and you certainly haven't heard the first from me!'"

In a lot of ways, Cooper was Miller's enabler—her trash-talk muse. "I only got mouthy a lot when Cooper was on the floor," says Miller, who insists she never went into a game planning to talk a bunch of mess, "unless I really, really didn't like somebody." It would just sort of happen. And when it did, Cooper would punctuate her teammate's conversations with what Miller describes as "drive-by" contributions. She says, "She'd hear me barking, and then she'd jog over and say something and then walk off. And I'm like, 'You heard her.'"

Other times, Miller would more explicitly appeal to Cooper's authority as the team's smack-talker in chief. Like if an opponent told Miller she talked too much, she'd say: "No, I really don't talk too much. Cooper over there—she talks all day. Don't you, Cooper?"

Yeah, I do. And tell that person next to you she ain't got no chance of stopping you!

"See, I told you."

But Miller didn't need anyone's help messing with opponents. Over the course of her NCAA career, she developed a distinctly exasperating style of smack talk, which borrowed as much from the college classroom, where she studied communications, as it did from her childhood experiences in the driveway and at mealtimes, when she'd nudge her siblings beneath the table. On the court, as at the dinner table, Miller would feign innocence, adopting a *who-me* posture, even as she needled. But there was shrewdness in her words: she knew what she was doing. Unlike teammate Cooper, Miller's modus operandi was not aggressive confrontation but constant irritation—she pelted opposing players with an interminable stream of infuriating small talk and inquiring-minds-type questions. "They should have called me the Mentalist," she says, with a laugh.

According to Mark Aoyagi, the performance psychologist whose résumé includes stints working with numerous athletes across the professional and Olympic ranks, asking "skillful" questions may well be "the most effective" form of talking trash because our minds tend to argue with statements but engage with questions. He says, "If someone says, 'You suck,' we are likely to think of reasons we don't suck. However, if someone said, 'Do you suck?' we are more likely to think of reasons why we might suck." In fact, he adds, "if I were advising someone on how to trash talk"—which he wants to make clear, for the record, that he would *never* do—"I would definitely advise taking advantage of questions." With Miller asking the questions, it was death by a thousand cuts, and it inevitably ended with opponents demanding that she please, please, *please* stop talking.

"Hey, how's your family?"

Miller, you don't know my family.

"That's why I'm asking. How're they doing?"

Shut up, Miller. Just shut up.

Miller's true trash-talk epiphany, though, came in the minutes before tip-off of a contest her freshman year. As she tells it, the Women of Troy were running their usual layup lines when Cooper instructed her to smack the backboard on her next attempt. She said, "Miller, slap that backboard one more time. Slap it!" Miller did as she was told, and then realized why: the opposing team, down at the other end of the court, couldn't take their eyes off of her. *Oh, my gosh,* she remembers thinking. *They're looking at us! They're looking at us!* The game hadn't even started, and she was already in their heads.

"Light bulb went on," says Miller.

FOR AVERY, HIS light-bulb moment—when he first appreciated the power of his provocations—came on a ferry ride from Prince Edward Island to Nova Scotia, through the Northumberland Strait.

He was only twelve or so at the time and was returning from a tournament with his youth hockey team. The insight had nothing to do with the contemplative scenery or meditative swaying of the ship. It was the fact that Avery's team and the opposing team, which was also traveling to Nova Scotia, had to be separated on different levels of the ferry on account of the young player's trash talk.

"I was saying things that twelve-year-olds weren't saying," says Avery. The root of that particular beef, as best he recalls, was telling an opponent "how hot his sister was." And as he rode back to Nova Scotia surrounded by his teammates, and with the other team stewing on another deck of the ship, "I realized that what I was doing had the ability to affect the outer circle; it wasn't just the inner circle, as far as me and the person I was talking to. It had a much greater effect."

As a pro, Avery quickly recognized the psychological ripple effect he could have on opposing teams. Specifically, Avery remembers playing in Toronto for the first time as a member of the Los Angeles Kings—and he could sense a kind of tense foreboding around his arrival. "They're anticipating what was going to happen. 'Who is this kid? What's he going to say? How bad is he?'" he says. "They kind of know I'm coming, and I can feel the energy around it."

He could feel all those eyes on him—and frankly, he liked the attention.

More than once, Avery describes his agitating antics to me as "self-serving." He says, "I enjoyed doing it so much [because] it brought the attention onto me and brought the attention off of everyone around me." But this wasn't simple narcissism, he's quick to clarify; his ability (and willingness) to become a competitive and emotional focal point provided a strategic edge. "I wasn't doing it so that everyone in the arena looked at me," he says. "I was doing it because it gave my team an advantage." Hyperaware of Avery's every movement, opponents were more likely to lose track of his teammates—or to go out of their way to slam Avery unnecessarily into the boards, as payback for his many transgressions. Even if those collisions—or other retaliatory cheap shots—didn't result in penalties, they often pulled opposing players out of position and created scoring opportunities for Avery's team. As the *New Yorker* put it, "Avery is a skilled player, agitations aside, but not so skilled that it would explain how much better the Rangers do with him than without him. The discrepancy testifies to the genius of the idiot."

"I always knew there was going to be a target on my back," says Avery.

But opposing players had targets on their backs, too.

It's an open secret in NHL locker rooms that players snitch on former teammates when they join a new organization, and Avery took advantage of that, trying to absorb as much information as possible about upcoming opponents. "I was always a fly on the wall. I tried to hear more conversations than I was a part of," he says. "I'm also not insecure about asking questions." Avery supplemented this locker-room research with newspapers, magazines, and any other relevant source. "I always had the ability to keep my act fresh. That information was my weapon system."

To hear Avery tell it, there was no one in the league he couldn't unsettle mentally. His trash talk became, effectively, a superpower. "It got to the point where there were no roadblocks as far as not being able to execute on the game plan," he says. And as his prowess grew, so did the anticipation period for opponents before they played Avery, which increased their psychological suffering. In time, the other twenty-nine NHL teams were circling those Avery games not just days in advance, but weeks or months. "Or even at the start of the season," he says. "They'd look at the calendar and go, 'Oh great.'" Long before the first puck dropped, Avery was worming his way beneath their skin. They were thinking about him, and he could feel it: the pulsing nervousness, the edgy and expectant dread.

In the minds of his opponents, the pest loomed ever larger.

———————

IN THE NAVY, there is a flight-simulation exercise in which pilots are asked to complete a series of tasks, with varying degrees of difficulty, while a range of unusual sounds play at random in the cockpit. As the exercise unfolds, instructors measure brain activity in the pilots' parietal lobes to see if they are recognizing the sounds. "Not surprisingly, the harder the task is, the less likely they are to have any reaction to the sound," explains a sports psychologist who works with the United States Naval Academy but asked not to be quoted by name, since we spoke without going through the military's proper communications channels. At a certain point, for some pilots, when the task is hard enough, they are no longer hearing the sounds at all. "They literally don't hear it." In fact, the pilots will insist that the sounds simply weren't played. "Which is really dangerous if you are in a cockpit and not hearing a radio when someone is telling you really important information."

According to Brian Decker, the former Green Beret, athletes—or any high-level performer, for that matter—will only be at their best when they are "totally immersed in their current environment." What he means by this: those performers must be appropriately tuned in to what is happening around them in order to pick up on "task-relevant cues"—the stimuli that relate to what they're trying to accomplish—and respond accordingly, while disregarding those cues that are unrelated to the task, which are mere distraction. In the jargon of athletes and sports psychologists, this is referred to as "focusing on the task at hand."

It sounds simple: *Pay attention to what you're doing!*

But it's not easy to remain so intensely present—to not think about a recent mistake, or worry about a future play, or otherwise allow your focus to wander beyond the immediate demands of performance, regardless of whether your opponent does something inflammatory, like jamming a finger up your ass or insulting your wife by name. Even the great and notoriously dialed-in basketball legend Rick Barry—a man who has never been accused of humility—admits to me, "It's almost impossible to stay at that high level" for the entirety of a game. Part of the problem, as the navy's flight-simulation exercise demonstrates, is that attention is a limited resource. What that means in the case of the simulator, per the navy psych, "is that when you are really saturated, when you're at your max capacity for attention, you don't tend to hear a lot of other things."

But the inverse is also true: if the pilots were to focus instead on the background noises—or if an athlete were to focus on task-irrelevant cues, like trash talk from Sean Avery—that would likely have an attentional spillover effect. Famed psychologist and professor emeritus at Princeton University Daniel Kahneman has written about this as "capacity interference." It's the idea of cognitive overload, of presenting someone with more information—greater attentional demands—than they can handle. And it gives us another way to understand the mechanisms by which trash talk threatens to affect performance. Per Kahneman, everyone has "a limited budget of attention that you can allocate to activities, and if you go beyond your budget, you will fail."

At Boston University, Edson Filho focuses in his research on human excellence and performance optimization. As he explains it, peak performance is defined by its efficiencies—the ability to eliminate wasted effort of any kind and to keep both the body and the brain operating with a kind of task-obsessed ruthlessness. Physically, this means there are no unnecessary movements: no hitches, no hesitations. And cognitively, this leaves the vast majority of one's attentional resources available to attend to other demands of the contest, such as thinking about tactics, anticipating what might happen next, or monitoring one's internal states to ensure they remain within an optimal zone of functioning—and they do need to be monitored.*

---

* According to John Raglin, athletes are "constantly tweaking the dials" when it comes to this sort of self-regulation. While sports psychology fetishizes the idea of being in a flow state, when time seems to stand still and everything happens effortlessly, he says those experiences are "so rare that you remember them." Far more often, "athletes are actively managing their resources. It's like, 'I've got to get a handle on my emotions. I've got to refocus,'" he says. "If anybody comes in there and screws with their instrument panel, then that's a serious thing—it's one more thing that they have to deal with."

When someone is performing at his or her best, you can see this reflected in that person's brain activity, via electroencephalography (EEG) or fMRIs, per Filho. "Part of being an expert is that you only recruit the parts of the brain that you need to recruit. You only use what you need to use," he says. "It is called neural efficiency." Meanwhile, if you were to look at the brain imaging of someone who is stressed, distracted, or otherwise dealing with cognitive overload, the picture would be much more chaotic, as "that person is accessing parts of the brain that he or she shouldn't have to access."

"That's the art of shit talking," says two-time NBA All-Star Danny Manning. "You want to see somebody lose focus."

Much of this happens unconsciously, of course. For example, when something distracts us, it is a stress to our system, and that often causes arousal. Our hearts may beat faster, our muscles may tighten, or our thoughts may race. (Any of which could have IZOF implications.) It's also possible that targets of trash talk deal with it by directing their attention inward: they will focus on their internal dialogue instead of the contest transpiring around them, perhaps obsessing over their mechanics, perseverating on a seed of self-doubt, or attending to a surge of unwanted emotion. Aoyagi says this is a poor reaction to trash talk that gets less attention: the "internal reaction, the turning in and beating oneself up." For those who allow trash talk into their heads like this, "there's some evaluation that starts to take place," says Michael Gervais, a performance psychologist who spent a decade working with the Seattle Seahawks. They may wonder, *Is this true? Is this not true?* "And that is where I want my competitor to have his attention—internal."

Smack talk hijacks the human impulse to make meaning, which is partly why Scott Goldman, a performance psychologist, suggests that "even the most innocuous trash talk" has the potential to provide a competitive advantage because it "still warrants some form of inspection, whether it is milliseconds or maybe even weeks." He says, "I've had a couple of players come to me and were like, 'I'm still kind of reeling on the statement that was said about me, you know, four games back.'" If you think that sounds far-fetched, talk to Chris Bosh. He has admitted that he couldn't sleep after Kevin Garnett called him "a mama's boy" during a game. It wasn't that he took offense to the allegation; it's that he found it so inscrutable. "I had the worst game of my career after that," Bosh said. "I was up just late at night like, 'What is *that* supposed to mean?'"

─────────────

AOYAGI REFERS TO attention as "the most critical dimension" when it comes to the mental aspects of performance because it connects so many other pieces of the sports psychology puzzle. For example, he tells me about the relationship between arousal and attention: "As arousal increases, attention narrows," he says.

This is important because there are various types of attentional states.

One way to visualize these differences is to imagine your attention as a kind of funnel or a cone. Within that funnel is a given amount of information, some of which will be task relevant, some of which won't. When the funnel is wide, your attention will be broad with an open awareness as you take in lots of information. When the funnel is narrow, your attention will be more tightly focused. One attentional state isn't inherently better than the other. But either a wide or narrow state can be more or less functional, based on the demands of a given task. For instance, a quarterback may want a broader awareness when he is dropping back to pass. To make the best decision about where (and when) to throw the ball, he needs to observe the routes of his receivers, read the defensive coverage, and be generally aware of the giant bodies closing in around him. A basketball player stepping to the free-throw line, on the other hand, needs a tighter spotlight of focus. In this example, "you want to be broad enough that you can take in yourself, your [physiological] activation level, the hoop, those things," says Aoyagi, but narrow enough that you can shut out such task-irrelevant cues as the jockeying of the rebounders in the paint, the distracting taunts of fans behind the basket, and the general hullabaloo of a raucous sports arena.

The key to attentional control, therefore, is not just the ability to put your focus where you want it to be, or even the ability to keep it there. It's also crucial to have attentional flexibility—the capacity to switch your focus, as appropriate—because there are performance-related consequences when someone's funnel of concentration is either too narrow or too broad. To illustrate this point, Aoyagi relays an anecdote that was shared with him by his late mentor Keith Henschen, a pioneering sports psychologist who worked for decades with the Utah Jazz. As Henschen explained, John Stockton was an OK free-throw shooter, but his shooting percentage would go up in critical moments of a game.* What this means, per Aoyagi, was that Stockton was "probably below his zone of optimal arousal" most of the time. As a result, his attention was likely a little broader than it needed to be when he was shooting free throws. "He might be taking in the stands. Not in an obscene way. Probably not even in a conscious way," he says. "But under pressure, he gets that little boost of arousal, and it actually pushes him into his optimal zone."

On the flip side, if a quarterback becomes overly aroused, his attention may become too narrow. Perhaps he homes in on a single receiver, to the exclusion of all the others, or doesn't see the safety creeping over from the other side of the field. And just like that: interception. Or think about a basketball player who responds to trash talk by turning the team sport into a one-on-one battle, driving into defensive traffic or jacking up contested shots, while seemingly ignoring a wide-open teammate beneath the rim. "That's because their attention is off task," says Aoyagi. "It is too narrow."

Understanding attention in this way also adds important nuance to the IZOF model—and to the performance implications of trash talk therein, says Aoyagi: "When you get someone past that optimal level of arousal, not only are you potentially activating that fight-

---

* I'm relying on Henschen's anecdotal evidence to make this point, since it's unclear how exactly he defined these critical moments.

flight-freeze response, but you are making their attention ineffective, as well." This is significant at the highest levels of competition. Why? Because while it's unlikely that many elite athletes—especially veterans in their sport—would be pushed so far beyond their optimal zones that they enter fight-flight-freeze, even small disturbances can prove costly. "Even the veterans, you might be able to get just enough under their skin to throw their attention off," says Aoyagi. "And that little fluctuation can make a huge difference."

The separation between elite performers in any sport is often infinitesimal. Football, they say, is a game of inches. Gold medals are won by fractions of a second. "It doesn't take much" to swing the outcome of a contest, per Indiana University professor John Raglin. "It's like you nick off that edge," he says. "We always talk about the margin of victory, which is a fraction of a percentage. Anything that subtracts from that can be the difference between a medal and not even being [on the podium]."

Just a small fluctuation. Any tiny lapse.

FORMER US MEN'S soccer goalkeeper Shep Messing understood the value of shaking his opponents' concentration. For him, it started in the opening round of the Olympic qualifiers before the Munich games in 1972, as the US men's team pursued its first Olympic berth in the qualifying era. A critical moment came as the United States played El Salvador to two draws and had to play a third match to determine who would advance. Held at a neutral site on a scorching hot day in Jamaica, that game ended, naturally, with the score tied at one goal apiece. "We went to penalty kicks," remembers Messing. With both teams on pace to net their five penalty shots, Messing knew it would all come down to him and figured, *fuck it, let's get nuts*.

With long, curly hair that was described by the *New York Times* as big enough "to hide a boa in it," Messing looked more like the fifth member of Black Sabbath than a world-class athlete. So one can only imagine what was going through the mind of El Salvador's Mario

Castro as he prepared to take his crucial penalty kick and looked up to see this mop-topped maniac running directly toward him, shouting all manner of obscenities. "I took my shirt off, bare-chested, started swinging the shirt around my head, and charged out at him, cursing," says Messing, who studied psychology at Harvard and hoped this display might be just enough to psyche out his opponent or to at least break his rhythm and concentration. The fans erupted, and the ref gave Messing a yellow card, as the goalie just stared Castro in the face. Per Messing, "I wanted him to know he's looking at the craziest guy he's ever seen in his life."

(Muhammad Ali took a similar tack against Sonny Liston, you'll recall.)

Messing still remembers the look on Castro's face. Scared stiff, he says. "This guy must have thought I was a lunatic." According to a contemporaneous report that quotes Messing, he also "slapped the guy on the back to encourage him not to miss," before returning to the net. But he needn't have bothered. Castro delivered "the worst penalty kick I have ever seen," in the goalkeeper's telling. The shot sailed so far over the crossbar that Messing barely flinched, "and we went on to the Olympic Games."

In the soccer world, there is a stigma around goalkeepers for being a bit touched—you have to be a little crazy to play the position, they say—and Messing used that reputation to his advantage throughout his career. "On corner kicks, I would constantly be talking to the opposition," he says. Or more accurately, he'd be rambling. Mumbling stuff to himself like, "I have no idea where I am" and "What the fuck is going on here?" Sometimes, he'd glare at a guy with a crazed look, get right up in his face, and say, "I haven't slept in a fucking week. I feel like I'm right on edge." Other times, he'd act completely poised and tranquil, before suddenly starting to jabber. That's when he'd approach an opposing player and grab him, in a gentle and sincere way, look him in the eye, and apologize. He'd say, "Look, I'm sorry for anything that I do. I'm off my medication. If I do anything stupid, I'm sorry."

That would usually earn a double take, per Messing. Get a guy to think twice about attacking the goal as aggressively as he otherwise might. "You definitely embrace the lunatic," he says. "You want to bring that out. So they're looking at you and going, 'I've got to stay away from this guy.'"

Over time, Messing adopted additional tactics to distract and upset opposing players, like pricking them with safety pins* or insulting international players in ways that were designed to exploit individual cultural sensitivities. "To a German, I'd say, 'Your sister is meeting me back at my hotel after the game.' That would upset the German more than the Mexican. The Mexican or Italian, if you question their manhood—that would upset them more, right?" At first, Messing came to this knowledge via academic means: he'd borrow books from the library. But once he started playing in the North American Soccer League (NASL), he'd simply ask his famous teammates for tips. Pelé or Carlos Alberto Torres would tell him what he could say to get under the skin of a Brazilian, while Franz Beckenbauer would snitch on fellow Germans. "Those guys thought it was hilarious," says Messing. "We had like eleven different nationalities on the team. I had the perfect market research right in my own locker room."

Still, the goalie's greatest—and most devious—psychological ploys in the NASL would often come right after halftime. That's when Messing would seek out an opposing player, as the teams were returning to the pitch, and say something to the effect of, "Fuck, I hope you're all right. There's a fire in your neighborhood." As for how he'd know such a thing, Messing would have done research into the off-field life of that individual before the game, and often he'd be

---

* Messing learned that trick from Pelé, when they played together on the New York Cosmos, a team in the NASL that became famous for signing foreign stars. "You could only get away with it one time in a game," he says. Inevitably, it would be on a corner, usually with the big central defender standing right in front of him. "You stab him in the thigh and throw the safety pin behind the goal." The guy wouldn't know what happened exactly, though he'd feel quite certain that Messing had done *something*. He says, "Guaranteed, he'd be furious for the rest of the game."

exploiting a personal relationship. "You'd always have a friend on the other team," he says. "I could say, 'My wife spoke to your wife.'" That would give the guy something to think about, and he'd have no way to check on it until after the game.

One time, Messing used this tactic to great effect during a 1977 divisional playoff match between the New York Cosmos and the Fort Lauderdale Strikers, with the score tied. It was the end of regulation, and the winner would be decided via penalty kicks. A good friend of Messing's, Ray Hudson, played for the Strikers. The two even had plans to go out together after the game. "I knew what street he lived on," says Messing. Before the shootout, the goalie approached his friend, and he said, "Ray, I hope you didn't hear. There's a gunman, and police are all over your neighborhood." Hudson didn't even ask how Messing had come to this information. "He freaked out," Messing says of his friend, who blew the kick, as the Cosmos advanced.

This technique—a kind of master's thesis in distracting smack talk for Messing—was more subtle than simply enraging a guy, if also more depraved. But that was why it worked so well, he says. "I tried to keep it at a level where they wouldn't be mad. They'd just be worried."

———————

IT WAS NEVER the aggressive or confrontational shit talk that bothered Danny Manning. As the number one overall pick in the 1988 NBA Draft, he knew opponents were going to come after him as soon he came into the league. "Everybody knows that you're the number one; there's no secret there," he says. "There are guys on every team that try to get under your skin, try to rattle you a little bit, try to intimidate you."

For him, all that noise was easy to tune out. The stuff that stuck in his craw, on the other hand, was more unexpected—it was the stuff he didn't see coming. Like when, in his first game as a professional, Manning found himself guarding Eddie Johnson of the Phoenix Suns, and Johnson was running him off double screens and pin downs and just getting disgustingly open. "He was laughing at me," says Manning, who also had to listen to Johnson offer the rookie words of faux encouragement on his way to scoring forty-five points that night. "Oooh, boy. Come on, young fella. You got to be better than that," he said.

Manning eventually tried to incorporate some of these confounding techniques into his own verbal game, like "saying encouraging things in a way, but actually talking shit." Or using his knowledge from a pregame scouting report to call out an opponent for being in the wrong spot on an inbounds play. "I'd be like, 'Come on, man, we're supposed to start this play over here. What are you doing? You don't remember this play?'" he says. "I wanted to be clever with my shit talking. I wanted to make guys think." Which was why, sometimes, he'd even compliment an opponent after he scored. Manning would say, "Hey, that's a good move!" And the guy would look at him side-eyed, like, *Huh?* Manning would say it again.

"That was a good move."

As the editor in chief of the *Journal of Sports Sciences*, a go-to performance consultant, and a professor at the University of Utah, where he chairs the Department of Health, Kinesiology, and Recreation, Mark Williams knows a little something about peak athletic performance—and its fragility. Williams, who is also the author (along with British sports journalist Tim Wigmore) of *The Best: How Elite Athletes Are Made*, focuses in his work on the psychology and neurology that underpin the acquisition of athletic expertise. And according to Williams, Manning was onto something.

In fact, per Williams and numerous other sports psychologists to whom I speak, complimenting one's opponents is an extremely sly way to mess with their heads. To explain what he means, Williams cites W. Timothy Gallwey's classic book on performance psychology, *The Inner Game of Tennis*. "The notion is, if you are playing tennis, and you go to your opponent and say, 'God, you are serving well today. What are you doing differently?' Then what it does," he says, is "it flips them into a more cognitively controlled phase, where they start thinking, 'Yeah, I am serving well today,' and they wonder, '*Why* am I serving well today?'"

It makes them think about what they're doing—about their mechanics—instead of just doing it. It causes reinvestment, which is the same thing that can happen in a threat state. It's problematic not only because ruminating on the well-practiced technical aspects of skill performance—on the things that are normally done unthinkingly, like swinging a bat or shooting a ball—can lead to a deterioration in the performance of that skill (or even the yips, when you lose the ability to execute the skill altogether), but also because it exhausts critical attentional resources that should be dedicated to other aspects of the competition. "We called that the Jedi mind f-u-c-k," says Cheryl Miller. "'Seriously, your follow-through, and the way you arc, you don't cock your arm all the way back—that's really working for you.' And next thing you know, she's thinking about her form, and now she's clanking."

Another potential benefit of this sort of polite and even praising trash talk is that it may cause an opponent to downregulate—to be less aggressive than they'd otherwise be. Former NFL offensive lineman Mark Schlereth refers to this verbal tactic as "pouring honey" on an opponent. He says, "I would constantly pour honey on people. Meaning, I would let them know how great I think they are and how great they're playing. Hopefully, the theory behind that was, they would get bogged down because they were standing in that sticky honey."

Part of what makes this tactic so effective—beyond the fact that it's "very difficult not to pay attention to compliments," per Kevin L. Burke, a sports psychology professor at Queens University of Charlotte—is that it defies expectations. In a competitive setting, we do not anticipate being greeted warmly or with praise by our rivals. When we are, it can stagger the mind—or at least slow it down. Daniel Kahneman has written about humans having two systems for thinking: fast (i.e., System 1) and slow (System 2). Fast thinking runs as a kind of autopilot, which can include things like well-practiced skills. However, as Kahneman writes, "System 2 is activated when an event is detected that violates the model of the world that System 1 maintains . . . you will stare, and you will search your memory for a story that makes sense of the surprising event." Polite trash talk—even when not outright complimentary—forces a performer to process information that's outside the norm and very likely unrelated to the competitive task at hand. As Florida State University psychologist Joe Franklin puts it, "We are always trying to make sense, automatically and effortlessly, of what we are taking in."

Former Colts quarterback Andrew Luck was known to stupefy opponents after they'd slammed him to the turf by congratulating the defenders, while NBA big man Zach Randolph would lull defenders into a competitive stupor with his charming (and disarming) small talk. He'd tell them about his off-season travels or ask if they had recommendations for a local restaurant—"and then he just drives past you and gets a basket," in the words of onetime NBA standout LaMarcus Aldridge. Per Steve Jones Jr., "It's a brilliant tactic that no one ever saw coming." Quarterback Philip Rivers was so unusual with his aggressively cuss-free smack talk that opposing coaches would warn their defensive units not to be unnerved by it. As a former NFL player who was in such meetings tells me, "You almost become a little bit numb to the generic trash talking. But when something out of the ordinary occurs, you almost have to be prepared because it's going to sound so strange." With Rivers, he adds, the coaches would say, "Get ready for daggunnit."

OPPOSING PLAYERS AREN'T the only ones looking to steal athletes' attention. Sometimes the biggest disruptors are the fans in the stands. When Sean Elliott played his first NBA game in Washington, DC, for instance, veteran Spurs teammate Terry Cummings cautioned the rookie to be aware of—and ignore—one heckler, in particular. Before leaving the locker room, Cummings said, "Hey, this guy is going to talk. Don't pay attention to him." Elliott scoffed at the idea that a fan could be so disruptive as to warrant this kind of warning. "I was like, 'OK, whatever,'" he says. But then the game started, and Elliott got his first taste of Robin Ficker. "He was on the front row! He was literally almost in our huddle," he says. "And he was yelling at the top of his lungs and stomping his feet. You couldn't help but look over there, and Terry was like, 'Don't look at him. If you look at him, he's going to start talking to you.'"

A Maryland-based attorney, who has often been disciplined for professional misconduct (and was eventually disbarred in 2022), and frequent failed candidate for public office, Ficker spent more than a decade as a fixture behind the opposing team's bench at Washington Wizards (née Bullets) home games throughout the 1980s and '90s, in which time he ascended in infamy until he became the sports world's preeminent heckler. It wasn't his intention to become a heckler, he says: "Since they were right in front of me, I started talking to them, asking questions." But once he started talking, he wouldn't shut up. Ficker was loud, he brought props,* and he always did his homework. "I knew their strengths and weaknesses on the court," he says of visiting players. "I would find out everything that was out there about a particular guy, or a particular difficulty the team was having, and then I would try to magnify it."

Ficker knew the names of players' girlfriends. He knew which guys were unhappy with their contracts (Scottie Pippen), or if anyone was behind on child-support payments (Lewis Lloyd). "I'd raise questions about that," he says. When Karl Malone purchased a new truck in the off-season, Ficker threatened to key his vehicle. "He became very upset at the thought of that," he says. The heckler wasn't trying to be cruel, just obnoxious. He'd ask players for their opinions about various things, or shout that someone was trying to reach them, when they were at the foul line: "Phone call for Reggie

---

* When he learned that a player might be arachnophobic, he'd sprinkle toy spiders beneath the opposing team's bench. To tease Charles Barkley, he'd bring bags of produce to the arena because of Barkley's refusal to eat vegetables. At some point, in one of those games, a visiting player was literally stuck holding an eggplant, per Ficker: "The coach told him to go in, and he didn't know whether to put it in his shirt or what to do."

Theus!" During timeouts, he'd talk over the opposing coaches and tell the players what they were doing wrong, while designing alternative plays on a whiteboard he carried with him. Players would give him hesitant sideways glances, which was Ficker's first indication that his words were hitting their marks, though it wasn't until teams started moving their huddles away from the bench and toward the middle of the court during timeouts that he realized how large an effect he was having. The heckler was eventually deemed so disruptive by the NBA that the league instituted a fan code of conduct, known as the Ficker Rule, which prohibited spectators from verbally abusing "players and/or coaches in a manner which interferes with the ability of the coach to communicate with players during game play or huddles."

Chris Kluwe never had the pleasure of being screamed at by Robin Ficker, but he was no stranger to hecklers. That's what happens when you spend eight years as a punter in the NFL. It never really bothered him, though. When fifty thousand people collectively insisted that he sucked, it became white noise, more or less. "It's just loud," he says. "It all kind of fades into itself, and you just tune it out." Which is why he insists "the most difficult situation I ever had to punt in" came in an almost empty stadium, during a late-season game at Detroit in 2008, with the Lions on their way to a winless 0–16 record. Kluwe remembers an eerie quiet that persisted throughout the game, with so few fans in the seats. "We were standing on the sideline, and we could hear conversations! Between people in the stands! It was the strangest thing," he says. Unlike the anonymous swell of a roaring crowd, Kluwe could make out individual voices, which he found much more unsettling. "When it's only a single voice, your ear naturally tends to focus on it. You are like, 'Oh, someone is saying something, I should pay attention to that,'" he says. "It was a significantly different type of focus required to tune out just that single voice."

Robin Ficker credits part of his powers to his "command voice," a result of his brief time at West Point, before he was kicked out of the academy for being argumentative. A profane and pioneering Detroit

Pistons fan named Leon Bradley, aka Leon the Barber, similarly stood out from the crowd, as he provided an unofficial and uncensored soundtrack at Cobo Hall and the Pontiac Silverdome. "He was the original, before Robin and all those other guys," says B.J. Armstrong, who grew up in Detroit. And while you might think it'd be easier for opposing players to ignore a celebrity heckler like Ficker or Leon because they know what's coming, the opposite is true: it becomes much harder. Even well-intentioned warnings, like Terry Cummings giving his Spurs teammates a heads-up about Ficker, could compound the problem. "You've now primed yourself to look that direction, or to *not* look that direction," says Aoyagi. But not looking is no better than looking because "the attentional mechanisms are the same." It's like when someone says, Don't think of a pink elephant. "What that does is it sends our brain on a search for a pink elephant," says Aoyagi. "Our brain holds that in our attention. So if you think, *Don't look at Robin Ficker*, your brain is now holding Robin Ficker in your attention."

Or Phil Rivers.

Or Sean Avery.

What Aoyagi is describing is known as the theory of ironic processes of mental control or the theory of ironic effects, which was developed by social psychologist Daniel Wegner to explain the difficulty of suppressing unwanted thoughts. Stuart Beattie, a senior lecturer of performance psychology at Bangor University in the UK, suggests that using ironic effect could be a smart way to not only distract an opponent, but also to plant negative thoughts in that person's head, which can similarly influence performance outcomes. You'd do this by telling someone not to fuck up, essentially, like Shep Messing telling Mario Castro not to miss before his penalty kick in the 1972 Olympic qualifiers. "Don't do this. Don't do that. That's how I would [talk trash] to people," says Beattie, "because when they're stressed and the last thing they think about is an ironic effect, they end up doing the very thought that they're trying to suppress."

IN ESTHER GOODY'S 1978 book, *Questions and Politeness: Strategies in Social Interaction*, social scientists Penelope Brown and Stephen C. Levinson introduced a concept they refer to as politeness theory, in which they laid out a series of linguistic strategies that demonstrate the various ways humans contort their communication methods to cause the least offense to other people. The goal of such politeness strategies, such as claiming common ground, seeking agreement, or showing deference, they suggest, is to help preserve others' social value (aka save face) even when the nature of an interaction is sensitive and potentially face threatening—which is to say: when it is likely embarrassing, or a potential imposition.

Would you mind terribly if . . .

Indeed, the "kernel idea" of politeness theory, per Brown and Levinson, is "that some acts are intrinsically threatening to face." And softening those potential face threats via politeness is what greases the interpersonal wheels, which is kind of a big deal, sociologically speaking. As renowned linguist John J. Gumperz put it in his foreword to a reissue of the book, which is now titled *Politeness: Some Universals in Language Usage*, politeness, "as the authors define it, is basic to the production of social order, and a precondition of human cooperation." In effect: it allows people to get along. Because when politeness is performed successfully, a person may not even realize they're on the receiving end of a face-threatening act.

But of course, this begs the question: What if you *want* that person to notice?

Is there not strategic value in being *impolite*, in that case?

In explicitly threatening another person's face?

Or outright insulting them, even?

In a word: yes.

As Aoyagi puts it, "the whole point of [trash talk] is trying to manipulate somebody else's attention. And that's what threat does; it grabs our attention."

Indiana University professor Michael Adams, who studies the English language, sees a dark side to Brown and Levinson's politeness theory. He says, "This is actually a guide in how to offend people and create conflict." Which is exactly what Jonathan Culpeper has been doing for almost three decades now. A professor of linguistics at Lancaster University, Culpeper has dedicated his professional life to understanding impoliteness. He's the author of *Impoliteness: Using Language to Cause Offence*, and he has compiled a reference website for impoliteness that basically reads like a how-to of verbal abuse.

As Culpeper explains it, face-threatening offenses are uniquely difficult for folks to ignore because they are so shocking. "In social psychology, they call this the fundamental attribution error," he says. "That is where you fail to attribute the cause of something to the context"—for example, an opponent demeaning you as part of a strategic effort, a fan shouting distracting disparagements, or even a friend with whom you're exchanging playful put-downs—"but just take it at face value and attribute it to the behavior." In other words, even when we *know* someone is likely to say something offensive, it's hard not to be, well, *offended*. "It's just overwhelming," adds Culpeper. Or as Austrian psychologist Fritz Heider, who is regarded as the father of attribution theory, put it: "Behavior engulfs the field."

As such, the more offensive something is, the more distracting it is likely to be.

Sean Avery understood that. Because it's hard not to take that shit personally.

———

IT MAKES SENSE that the Atlanta Thrashers made Avery such a central topic of team conversation before the 2007 playoffs because they knew what was coming—on an abstract level, at any rate. The devil is always in the details—and they wanted to be ready for it. To not be caught off guard.

Little good it did them.

In that series, as was ever the case when Avery was on the ice, no player would be spared his abuses—Avery went at everybody in his time in the NHL; well, everybody except Joe Sakic*—but the Rangers pest seemed to take a special shine to the Thrashers' star winger, Ilya Kovalchuk. A former number one overall draft pick, Kovalchuk was a dangerous offensive player and a prolific scorer. But you wouldn't have known that from listening to Avery. Namely, he homed in on what he believed to be the Russian player's insecurities, his secret fears. "There's always been folklore around Canadians being able to win and Russians not being able to win," says Avery. And despite Kovalchuk's tremendous talent and personal accomplishments, this was his first playoff appearance. "At that point, he hadn't won."

As the series unfolded, Avery leveraged this information. Over and over, he told Kovalchuk that he was a loser—that he'd always be a loser—because Russians are losers. Not like Avery. Because Avery was Canadian. He'd already been on a Stanley Cup–winning team. His first year in the league, in fact. "He probably had those insecurities because he'd heard those whispers," says Avery. "I took all of that information and created a storyline, and I targeted it all at him. That gave me the ability to sell it, and I guess he started to believe it."

You're going to fuck up. Don't think of a pink elephant.

According to Avery, the NHL playoffs present a perfect hunting ground for pests because of the best-of-seven series format. With that repeated exposure, the indignities compound. As Avery explains, "When you play seven times over a two-week span, that's like a cut that can't heal. Like, it just doesn't fucking go away."

It didn't take long for Kovalchuk to show cracks.

---

* As the story goes, Avery was on the bench for the Detroit Red Wings, his first NHL team, when Joe Sakic skated by. Avery stood up, planning to subject the veteran to his usual invective, but Brett Hull grabbed the back of his sweater. "You are not allowed to speak to Mr. Sakic," said Hull. Avery confirms this. "That story is true," he says. "It's somewhat ironic that it was Hully, because he was the king of trash talk—but to his own teammates."

With less than a minute remaining in game two and the Rangers leading by a goal, the Thrashers star made a beeline for Avery and hit him in what was described by the Associated Press as "a nasty play," which resulted in a costly penalty that nullified a Thrashers power play. The following game, early in the third period, two Rangers players—one of whom was Avery—checked Kovalchuk into the boards. And while the check may have had a little more oomph than was strictly necessary—a little extra fuck-you of a shove at the end—it wasn't egregious. Kovalchuk just lost it, though. As Avery retreated toward his defensive zone, Kovalchuk turned and skated after him, not even looking for the puck. When Avery saw him coming, he clocked the single-mindedness in Kovalchuk's eyes instantly—and recognized the situation for what it was: an opportunity to deprive the Thrashers of their best player in a game they desperately needed. Avery shook off his gloves.

The TV broadcasters could barely believe what they were seeing.

"That's the height of frustration right there," one said, as Kovalchuk threw the first punch. "Avery has gotten to Kovalchuk."

"You're right," the other replied. "When a highly skilled player like Kovalchuk drops his gloves, you know he's lost his focus."

The star player had indeed given in to anger and impulse. For his transgressions, he was sent to the penalty box with a ten-minute misconduct penalty, as the Rangers went on to win that game 7–0 and the series in a four-game sweep. It wouldn't be the last time Kovalchuk tussled with the Rangers pest, either. In 2010, then a member of the division rival Devils, Kovalchuk once again attacked Avery, baited into a fight toward the end of a close game. Afterward, he conceded, "I should stay away from him."

As if the thought just occurred to him.

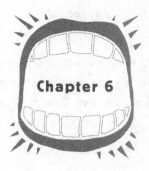

THE LAST
10 PERCENT

FORMER NFL WIDE RECEIVER Steve Smith Sr. tells me a parable. It's about a lion and a gazelle who live in the Serengeti. The gazelle knows that when the sun comes up each morning, it must run faster than the fastest lion or it will be eaten and die. Meanwhile, as day breaks across the African plains for the lion, it knows that it must run faster than the slowest gazelle or it will starve. "The point of the story," Smith says, "is when the sun arises, you best be running."

Smith shares this as a metaphor for how he felt before every game—for what he believed to be the boiled-down, zero-sum essence of game-day competition, in terms of pitting his best effort against his opponents' and his willingness to make that challenge explicit. You have to be "all-in," he says. "And when I mean I'm 'all-in,' that means I prepare and train in the off-season for this very moment, to look whoever in the eye and tell them what I'm going to do about it." In so doing, Smith would not only ramp up the psychological pressure on his opponent—because sometimes a gazelle runs a little slower when it's looking over its shoulder—but on himself, too. Which was no accident. As the wide receiver walked away, a private smirk would creep across his face, and to himself, he'd say, "Now, don't fuck this up."

———————————

ONE OF THE most famous studies in behavioral psychology involves a rat and a box. The experiment was devised by a man named B. F. Skinner and deployed what is known as operant conditioning. In the experiment, a hungry rat was placed inside the box, wherein there was a lever that, when pressed, would reward the rat with cheese. In time, the rat learned to press the lever whenever it was hungry, and the rat became successfully conditioned.

The experiment had huge implications for the field of behaviorism, as it made a case for nurture versus nature (i.e., that behaviors can be learned and changed, based on one's environment and/ or experiences). But according to Scott Goldman, there is a complicating factor that is often ignored when considering the meaning of Skinner's box. "The thing that everybody forgets in those research studies is that the rat won't press the lever unless it's hungry for the cheese," he says. "And that's the part of the study I tend to gravitate toward." This overlooked fact has enormous implications for things like drive and motivation, per Goldman. He makes an analogy to sticking one's hand in a vat of boiling water. "The discomfort somebody is willing to tolerate differs depending on the reward or the purpose of tolerating it," he says. "If you were going to offer me five bucks to put my hand in scalding hot water, I'm not interested. But if you're telling me it will ensure the safety and security of my children, you got it. No problem."

In the case of high-level athletes, adds Goldman, who is also the cocreator of the Athletic Intelligence Quotient, a test of "sport-specific cognitive abilities," which is used across professional and college athletics as an assessment tool, teams invariably want to select players "who are willing to tolerate the discomfort of whatever the sport activity is, whether it is training or performance in a big-time moment." They want players who are hungry for the cheese. But appetites have a way of changing and motivations along with them. For example, if a player comes into a professional sports league and is motivated by a specific goal—say, achieving financial security for his family and their future generations—that's great and laudable. But what happens when that player signs a lucrative second contract with many millions of dollars in guarantees? Will he still be as hungry to compete as he was before? Will he be willing to endure as much pain and discomfort in service of his career? Will he still feel that lion chasing him, or will he maybe feel it's time to slow down?

For some, that's where trash talk can come in because trash talk can have a major impact on player motivations. According to Goldman, talking shit is a great way to not only remind a person about what they might be hungry for—because folks can lose focus over time—but also to "shift that hunger to a different need" and thereby create new motivations. He says, "Again, to get the rat to press the lever, they need to want the cheese. But the cheese doesn't have to always be out of hunger; it could be out of desire—*I love the taste of cheese*—or out of self-actualization." Or out of reputational concerns, personal pride in one's efforts, the need to stay relevant, to not be embarrassed, whatever.

Muhammad Ali biographer Jonathan Eig speculates that the boxing great may have talked more shit as he aged in an effort to create psychological stakes for just this purpose. "I think it may have been something that he used to help stay motivated," Eig says. "When he was younger, he loved to train. He trained really hard. As he got successful, it became harder and harder for him to maintain the discipline." But he remained terrified of losing face in public— of being humiliated—and so he talked his boastful mess and even invited crowds and members of the media to watch him in the gym. For Ali, in particular, this was a sensible strategy to decrease the likelihood he would slack off during those training sessions, per Eig. "He did not want to be embarrassed."

NOT ALL MOTIVATION is created equal.

For instance, psychologists distinguish between what's called intrinsic and extrinsic motivation. At the most basic level, these distinctions describe the difference between someone's drive to engage in an activity as a result of either internal or external factors. Consider an athlete who competes in a sport because that person finds it inherently rewarding to do so—or, for that matter, a rat who presses a lever for the simple love of pressing that lever—versus an athlete who competes primarily to gain potential rewards (like fortune and fame) or to avoid potential consequences (like public shame).

Relying on extrinsic motivation and external motivating factors is regarded as suboptimal because it represents a less sustainable fuel source, so to speak. According to Brian Decker, intrinsically motivated athletes do not compete against others so much as they compete against themselves. "They're trying to achieve mastery," he says. Even still, a potentially motivating external factor—like trash talk—can play an important role in helping some athletes achieve peak performance. "Trash talking is a way to actually increase somebody's full embodiment and engagement because it ups the ante from a social standpoint," says Michael Gervais. It prepares a person to perform at a high level and strips away potential excuses for not giving one's best. "It definitely can increase internal drivers. Like, you can see it. OK, there's something on the line now. There's a little ego involved, there's a little extra skin in the game." In this way, Gervais adds, external factors can be "facilitative" in achieving "an ideal competitive mind-set"—just as they can help some players reach their zones of optimal functioning—and can therefore act as important tools of engagement. Sociologists David G. LoConto and Tori J. Roth refer to trash talk, in particular, as "a means of creating a competitive stance."

It certainly was for Gary Payton.

As Payton tells me, there were some nights when he just didn't want to play basketball. For whatever reason, his competitive juices weren't flowing. But he knew how to get himself going: he needed to start some shit. "Talking trash was one of the things that would motivate me," he says. One of his tricks was to approach a referee before tip-off and request that the official give him a technical foul at some point during the game. Per Payton, "I'd say, 'Yo, look here, I'm going to get on you tonight. You make a bad call? I'm going to get on you. When I get on you, just give me a tech.'"* Other times, he'd pick out a single fan in the stands—literally anyone, so long as that person was brave enough to heckle Payton—because that would provide him with the necessary tension to deepen his investment in the game. "A fan that says one thing to me—he'll go at me, and then I'll go at him, and I say, 'OK, that's what's going to get me motivated.'" Opposing coaches recognized this tendency in Payton—the way in which he would occasionally flail for that emotional charge—and they would admonish their players not to talk to the Sonics point guard, especially on those nights when he seemed disengaged. Payton says, "They'd be like, 'Y'all, shut up. Don't let Gary get involved in the game.' As soon as somebody says something to me, they be like, 'Shut up! Shut up!' But by that time, it's too late."

He'd already sniffed the cheese, and now he was hungry.

This need for confrontation—for an external kick in the ass, by way of personal challenge—at least partially explains why Payton was so relentless in his verbal assaults, per Cheryl Miller. "He had to get you going because it got *him* going," she says. Payton challenged and baited and demeaned his opponents, until they responded, because in their response, they gave him what he craved.

Draymond Green seems to operate in much the same way. The Golden State Warriors stalwart and all-world shit stirrer has admitted that he largely talks as much mess as he does to provoke a response. He barks, so that you'll bark back. According to Gene Steratore, who officiated Green when he was still in college at Michigan State University, the NBA star has always required this kind of strife. "My opinion of Draymond was that he wanted an adversary.

---

* "Most of the time, he didn't have to ask," says former NBA ref Bennett Salvatore.

He wanted to create one. That was part of his dynamic. That's what fueled him."

Edson Filho, the Boston University sports psychologist, warns athletes with whom he works that these kinds of pump-yourself-up-by-attacking-others strategies are precarious because they depend on the reactions of those other people. He says, "You are not self-regulating. You are feeding off of somebody." Or as Steratore puts it, "You have to swing back to give me my full satisfaction." But the reality is that precious few players are able to resist the provocations from players like Payton and Green, despite their coaches' warnings.

Hockey pest Sean Avery similarly thought of his creep-beneath-your-skin tactics as more than mental warfare; they were a way to raise the stakes on his own performance. "People don't understand," he says of trash talk. "It's actually a great tool to use to self-motivate because you have to back everything up." What's more, Avery knew that opponents would be gunning for him extra hard each time he laced up his skates as a result of his agitating style, and he welcomed that challenge. "I used that as a way to hold myself accountable, to make sure that I didn't take nights off," he says. "I always knew that there was going to be a bull's-eye on my back."

By talking so much shit, Avery made every game matter.

AS AN NBA REFEREE, Eli Roe worked a lot of forgettable games. But there are some nights that will always stick with him. One such contest involved the Denver Nuggets and Sacramento Kings. It was 2015, a mid-January affair, and what made that game remarkable had nothing to do with the quality of the clubs or their respective place in the Western Conference standings. The thing that made the game memorable was an offhand remark by DeMarcus "Boogie" Cousins, who would be selected to his first of four straight All-Star teams that season, in front of his teammates on the Kings bench.

Boogie was a player who was known for getting on foreign guys, per Roe, and on this night he was matched up against a second-year forward from Bosnia and Herzegovina named Jusuf Nurkić. As the third quarter was getting underway, Roe tells me, "DeMarcus had a chance to make fun of him in front of his players' bench." The ref didn't think much of it. "Like I told you before, that stuff would happen with foreign players." As it happened this time, Nurkić grabbed an offensive rebound on that possession and scored on a seven-foot hook shot. Says Roe, "DeMarcus shook his head. Almost like, lucky shot or whatever. You know, still kind of dismissing Nurkić." Barely a minute later, coming off a missed shot from Cousins, Nurkić scored again. And on the following possession, Nurkić forced Cousins into committing a turnover, as he stole the ball.

Sacramento called a timeout.

As the quarter wore on, the competition between the two players intensified. According to Roe, it was evident that Cousins, who had a reputation for occasionally taking some possessions off, was fully engaged in the game. "He was like, 'OK, I'm fucking playing now,'" the former ref says. "But for whatever reason, during this six-, eight-minute stretch, Nurkić was just on fire. He was hitting these sixteen-footers, he was hitting little baby hooks, he'd blow by him and get a layup, or whatever."

This back-and-forth was exciting for Roe to witness, in part because it was so unexpected. He says, "You would think these are two sub-.500 teams on a random night in January. They're just going to go through the motions, most of the game." But once Cousins started talking crap—demeaning his opponent in front of his whole bench—the game took on a different character altogether. "During that eight-minute segment, Cousins and Nurkić were playing their fucking asses off. They were *into* it," he says. "If Boogie would have never said anything, then it would have never developed into that. And now they're both playing really hard and really intense, and it's only because of the trash talking."

HERE'S THE THING: sports are actually boring.

Not for the fans, of course—those face-painted folks who look to their hometown teams for emotional connection and spiritual release; those of us who follow the storylines as closely as the standings and ascribe personal and cultural meaning to the achievements of strangers in borrowed laundry. But for those strangers themselves? The players? *Booooring.* Which is why it's no surprise that a player like DeMarcus Cousins may simply go through the motions from time to time.

"The average fan forgets how mundane sport can become, particularly to professional and high-level athletes that have done it so many times," says Mark Aoyagi. In discussing the sheer length of an NBA season, B.J. Armstrong tells me, "It's impossible to be at your best for eighty-two games. But what's not impossible is to *try* to be at your best for eighty-two games." Which speaks to the need for compensatory strategies—for anything that can spice up the competition or "introduce a little fire into this," as Aoyagi puts it.

For plenty of folks, trash talk is just that spice.

Draymond Green has talked about the need to manufacture drama amid the regular-season tedium to prevent emotional letdowns. "I gotta start talking junk to everyone—to pump myself up and to get my teammates going," he says, "because I know, once *you* start talking, it's a battle." He's hardly the first to do this: baseball legend Jackie Robinson used to deploy bench jockeying in the same way. Whenever he noticed lethargy creeping into his ball club—during a day game after a night game, perhaps—that's when he'd start riding the opposing team, looking to create a spark in his own dugout. In fact, Robinson had this to say about such verbal abuse: "It wakes a club up."

The problem is, as Cousins discovered: sometimes it wakes the other club up, too.

The idea that trash talk can backfire—and not just because a shit-talker may fail to deliver, but also because it might motivate that person's opponent—is almost too obvious to mention. There are countless examples, from Babe Ruth's called shot (when nearly all of Wrigley Field along with the entirety of the Cubs bench was riding him) to Reggie Miller vampiring energy from Spike Lee in Madison Square Garden to Damian Lillard exploding during the NBA's 2020 bubble season by dropping fifty-one, sixty-one, and forty-two points in successive games, after being trolled by opponents Paul George and Patrick Beverley for missing two end-of-game free throws. It's largely for this reason that Basketball Hall of Famer Rick Barry would never talk smack to his opponents. "Why would you want to give somebody any motivation whatsoever, any fuel to get the fire burning more?" he says. "I know if somebody started to do that to me, that just made me want to go ahead and kick their ass even more."

And yet, it must be mentioned.

That's what Georgetown professor Jeremy Yip and his collaborators discovered when they examined trash talk in the workplace. Specifically, in their pilot study, the researchers placed participants in a competitive setting, instructed them to send either trash talk or a neutral message to their opponent, and then asked them to predict what sort of effect that message was likely to have on their target's motivation. Most participants who sent the trash-talking message believed it would diminish their opponent's motivation—but that is, as Yip and his colleagues describe it, "a failed mental model." In reality, they found that targets of trash talk not only maintained their motivation levels; they increased them. "Our work showed that if you are a target of trash talking, you are more likely to exert greater effort—you perform better on effort-based tasks—than those who are interacting with someone who communicates more neutrally," says Yip. "People did not anticipate that there would be an elevated level of motivation."

It's not just office workers. Robin Ficker insists his heckling has never backfired, not even against players like Reggie Miller. ("I don't think I helped him," he says. "If they're talking to me and interacting with me, they're basically distracted.") Anecdotally, Scott Goldman has witnessed a similar blind spot at high levels of sport, even among elite athletes, which is why he always feels compelled to warn the trash-talkers with whom he works. He tells them, "Be careful. Because that blade cuts both ways."

But Yip's pilot-study participants aren't entirely wrong in their expectations, either. After all, it sure seems as though trash talk can succeed against some folks via causing distraction or overarousal, even if it's not wholly obvious on a population-wide level—and it's not. In fact, almost all of the quantitative studies of trash talk I've come across—and there haven't been all that many, to be fair*— could be read as proof that trash talk *doesn't* work. That's because, when examining the impact of trash talk on a group of people who are engaged in a task—say, shooting free throws or playing video games—researchers usually find no overall decline in performance versus that of a control group. It's only when you dig a little deeper into these experiments that you see the more meaningful discoveries. For example, in a study led by Christopher Ring, a psychology professor at the University of Birmingham in the UK, the results of which were published in a 2019 issue of the *Journal of Sports Sciences*, researchers found that trash talk had no effect on the success rate of a group of free-throw shooters. At the same time, the study confirmed "that attentional processes and affective responses can be manipulated using verbal behaviour," which is to say, participants who were subjected to trash talk were angrier and more distracted.

There was a similar outcome in an experiment involving the football video game *Madden*, run about a decade earlier by researchers at Florida State University, which explored the effect of trash talk on efficacy beliefs, specifically.** They found that individuals who were forced to remain quiet during competition had lower efficacy beliefs

---

*   Where's the grant money, scientists?!
** A term coined by psychologist Albert Bandura, *self-efficacy*, according to the American Psychological Association, describes "an individual's belief in his or her capacity to execute behaviors necessary to produce specific performance attainments"—that is, to succeed at a given task.

(which is to say greater self-doubt), while those who were allowed to talk had higher efficacy beliefs. Edson Filho coauthored a paper based on that study's results. He says, "There is a big link between efficacy and performance. It actually is the biggest link." And yet, again, despite these shifts in self-efficacy, the researchers found no overall difference in performance based on who was or wasn't talking shit. This seeming contradiction is less problematic than it seems, per Filho. For one thing, it's possible that, given a large enough sample size, trash talk will inspire as many people to improve their performance (via increased motivation) as it will hurt others, and those changes will effectively negate each other in the final results. It's likewise possible that, in any given participant, the negative effects of trash talk will be mediated by that increased motivation (i.e., that you may be distracted, but also exerting greater effort). Ring and his collaborators nod to this possibility in their paper when they write: "Motivation-related changes in effort may have compensated and masked the effects of disruptions to attention associated with verbal antisocial behaviour."

Filho also makes a comparison to the "hot-hand belief" in basketball, which is the idea that a player is more likely to make a future shot if they've made past shots. "Sometimes when you have some data, the mean is error," he says. "But that doesn't mean the effect is not there. When you look at every player, there is not an effect. There is regression to the mean, and the mean is zero." But for an individual player, on a case-by-case basis, it may well exist. "For Michael Jordan, if you look only at Michael Jordan, once he is in a hot-hand state, he is in a hot-hand state," he says. "It might be the same thing with trash talk. It might not impact everybody."

It is, in other words, all about the individual.

With that in mind, it can be convincingly argued that the most important takeaways from studies such as these is not whether or not trash talk can be seen to hurt performance across a group of people (it can't), but that the studies can identify clear mechanisms at play—like changes to one's emotions, attention, or efficacy beliefs—that explain the pathways by which trash talk *could* affect an individual's performance. Mark Williams, the University of Utah professor, agrees with this general assessment. "There is a huge amount of research that has looked at, for instance, the effect of anxiety, physical workload, mental fatigue, [and] environmental conditions" on performance, he says. "And ultimately, these stressors do tend to draw on what might be deemed to be limited attentional and/or cognitive capacities, so there is no reason for me to think [trash talk] would not work in a similar manner."

The question becomes, then, not *whether* trash talk works, but *how* it works on any given person. For example, will angering your opponent provide you with a competitive advantage by emotionally distracting that person with task-irrelevant goals like retribution, or will the target of your trash talk use their elevated emotions as a trigger to intensify their focus, up their effort, or otherwise reach an optimal zone of functioning? According to John Raglin, who studies the IZOF model, "There are people that, when they're threatened or insulted, it gets their goat up, and that drives them to further their performance, or it motivates them to try harder or it focuses their efforts and gives them an additional emotional energy." And the last thing an athlete would want, per Brian Decker, is for an opponent to upregulate.

An effective trash-talker must know not just who to go after, therefore, but also who to leave the hell alone.

WARREN SAPP HAD a routine. Every week, on the Friday before a game, his PR staff would hand him a homemade booklet, usually about forty or fifty pages in length. This was his reading material for the next two days, culled from newspapers and magazines across the country—but especially from the hometown publications of whichever NFL team he'd be playing that Sunday. He wanted to know what people were saying about him. "Any little slight. Any little anything," he says. "There's always somebody who don't want to say that you're the best at what you do. There's always somebody that says, 'This will be the week.'"

Which was exactly what Sapp wanted to hear.

This was a practice that started for Sapp in college, when he played for the University of Miami. There he met John Hahn, a young sports information director, who would go on to spend more than fifteen years working communications for the Detroit Red Wings, and Sapp credits Hahn for teaching him how to use negative comments in the press for his own competitive gain. "He taught me that," he says. "He's the one that trained me on, 'Did you see this?!'"

They even had a name for this activity, Sapp tells me: "Find the hate."

It wasn't always easy. These were the days before widespread adoption of the internet, and playing in the Big East Conference, Miami's rival schools were located all along the East Coast, from Blacksburg, Virginia, to Boston, Massachusetts, to Upstate New York, in Syracuse. "Trust me! My people did a good job of finding them articles and cutting them up," he says. "These were printed papers that they threw at people's living rooms. I wanted to know what the hell you had to throw in somebody's living room that you're going to say about me."

Sapp mentions this to me as part of a conversation about motivation—and he refers to these weekly booklets of hate as "an accelerant." He says, "Build a fire, pour lighter fluid on it, and then throw the match. Now *that's* a fire."

Because Sapp was a voracious reader—and not just of the shitty things people muttered about him in the media—he'd occasionally ask his staff to go through the clips and underline or otherwise call out the most provocative or insulting lines from that week's batch of articles, the really disrespectful shit. That way he could more easily skim the material and find the juiciest bits. He says, "If I was reading a good book, I'd be like, 'Yo, I got my book this week, man. Can you highlight some of the hate for me?'" *Find the hate. Highlight the hate.* Still, Sapp never lost his appreciation for what the booklets provided for him; he never took it for granted. On the contrary, he came to rely on it, this pregame injection of venom from those who doubted him. Each week, he'd thumb through the pages with the same anticipation: "Let me see what they said, what they've been saying about Sapp."

The way he talks about it, it almost sounds illicit.

"Let me get some of that," he says. "I *need* some of that."

––––––––––––

DAMIAN LILLARD REMEMBERS his high school coach laughing at him when he shared his plans to one day play in the pros. Draymond Green can name all thirty-four players who were selected ahead of him in the 2012 NBA Draft. Tom Brady, who has likewise never forgotten how many teams passed on him (or how many times they did so) when he was taken in the sixth round of the 2000 NFL Draft, with the 199th pick, has made a career of listening to his critics—and then shutting them up. (In some ways, milking that underdog mythology for motivation became even more important to Brady as he achieved unimaginable on-field success and off-field fame. During the 2019 AFC Championship game, New England Patriots wide receiver Julian Edelman could be found on the sidelines feeding this need by screaming at his quarterback, "You're too fucking old! You're too old!")

These are just some of the tricks we play on ourselves.

"In the mind of an athlete, you take so many things and you twist them to motivate yourself," says Steve Jones Jr., the basketball coach. "And that may motivate you for two, three, four, five months, or for the rest of your career, the rest of your life. You can build a mountain of disrespect, even if no one's disrespected you."

Kobe Bryant always understood this. Before a summer invitational tournament while he was still in high school, for instance, the young hooper worked himself into a mania about how he was going to destroy Tim Thomas, one of the next day's opponents, who had the gall to be regarded as the top player in the country at the time.

"I'm gonna *kill* this dude," former NBA star Richard "Rip" Hamilton remembers Bryant saying, as he paced their shared room, refusing to sleep. As a pro, too, the Lakers guard would serially invent boogey-men for himself—which served as motivational grist—and then do everything he could to torture those people he decided to place in his crosshairs. You didn't have to be a big name to make the list. He attacked also-rans like Jimmy King, who had been a member of the University of Michigan's fabled Fab Five but sputtered on the NBA stage, and training-camp invitees like Paul Shirley. Per Jeff Pearlman, author of *Three-Ring Circus: Kobe, Shaq, Phil, and the Crazy Years of the Lakers*, "Paul Shirley was not going to make the Lakers. He was the last guy in camp, he had no shot." Which makes it all the more amazing (or bizarre) that Bryant still found it necessary to personally terrorize him. "Kobe swats his shot one day and points to his dick, and he was like, blah, blah, blah." Shirley was confused more than anything. "He was like, 'I'm no threat to you whatsoever. Why are you talking trash to me?'"

Tiger Woods is another elite-level athlete who has been known to warp reality to his psychological purposes. In 2019, for instance, Mexican American golfer Abraham Ancer said, "I would like to play Tiger," when asked who he'd choose to compete against in the Pres-idents Cup, if it were up to him. It was a logical response: Woods was his childhood hero. What an honor that would be! But the way Tiger responded, you'd have thought Ancer had taken a dump on his favorite driver. As fate would have it, Ancer and Woods would be paired together. And after Woods won, he said, without a hint of good humor, "Abe wanted it, he got it."

When *The Last Dance* documentary, about Michael Jordan and the Chicago Bulls, premiered in 2020, much was made about the series' depiction of Jordan as a competitor and his proclivity for find-ing or inventing slights. (Some say he picked up this trait from his college coach, Dean Smith, who remembered every word ever written about him and his team.) As author Mark Vancil says in the film, "He constructed reasons to play hard every night. These little slights were deep indignations to him." The athlete-podcast landscape is similarly littered with stories from former players who learned that lesson the hard way—that you don't talk shit to MJ. You don't give him a reason. "Jordan was off-limits," says Cheryl Miller. Which isn't to say fellow players didn't know things about him that could have been used as trash-talk fodder—personal knowledge about his off-court habits, for example—they just knew better than to say anything. "They had dirt on him," says Miller. "But nobody was game enough to bring it up because they knew Jordan had a long memory and he would file that away."*

This was the same man whose Hall of Fame speech was basically a laundry list of personal grievances. Anything you said could and would be used against you. In 1997, with Jordan on the cusp of his thirty-fourth birthday, George Karl made a comment to the press about how the all-time great player was becoming more of a jump-shooter as he aged—which was really a statement of fact more than anything. But not to Jordan. He interpreted this as a public humiliation of the highest order and vowed to make the coach eat his words, which he did, scoring forty-five points on the road in Seattle. Karl tells me, "At the end of the game, he walks by, 'I'm a jump-shooter, huh?'"

It didn't have to be verbal. Jordan could find motivation in any perceived disrespect—in anything he saw as an attempt to embarrass him. Sean Elliott tells me a story about working at Jordan's basketball camp as a counselor. At night, the counselors would scrimmage, and the campers watched. In one game, Elliott was shooting especially well, and so when he received the ball on the left wing, guarded by Jordan, he gave a ball fake, and Jordan fell for it. In the stands, the campers reacted. "The kids said, 'Ooooh,'" says Elliott. "They went just like, 'Oh, he got you!'" Rid of his defender, Elliott drove to the middle. "I should have tried to dunk it," he says, but there was a big guy in the way, so he put up a soft hook shot instead. "For most

---

* There was at least one athlete brave enough to prove himself an exception to this rule: Gary Payton.

people, that play works." But not this time. Despite biting on the ball fake, Jordan recovered almost instantly. Says Elliott, "This dude came from behind, and he blocked my shot so hard the ball damn near burst. It was a message, like, 'Don't embarrass me in front of my campers.' He wasn't letting *anybody* laugh at his expense, boy."

YOU COULD CALL it pathological, this need to twist events in one's mind—to make mountains out of molehills—and to even fabricate when necessary. Cheryl Miller sees some sociopathy at play, too—or at least she did with Gary Payton. Says Miller, "Gary was a sociopath when it came to trash talk. I mean he enjoyed it. He reveled in it. He got some delight from torturing people."*

But even if these willful distortions of reality don't rise to the level of a personality disorder, there's an undeniable level of pettiness that runs through it, which makes sense. That was one of the other curious findings Jeremy Yip and his collaborators turned up during their research: targets of trash talk "become motivated to punish the trash-talker and see the trash-talker lose rather than to maximize their own rewards of winning a competition," in his words. Put another way: if you talk shit to someone, that person will no longer care as much about winning as he or she will about ensuring that you lose. The other person will even be willing to incur a cost, as part of the deal, so long as you, the opponent, incur an even larger cost.

That is to say: people become petty as hell.

Maybe that shouldn't be so surprising. As Bertrand Russell once observed, "A great many men will cheerfully face impoverishment if they can thereby secure complete ruin for their rivals." And while that may speak to a somewhat depressing feature of humanity, perhaps there's an upside, too. If you're the sort of person who's looking for a reason to get your hackles up, then it follows that finding a way to be petty—for which the *Encyclopaedia Britannica* dictionary gives

---

*   Payton laughs when I read him this quote from Miller, because he did truly love talking shit.

as one of its definitions: "treating people harshly and unfairly because of things that are not very important"—could be quite functional.

When I mention this idea of pettiness to Yip, he says he hadn't thought about the effects of trash talk in those terms, but he doesn't disagree. He says, "It would be interesting to know, with these athletes, are they actively monitoring their Twitter feed? Like, do they care what is being said in the lead-up to the game?" For some, social media could provide a bottomless well of disrespect—and, therefore, potentially, petty motivations. I mention Kevin Durant and his enigmatic Twitter presence, replete with burner accounts, which he's used to respond to online trolls. Yip laughs, says, "That is such a waste of time."

If nothing else, it's super petty, I say.

"Yeah, it is," he says. "Don't tell him I said that."

THERE'S A PERSISTENT myth in American political discourse that the first-ever televised presidential debate—between Richard Nixon and John F. Kennedy in 1960—was a political windfall for the eventual thirty-fifth president of the United States, JFK, because the image broadcast into people's homes showed him as attractive and luminous, while his opponent, who refused makeup, was sweaty and ogre-like. As legend has it, viewers couldn't see past these superficial differences to the substance of their disagreements. "That's one of the greatest urban legends in the history of America," says Sam Nelson, the director of speech and debate programs at Cornell University, who has more than twenty-five years of experience as a competitive-debate coach.

In reality, Nixon's mistake wasn't turning away the rouge but in hyping up his own performance before the fact, per Nelson. "He had been a debater at Whittier College, in California, and he supposedly said, 'I'm going to mop the floor with Kennedy. Kennedy doesn't know what he's doing.'" Overly confident, Nixon barely prepared.

The problem wasn't that Nixon was wrong to believe in himself—in reality, he performed just fine under the bright TV lights. But what he didn't do was "mop the floor" with his Democratic opponent, as predicted. Kennedy did OK! And in so doing, he blew past many people's low expectations for him. He looked good, if only because everyone expected him to look so terrible. "Almost everybody thinks that Kennedy won the debate, just because he held his own."

This is a lesson that remains top of mind for Nelson whenever he's approached by candidates for public office. They come to him, seeking counsel, before taking the debate stage. Here's what he tells them: "Spin down expectations."

"You actually do the opposite of trash talking," he says. "You talk about how you're not very good at debate." You let them underestimate you.*

It's a strategy that can work for athletes, too.

Wade Schalles is the Guinness World Record holder for most victories and pins by an amateur wrestler. As a high schooler, however, he knew he wasn't an intimidating presence—he'd always been on the scrawnier side. Still, Schalles believed it was possible to use his physical size for psychological advantage. During weigh-ins, when most people sucked in their stomachs and puffed out their chests, he did the opposite. "I would round my shoulders and kind of slink onto the scale, and people would go, 'Oh, I have that skinny kid? I'm going to crush him,'" he says. "I knew I couldn't impress anybody with my body, but wait until I get my body wrapped around your neck."

This describes the risk athletes—especially elite athletes—face going into many competitions: that they will be *overly* confident. Stuart Beattie, the senior lecturer of performance psychology at Bangor University in the UK, refers to this as "cruising," and it's exactly

---

* Intentionally or not, this set-the-bar-breathtakingly-low dynamic benefited Sarah Palin when she participated in the 2008 vice presidential debate and basically only had to refrain from vomiting onstage for her performance to be deemed a success.

what guys like Kobe Bryant and Tiger Woods were guarding against in their search for even the smallest motivating factors, in harboring the unlikeliest grudges and identifying the pettiest slights. Beattie makes an analogy to driving in a car. "Let's say you have an appointment, and you're going to lose something big if you don't make it," he says. "To start with, when you jump in the car, you'll be chancing red lights, you'll be getting your foot down, you'll be investing so much effort in trying to get there." But what happens when you're catching only green lights and making great time? "Halfway through the journey, what do you do? You slow down. You relax. You take the foot off the gas." It's not a character flaw; it's human nature, Beattie explains. "That's the whole thing about self-efficacy and the cruising aspect. Once you feel confident about obtaining something, you back off. Your motivation to achieve that end drops." But those efficacy beliefs could be based on false or incomplete information. Like, what if there's unplanned roadwork ahead? Or what if that skinny kid is a much better wrestler than he's letting on? "Sometimes that's our undoing," he says.

For this reason, having an element of doubt—which can be real or imagined and can come either by having someone doubt you or by talking such a big game that backing it up feels like anything but a sure thing—can be good or even necessary.* "You need that element where you have engagement," says Ashley Merryman, coauthor of *Top Dog*. "If you absolutely think this is a cakewalk, you can underperform. That's when you can lose. That's when Goliath loses because he takes it for granted that he's going to win. He's not sufficiently motivated."

If you're competing against a Michael Jordan type, that's exactly what you want to happen. You want that person to view you as no threat whatsoever—as not even rising to the level of challenge. "Don't roust him," Len Elmore would say, whenever he worried his talkative

---

* Assuming your efficacy beliefs are in no danger of tipping too far in the wrong direction.

teammates might inspire the opposition. Sean Elliott would be apo-
plectic anytime some fresh-faced fool hazarded a degrading comment
in MJ's direction. "There were times when guys talked trash to him,
and you'd be like, 'Are you out of your mind? What are you doing
talking to that man?'" he says. "We actually said several times, like,
'Don't say anything to him. Why would you poke the bear?'"

JOHN MCGRAW KNEW what he was doing. The diminutive
baseball man and vicious bench jockey began his managerial career
around the turn of the twentieth century, and when he'd arrive in
visiting cities with his team, he wouldn't have his players dress for
games at the ballpark, like most clubs did. Instead, he ordered his
players to put on their uniforms in their hotel rooms. From there,
he would lead his team through the streets via horse-drawn carriage.
Opposing fans reacted to this spectacle by throwing tomatoes and
even rocks at the rival club—the invaders—as they paraded through
the streets of their hometown. According to baseball historian and
McGraw expert Steve Steinberg, this was done, in part, to stimulate
attendance. But it also served as a kind of visceral (if possibly painful)
bulletin-board material.

Did you hear what they said about us?
Ow, that hurts!

The basic idea behind bulletin-board material is that it's possible
to rev up one's team by exposing them to negative comments from
outsiders. It's not so different than Warren Sapp's book of hate, or
Michael Jordan's knack for nursing a grievance and then leveraging
it for in-game effort; it's simply scaled for team-wide consumption.
McGraw wasn't the first to understand there could be competitive
benefit to this practice, and he definitely wasn't the last. In football,
in particular, it remains common for coaches to lean on defend-our-
honor narratives within the locker room—thereby offering players a
potential motivating spark, shaking grizzled vets out of the tedium

of their routines, and instilling an us-versus-them mentality.* Bill
Belichick is considered by many to be a master. Before Super Bowl
XXXIX, for instance, in which Belichick's Patriots would be taking
on the Philadelphia Eagles, the head coach made a speech to his players the night before the game. "Let me just read you a little something here," he said, pulling out a piece of paper. What he read was
the Eagles' victory parade route, as already mapped out through the
city of Philadelphia. "It's eleven o'clock, in case any of you want to
attend that." Other times, Belichick wouldn't have to say a word; he'd
just flash incendiary headlines on screen during film-study sessions.
The message was always clear. "We definitely bought into it," former
offensive lineman Damien Woody, who spent four seasons with Belichick, has said. "It would get you fired up, pissed off, all that stuff."

Mark Schlereth says there isn't a team in the NFL that doesn't
employ bulletin-board material. (Although maybe there are some
that shouldn't.**) He remembers Joe Gibbs, his head coach in Washington, reading the team article excerpts in which an opposing coach
made disparaging remarks about Washington's offensive line the
night before Super Bowl XXVI. "Joe Gibbs was *livid*. I've rarely ever
seen him so mad," per Schlereth, who adds that Mike Shanahan, his

---

* According to Yip, groups often bond when exposed to disparaging remarks
from outsiders, because it increases the perception of a rivalry relationship.
Kristen Lindquist, a professor of psychology and neuroscience at the
University of North Carolina, Chapel Hill, credits these effects to some
of our most basic and primal instincts as humans, like tribalism. "One of
the most salient things to humans is the groups they belong to," she says.
"There is a lot of reward associated with feeling like your group is superior
and denigrating the other group. I would imagine that a huge part of trash
talk is helping to create a sense of us versus them."

** Before Adam Gase's third season as head coach of the Miami Dolphins, he
prepared a preseason slideshow in which he'd compiled all the disrespect
the team was receiving from expert prognosticators. But when he shared
the presentation with Scott Goldman, then the director of performance
psychology for the Dolphins, Goldman suggested he scrap it. "It was just
too much," says Goldman. "What happened was, there were so many
headlines on the slides, and it was so visually clear, it just made it seem very
factual, like maybe they got a point here!"

coach with the Denver Broncos, would use similar tactics. "If some-body said something about us as a football team that he found offen-sive, he wouldn't hesitate to bring it up."

From Schlereth's perspective, the upshot of bulletin-board material was less about some last-minute infusion of energy—like a movie-scene locker-room speech—so much as it was the ongoing and arousing effect it could have on a team during the week before a game: during drills, film sessions, and the like. As he explains, there are often a handful of players in any given locker room who exert less than maximum effort, whose attention wanders—which makes sense when you consider that NFL teams have unwieldy fifty-three-man rosters—and if getting those few guys good and pissed off somehow increases their engagement and sharpens their focus, that's a net posi-tive. "If you heighten their preparation and heighten their awareness, how much better are you going to be in the long run as a football team?" he says.

Former NFL punter Chris Kluwe saw this as tapping into what he calls "the last 10 percent." Says Kluwe, "You expect guys to play at 100 percent capacity, right? But for certain guys, sometimes they think their 90 percent is their 100 percent." The key is to unlock that last 10 percent.

———————————

GARY PAYTON DIDN'T like to practice—at least not in the pros, not as he got older. But don't take my word for it. As Payton says, "I didn't like to practice." The same was true for his Sonics teammate Shawn Kemp. As the coach of the Sonics, George Karl recognized this about his star players, he tells me. It became obvious, as the guys would just go through the motions, hoisting up ill-advised shots. Moving up and down the floor with a total lack of intensity.

Karl knew something had to change. He needed to find a way to make practice matter, to get the competitive juices flowing. At times, he'd try to motivate his team by talking shit to them. He says, "Gary and Shawn had to live with me getting on them about being lazy in practice. Fucking practice up because you're not playing hard." But that wasn't really the answer, as the players would talk shit right back to him, and before long the sessions would devolve into three-way bickering contests. Sportswriter Phil Taylor says the same could happen during games. "I loved sitting courtside at Seattle games," he says. "George Karl and Shawn Kemp and Gary Payton—I mean, they would be trash-talking to each other, much less their opponents." He remembers one game when the coach seemed unusually exasperated and said something to Kemp to the effect of, "Shawn, if you could just make a *pretense* of playing defense." Kemp replied with a series of expletives.

Other times, Karl would lose patience and toss Payton out of practice. But he'd still get an earful. Says Taylor, "His trash talk to Karl would often be about his growing paunch. Like, 'Man, they told me you played! That can*not* be that you played ball.' And stuff about his hairline." Eventually, according to Taylor, even Karl came to understand that "Payton was not somebody you really wanted to verbally joust with."

The coach admits as much himself.

"Gary and I trash-talked each other," says Karl, "but Gary would win those battles." If Karl took his point guard out of a game, he says, Payton would talk trash to him from his seat on the bench. "And if I didn't put him back in, he'd be trash-talking everybody on the fucking bench. He motherfucked *everybody*." When that happened, Karl says, a "cloudy energy" would descend over his team—which sometimes he preferred to just avoid. He says, "I'll be honest with you, there were games I never took him out because I didn't want to hear his chatter. People would say, 'Why did you play Gary Payton for forty-eight minutes?' Well, I didn't want to hear his shit!"

But the coach didn't want to silence Payton. He understood the star guard was at his best when he was talking trash—that it was fundamental to his game. Rather than fight against his player's proclivities, Karl eventually learned to leverage them to his—and the team's—advantage. As it turned out, he *could* use trash talk to make practice matter, just as long as he wasn't the one talking the trash.

David Wingate joined the Seattle SuperSonics for the 1995–1996 season. A ten-year veteran, Wingate was essentially the last man on the bench, according to Karl. "He knew he wasn't going to play very much," he says. But he nonetheless held an indispensable role on the team. He was the designated shit-talker. Says Karl, "If Gary didn't want to practice, instead of me motherfucking Gary, we had David Wingate motherfuck Gary. They'd be chirping back and forth. I was amazed how many times David Wingate got Gary to come practice."

When I ask Payton about this, he lights up at the mention of Wingate's name.

"David was my best friend on the team," Payton says, and he fondly remembers their on-court battles. "David used to go at me. He'd grab on me and hold on me," and talk all kinds of mess, per Payton. *Come on, come on, you ain't got it. They call you a superstar? You ain't no All-Star.* "I used to love that. I used to love going back at Dave because Dave pumped me up in practice. And when he pumped me up, that means I'm going to get some extra work." The point guard knew he was being manipulated, but he didn't mind because he also knew it was to his benefit. Wingate did what his coach never could have on his own: he made Payton want to compete.

PEOPLE LOVE TO hear stories about Larry Bird as a shit-talker—there's just something about a pasty white guy from Middle America talking a bunch of foulmouthed mess. Like how he'd call for the ball when Michael Jordan switched onto him on defense by saying, "I got a little one on me." Or how he'd shout, when he and Dennis Rodman were muscling each other in the post, "Hey, give me the ball! Quick, before they realize no one's guarding me." Or how he developed a habit of telling defenders exactly how he was going to embarrass them on the court, just as Satchel Paige would broadcast his pitches from the mound. Bird would tell opposing players which way he was going to drive, or how many times he was going to pump-fake, or whether or not he was going to bank it in. Sometimes he'd ask defenders if they were ready. And after he scored, he'd say, "Oh, I thought you said you were ready."

It can read as semiplayful, these statements, but Bird inspired plenty of enmity, too. He'd taunt big men like Patrick Ewing—saying, "You can't guard me"—and mock the declining skills of legends like Julius Erving, as they finished out their careers. (Dr. J got so fed up with Bird that he physically attacked him.) According to former Boston Celtics teammate Robert Parish, "Bird was degrading. He'd make it real personal."

But perhaps the best way to understand Bird as a talker is this: he was a competitor in constant search of a fresh challenge. Like Jordan sniffing for any hints of disrespect, which he could warp into motivational fuel, Bird hunted for reasons to raise his game.* Sometimes that involved pestering ball boys in visiting arenas to find out what the scoring record was in that building (so he could break it), and other times it involved demeaning his opponents in graphic terms, or telling them just what he was about to do to them, in direct and unambiguous provocations—because he knew that would put the pressure on them to stop him, and on himself to succeed. "So much of it with him, I don't think it was about other people. It was always to put pressure on himself," says Jackie MacMullan, the longtime *Boston Globe* journalist, who collaborated with Bird on multiple book projects. "You're putting a lot of pressure on yourself when you say things like that."

---

*   Even Jordan recognized the parallels, and he forbade his teammates from engaging with Bird on the floor. When the baby-faced B.J. Armstrong first joined the NBA, Bird took a run at him by saying, "I can't believe they're letting kids from junior high into the NBA." With Armstrong about to respond, Jordan stepped in. He said, "Not a single person. Not one word. No one talk to Larry Bird." To which Bird replied, pleading in his Indiana drawl, "C'mon, Michael. Let these guys get involved in it. Come on."

In his playing days, George "the Iceman" Gervin was similar in this regard. His goal was to achieve consistency from game to game, and he found it useful to see little challenges everywhere. It could be as simple as an opposing player saying to him before a game, "Ice, man, don't get thirty on me." Which would be meant as a joking compliment, but Gervin would think to himself, *No, I won't get thirty because I'm going to get forty.* Or it could be the way a defense schemed against him. Or maybe an opposing coach would do something to make him mad. That's what defensive stalwart Michael Cooper says happened against him and the Lakers, when Gervin dropped forty-plus on him. "But he wasn't looking at me, he was looking at Pat Riley," says Cooper. One time, the Indiana Pacers made the mistake of marketing an in-game promotion, wherein all the fans would win fried chicken if the Pacers kept Gervin under thirty points. They even assigned Dudley Bradley, known as the Secretary of Defense, to guard him. No matter. Gervin scored twenty-five in the first half and fifty-five for the game. "No chicken tonight!" he screamed to the fans.

When Gervin played against the Boston Celtics, he didn't have to look as far as the marketing department to find a suitable challenge—he just had to locate Larry Bird. The Celtics star would always have a few choice words for the Iceman, as he did for almost everyone. Says Gervin, "Because Danny Ainge used to guard me, he used to say, 'Ice, give him fifty, man, because he's scared of you.' That's what Bird would say to me."

It wasn't reverse psychology; Bird *wanted* Gervin to go at Ainge with everything he had because he knew, in talking that trash, he wasn't just putting the spotlight on his Celtics teammate, but on himself, too. Someone had to match the Iceman if his team was going to win, after all. Says Gervin, "That was his motivation."

———————

IN 1897, A man named Norman Triplett watched a bunch of competitive cyclists hurry around a track. He recorded his observations and published the results the following year in the *American Journal of Psychology*. Triplett's efforts are widely considered to be the first-ever sports psychology experiment, and they gave rise to a concept we now know as "social facilitation"—a phenomenon that describes the human tendency to perform better when in the presence of other people than when alone. (Imagine running as fast as you can on an empty track versus running with someone next to you, and you'll get the idea.) Or as Triplett put it, "the bodily presence of another contestant participating simultaneously in the race serves to liberate latent energy not ordinarily available."

Or put another way still: a rival will push you further than you can go on your own.

"The actual Latin meaning of competition is together we strive. That's actually the true nature of competition," Mark Aoyagi says, in reference to the concept. "It's about recognizing that my fellow competitors are not my enemies. They are my facilitators of me getting the best out of myself."

That's what B.J. Armstrong says trash-talkers like Larry Bird and Michael Jordan understood implicitly, and what he eventually came to appreciate in his time in the NBA. It was a smack-talk revelation: that the most confident trash-talkers were simply looking for ways to stay motivated and perform at their peaks. They weren't trying to diminish their opponents, necessarily; rather, they often wanted to draw the best out of them. In their verbal challenges, they invited opposing players to raise their levels of performance—because that, in turn, would bring the best out of themselves. It would ensure that someone poked the bear. "That's what I understood about trash talking," says Armstrong. "The best trash-talkers are the people who want you to be at your very best because what they're really saying is, 'My best is better than your best, so let's get to our best and see what happens.'"

Section III

THE ANSWER TO TRASH TALK

Chapter 7

HOW TO RESPOND (OR NOT RESPOND)

WHEN DR. CHARLES "Andy" Morgan first visited Camp Mackall, an active training facility for the US Army buried deep in the North Carolina woods and home to one of the military's SERE school compounds, he didn't know what to expect. A Yale psychiatrist, University of New Haven national security professor, and expert in forensic psychology, post-traumatic stress disorder, and human performance under highly stressful conditions, among other things, Morgan traveled to the facility at the army's invitation. He was interested in potentially running lab tests on students as they participated in the SERE program's culminating field-training exercise: a multiday prisoner-of-war-camp simulation meant to mimic the stresses, deprivations, and other abuses of actual captivity.

SERE—which stands for Survival, Evasion, Resistance, Escape— represents the military's most intense survival course, reserved for those soldiers who are most likely to find themselves isolated behind enemy lines. At Camp Mackall, the captivity portion of the training, which follows about two weeks of classroom and field instruction, runs around the clock for several days, while SERE's cadre, in the guise of enemy captors, spend that time trying to break down both individual and group resistance via a range of physical and psychological stressors, including a whole lot of deeply personalized shit talk designed explicitly for mental and emotional manipulation. It's also the only school in the military in which instructors are allowed to hit their students. Still, Morgan was skeptical. On the day of his initial visit, there was nothing going on. It was gray and foggy, and an eerie stillness hung like gauze atop the loblolly pines that sprung from the brown Carolina earth. As he was guided across the wooded grounds, which had all the welcoming ambiance of a concentration camp, he was privately dubious the level of stress produced during the SERE exercises here would be any different than what he could generate in a lab back in Connecticut. The students—most of whom at Camp Mackall attend SERE as part of the yearlong Special Forces Qualification Course, aka Q Course—knew going in this was only a simulation, a training exercise. Wouldn't they see through the whole role-play thing, and, even subliminally, call bullshit? He doubted their hormone response would approach the real-world levels he had been promised.

Boy, was he wrong.

WHEN SERE IS in session, you can smell it. Morgan describes the stench as an unmistakable blend of garlic and onions that pervades the exercise from the point of capture on. There's a reason for this distinctive, nostril-puckering aroma: it's the smell of fear. "We have two different kinds of sweat glands, the apocrine and the eccrine glands," he says. "The apocrine glands are the ones you can really smell. You can *smell* fear. It's part of the stress response, so people do not smell good." For Morgan, the first indication SERE might be eliciting truly elevated levels of stress, though, was when he saw grown men cry. "Just like tears running down their face because they're in a dilemma and they don't know what to do," he says. "That was a good sign." As was the fact that the red and itchy splotchiness of poison ivy was disappearing from students' bodies within hours. "It was like they were on prednisone because all the poison ivy vanished, and it's an allergic reaction," he says. "I knew at that point the [stress hormone] cortisol had to be high enough to shut off their immune system."

On top of that were the symptoms of dissociation students were reporting, which Morgan describes as similar to the sort of horror-movie visual tricks that cinematographers use to convey something scary, like a camera both reeling back and zooming forward simultaneously. Other symptoms include the world looking distorted: bigger or smaller. Sounds warping, colors changing. Having the feeling of being separated from one's body and looking at oneself from above. "Just for them to be checking all those things off, which sound really crazy. Like, other people look mechanical, motionless, or dead. I feel that I'm seeing the world through a wide-angle lens, or through tunnel vision, or my arms and legs feel longer or shorter than they really are. Time is moving in slow motion, or everything is happening as if it's in one single moment. Those kinds of things," says Morgan, who had every reason to believe the students were experiencing serious alterations to their physiology and cognition. "These weren't people who were prone to exaggerating."

Then he got the data back. At various points in the exercise, Morgan and his team would draw blood and collect spit samples from students to test their hormone levels, and that's what cinched it: the stress was off the charts—literally. Says Morgan, "When we first got our data on [cortisol] in the first paper we published, we actually removed like thirty people because the reviewer said, 'Well, these are outside the physiologic ranges. We've never seen it this high in people before.' But it didn't change the findings."

Bottom line: the stress was legit.

Brian Decker didn't need any lab results to know that. The former Green Beret, who is now vice president of team development for the Carolina Panthers, went through the course himself—"I lost seventeen pounds in seven days," he says—before eventually serving as commander of Camp Mackall's SERE school, where he overlapped with Morgan, who, despite his initial skepticism, has spent twenty-plus years studying stress-related trainings such as SERE. Of the cadre's efforts to expose psychological vulnerabilities in each student, Decker says, "You're malnourished, you're hungry, you're getting put into small boxes, you're getting buried in the ground, you're getting sprayed with water—it is shit talking at the highest level that can be done." On its face, the pressures and abuses of SERE school may seem wholly disproportional to anything an athlete might face on the field of play, and there are unquestionably critical degrees of difference. As Decker says, "I always tell people, 'Listen, there's nothing I'm ever going to do in sport that will ever compare to what I was exposed to in the military. Never.'" And yet, in both cases, it's all about building resiliency and demonstrating mentally tough behaviors in stressful situations; it's about learning to respond appropriately, in spite of external pressures, distractions, and provocations. (A good rule of thumb for SERE, I'm told, is that the more a student is being abused, the worse that person is doing, in terms of applying the proper resistance techniques, which is to say: they aren't responding in the right way.) Decker, who also spent three years in charge of the assessment and selection process for Special Forces while in the military, clearly saw the connections once he transitioned to life in the NFL,* and he's made a successful second career by incorporating the lessons of SERE and Special Forces into the training philosophies of professional football teams.

For all these reasons, I feel confident I'm in the right place when I arrive at Camp Mackall early on a late-summer morning, the dark of night still choking the sky. It has been six months since I first contacted the army's press office, because I want to know more about the training methods and psychological principles that underpin SERE,

---

* He's not the only one: the US Army is the largest employer of sports psychologists in the country.

in hopes of uncovering insights about what it takes to handle even the most aggressive and threatening shit talk: specifically, how the course not only helps soldiers cope with potentially overwhelming stress, but also prepares them to optimize their performance under pressure—and to my surprise, the army agrees to host me. I've been driven to Mackall by my chaperone for the week, Janice Burton, a chatty and hard-charging deputy public affairs officer for the John F. Kennedy Special Warfare Center and School (SWCS), which is based about an hour east, in Fort Bragg, and more informally referred to as "Swick." (On our drive, Burton tells me about her husband's experience with SERE years earlier, during which he was forced to maintain a prostrate stress position in the cold December dirt or suffer humiliating and painful slaps at the hands of a small, kneeling woman playing the role of a Korean captor.) Today, we arrive to find an artificial-turf field splashed with the harsh yellow glare of generator-powered floodlights. On the field, Special Forces candidates at the very front end of their assessment and selection process are being evaluated on their ability to perform basic physical fitness requirements—push-ups and sit-ups and the like—to help determine which of them will advance to the Q Course. As I climb out of the car, I notice the muggy morning air smells more than anything like pine trees and what I assume are generator fumes. For this group, the garlic and onions come later.

The goal of the verbal abuse at SERE—which is combined with all the other stressors of simulated captivity, like sleep deprivation, frequent humiliation, a creeping sense of starvation, generally harsh conditions, and a concentrated stream of what they call "physical coercion"—is to elicit emotional reactions from students. To make them mad, or sad, or scared or even question their purpose. "The cadre is really looking for anything that will get an emotional response because the one thing they've learned over time with captured individuals is, once you find an emotional response, you have leverage. If you can get people to make decisions out of emotion, they stop thinking clearly about what they're doing," says Morgan. "It means I control you, and I can begin to shape your responses, almost like operant conditioning."*

On a practical level, a soldier who exhibits emotionality is no longer focused on resistance—the task at hand—and is therefore easier to manipulate into doing whatever a captor wants of them: divulging information, perhaps, or being used for propaganda purposes, or turning against fellow soldiers, which can lead to feelings of isolation and the further breaking of group cohesion. "It's much more difficult to leverage a group when they're all together," a SERE instructor tells me. "But if I can pit them against each other and break an individual off, now maybe I can exploit that individual."

As you can imagine, SERE instructors engage in some of the world's most provocative shit talk: it's for a reason the army doesn't allow outsiders to videotape or otherwise record the exercises. "What do you think they're saying to African Americans, or women, or anybody?" says Morgan. While instructors must steer clear of certain banned words, like the N-word, they are otherwise allowed to say basically anything that pokes at those kinds of sensitivities—or any other sensitivities that may exist around race, religion, gender, status, sexual orientation, physical appearance, and so on. Often instructors will key in on those people who stand out within a group, for whatever reason—they could be the youngest, the oldest, the only female student. As instructors get to know a group, they can pick up on more subtle differences, too. A commander of the 7th Psychological Operations (PSYOP) Battalion, Lieutenant Colonel Sharon Engelmeier was both the oldest and highest-ranking student when she attended SERE several months before my visit to Camp Mackall. (The experience happened to coincide with her fortieth birthday.) Engelmeier tells me her instructors tried to isolate her and remembers specifically

---

* Cheryl Miller tells me almost the same thing about eliciting emotion from one's opponent on the basketball court. She says, "If it gets emotional, and *you* get emotional—but I understand that I got you to that point—then I control you."

being called out for having a deep voice. "I remember at the time thinking like, 'Why did you just say that? I'm not even going down that path,'" she says. "I could see they were poking at me."

And they would continue to poke.

And poke.

And poke.

And then maybe dunk her head in a bucket of water.

The basis for much of the mental and emotional torment that takes place at SERE comes from a kind of playbook called the SOP, or standard operating procedure. The SOP lays out scores of scenarios—or dilemmas, as they're also known—which are designed to mind-fuck the students in a variety of ways, including but not limited to picking at sensitive areas, tempting individuals to recede from the group for self-preservation reasons, cajoling students to second-guess their most deeply held beliefs (such as their faith in God or government), and exposing preexisting prejudices to create intragroup fault lines. For example, Morgan tells me about a scenario in which a male student is made to believe his captors are torturing a female classmate, and the abuse will only stop if he talks. "You could tell that, for some of the guys, it's like, 'Screw her! She's a woman. She shouldn't be here in the first place,'" he says. "Then you'd have others who just look absolutely lost because they don't know what to do." Meanwhile, the female student can be made to resent those who don't come to her aid.

Most SERE classes can expect to experience a few standard scenarios, like having to watch their captors burn an American flag or tear out pages of the Bible. "You see some primitive things kick in," says Morgan, who at times feared students might actually riot, as they watched the flag go up in flames—but the dilemmas are not chosen at random. Instructors select scenarios based on the specifics of each student—based on their individual behaviors, potential insecurities, and even personal lives. As Colonel Stuart Farris, who is chief of staff for SWCS when we meet, says, repeating a mantra he learned at SERE years earlier: "To know you is to exploit you." To that end, instructors will incorporate any and all information they can acquire about a student, which is as likely to come via social-media research as postcapture interrogation. "Anything they find on the web is fair game. You can see sometimes students suddenly realizing that what the instructor is saying comes from online," says Morgan. When that happens, "they become quite alarmed."

Even still, it's impossible to predict where any given scenario will lead. Morgan compares the SOP to a Christopher Guest script, like *Best in Show*, in which key themes and goals are made explicit, but the actors are encouraged to improvise within each scene. Likewise, the best instructors freelance within the confines of SERE, looking to exploit any psychological weaknesses, any emotional reactivity. Morgan describes these shit-talking efforts as a kind of art form, when done well. He says, "Depending on how poetic and ingenious they are, they become beautiful at it." But even the most exquisite and inventive abuses are always deployed as a means to an end, as part of the course's critical educational component. Says Morgan, "There's a very specific intent to find any vulnerability in you. They're trying to get a finger somewhere under your skin, and they'll use any kind of trash talk [to do it]. Most of it, like 80 percent of it, won't be effective. They just keep poking until they find something. They find the one that works for you."

FORMER NBA STAR Gilbert Arenas had a habit of talking smack before a game even began. It was when the starting lineups for either side were bumping fists and exchanging pleasantries around midcourt—just before tip-off—that's when he'd spit out some incendiary shit. He says, "We'd be shaking hands, and I'm like, 'Aight, we gonna treat these dudes like some hos. Go ahead, get a little pussy, and then get on out of here.'"

The idea behind these insulting forays was mostly exploratory, Arenas tells me. "Just to see their reaction." Like the cadre at SERE, he was probing for information. "You sit there and just jab. Jab until you get a reaction."

And there was almost always a reaction.

In its presentation of a challenge—and in its often-degrading provocations—trash talk all but demands a response, in one form or another. This impulse to respond is likely guided in part by what Jonathan Culpeper, the impoliteness scholar, explains to me as the principle of reciprocity. To illustrate his point, Culpeper makes an economic analogy. "It's like a debit-credit balance sheet," he says. "If I approach you in a very polite way, I actually put you under pressure to reciprocate back to me at roughly the same level because I've given you a credit in my politeness." If someone is impolite to you, however, then you are given a debit, he says. "Now, if you don't do a debit back to level it out, you're left with a debit on the sheet—meaning that you take the hit. You're left with this damage to your identity, your face."

Thus the desire—nay, the imperative—to respond. As Warren Sapp puts it, in discussing the dozens, "Whenever you get sliced or cut, you got to get back."

Many athletes talk about this need to respond as a matter of respect, which is a concept that has become almost sacrosanct in leagues like the NBA. Danny Manning admits that, when he was a rookie, he was motivated in large part by earning the respect of his peers. "That's one of the bigger driving forces for a player," he says. The few times LeBron James has made trash-talk headlines it has been because he regarded his opponent's banter as somehow disrespectful. "For me personally, as long as it doesn't get disrespectful, I'm fine with it," James has said.

But, with all due respect to King James, that's a silly thing to say. For one thing, to engage in trash talk is to be inherently (or at least superficially) disrespectful. But even more than that, to vocally demand respect is also to broadcast a sensitivity and leave oneself open to attack. "The immediate response to trash talking is it becomes a threat to your ego," says B.J. Armstrong. You feel disrespected, like you need to defend your honor. "That's why you respond." It's this same instinct to get even—to demand satisfaction—that has allowed cultures of honor (which put premiums on notions of masculinity and reputation) to persist across geography and generations. It's the instinct to *take this shit outside.*

But it's a trap.

"In places like that [with honor cultures], people will kill you out of pride—if nothing, just to save face," says Brian Decker. "Whatever mechanisms and processes are at work, [they] are the basis by which you can shit-talk people because what it will get them to do is it will get them to abandon their game."

As a player, Brian Scalabrine understood the temptation to shut up a shit-talker was, more than anything, a prideful reflex, and he used that to his advantage. "Most NBA players, they love to prove other people wrong," he says. That's why Scal would yell statements of fact to his teammates that were very much meant to be overheard by the opposition. Things like, "We know Mario Chalmers can't go left!"* Even the biggest-name players can fall into this ego trap. A former teammate of Isiah Thomas's tells me the Hall of Fame point guard would start playing one-on-one instead of facilitating for his teammates when opponents talked shit. "If guys talked trash to him, he would just start shooting the ball every time," says the former player. "He just had to prove he was the best." According to Arenas, Russell Westbrook has proven to be susceptible to trash talk, as well, because he can't help but engage when someone challenges him verbally, and then he "becomes like a Ferrari in traffic."**

Personal pride and individual egos can similarly be exploited at SERE school, as students often betray their emotionality in small,

---

* Chalmers is sitting with us in a BIG3 locker room in Las Vegas when Scalabrine gives this example.

** During the 2021–2022 NBA season, Russell Westbrook also betrayed a measure of prideful sensitivity when he took public umbrage with folks calling him Westbrick, in regard to his shot selection and propensity to occasionally miss badly. He said, "The moment it becomes where my name is getting shamed, it becomes an issue."

unintentional gestures. "It's almost like something in their eyes changes," one instructor says. "They get a little more rigid. Maybe their hands get a little harder," like the clenching of a fist. "Even though they know that's not the proper response, it's the response that is natural because we're a more prideful group. We want to defend our honor." Andy Morgan tells me about a class of Navy SEALS from the early 2000s, in which the students weren't abused at all—at least not physically. Instead, they were tied up, placed in a shower stall, and left to listen to Islamic prayer music. "The messaging was, 'We're not even interested in you. You're not even important enough to be interested in.' And it was enormously effective," he says. According to Morgan, the students were so insulted by this dismissive treatment that half of them refused to speak with a fictional TV reporter when given the chance, which would have been an opportunity within the training exercise to get on the international news and communicate something back to the US government. "They were so mad that they were useless," he says. "The teaching point at the end of that iteration was, you have to get over yourself."

At the end of every iteration of the survival course, there is a teaching point of some kind for each student, some sort of tangible takeaway. The students need to be made aware of their own buttons, because if they want to respond in mentally tough ways, they first need to know where they're weak. As a senior SERE instructor who has logged thousands of hours interrogating students under the duress of simulated captivity puts it to me, "You want to teach people to control their emotions." This is what happens on the debrief day, after however many interminable hours of physical and psychological torment in the hyperstressful environment of SERE, when the students sit down across from their instructors. "They meet the interrogator and they go, 'Man, I just wanted to beat your face in,'" says Morgan. "And [the interrogators] are like, 'Yeah, but here's what I was doing that was getting you so angry. Did you know it? You should work on that because, man, you have got a big red button that says PUSH ME HERE AND I BECOME IRRATIONAL.'"

The specifics of those buttons vary from person to person, of course—one soldier might be sensitive about his religion, another might lose his composure out of fear—but in a way, the differences are almost irrelevant. Everyone has flaws and points of imperfection, things they can work on. The key is to have enough humility to acknowledge your personal and psychological deficiencies, whatever they might be—to embrace them even—and not let them translate into potential liabilities that other people can exploit. Because they almost certainly will if you let them.

AT THE END of the movie *8 Mile*, in the climactic rap-battle scene, the character played by Eminem does something nobody sees coming: he uses his turn on the microphone not just to take down his opponent, but also to preemptively cop to all sorts of embarrassing shit he knows could be used against him. "I am white, I am a bum, I do live in a trailer with my mom," he snaps, in an attempt to blunt those lines of attack, among others. A psychologist and antibullying expert named Izzy Kalman brings up this scene to me as part of a discussion about how to disarm the disruptive and face-threatening effects of trash talk. Kalman says of Eminem, "He insults himself so badly that his opponent can't possibly insult him worse than he insulted himself."

But it's not just that the rapper took the words out of his opponent's mouth; it's that he demonstrated a level of self-awareness—coupled with a willingness to be brutally honest about his own strengths and weaknesses—that prevented these areas of possible insecurity from being weaponized against him. By understanding how he was likely to be attacked and confronting those embarrassing truths head-on, he stripped them of their power. Hockey pest Sean Avery may not be much of a rap-battler—and he definitely never went to SERE school—but he likewise credits his effectiveness on the ice to his ability to make preemptive peace with his own shortcomings. "I'm extremely self-aware," he says. "I don't think you can do this unless you're self-aware." In Avery's case, he accepted early on that he'd always be one of the shorter players on skates. "I know I'm short and I've always been short. I came to grips with being short at twelve years old," he says. Individuals who don't want to admit such things about themselves, who repress their insecurities instead, are doomed to remain sensitive and therefore vulnerable to attack. In those cases, "you're the joke," says Avery. "You're the punch line."

Benny Kauff was an athlete who fell into that latter category. When he signed with the New York Giants in 1916, the brash young ballplayer crowed, "I'll make them all forget that a guy named Ty Cobb ever pulled on a baseball shoe." David Jones, an editor for the Society for American Baseball Research (SABR), has called Kauff "the Deion Sanders of the Deadball Era" for his sartorial splendor and swaggering predictions, and the local media ate it up, rewarding his boastful talk with glowing newspaper coverage—for a little while, at least.

On the field, Kauff was good, not great. He had holes in his game like almost everyone else. The problem with Kauff, according to Giants manager John McGraw, was that the peacocking player was too prideful—or otherwise unwilling—to confront those areas where he was deficient. Per McGraw, he "could never grasp the idea of trying to find his faults instead of trying to hide them." Kauff's inability to acknowledge his own flaws left him even more exposed— like a bald man swearing he hasn't lost his hair while his toupee flaps in the breeze—and opposing pitchers were able to attack precisely those areas he pretended didn't exist.

Within the military, there can be a similar instinct for folks to turn a blind eye to their own imperfections, to deny any weaknesses. "There's a degree of humility and a willingness to be vulnerable that I think may be lacking," says Colonel Farris. "Everyone wants to act like a tough guy." I hear the same thing from others at Fort Bragg, including Colonel Matthew Tucker, commander of the army's Second Special Warfare Training Group, which houses the schools for advanced skills, like free-fall parachuting, sharpshooting, and combat diving, and Curtis Price, deputy to the commander. "The stress we don't put our guys through very well is ego stress," says Price, as we sit in Tucker's office. "That's the one that we've got to work on."

In this sense, at least, SERE often succeeds where other courses fall short: it cuts through the culture of bullshit and bravado that too often clogs the military's ranks, and it forces students to learn about themselves in an extreme and hopefully unforgettable manner—at their most unvarnished, their most vulnerable. "We teach people to be honest," says Major General Patrick Roberson, who is the commander and commandant of SWCS at the time of my visit. "You're learning a lot about yourself. You learn a lot about your limits."

The whole idea of SERE is to push students to those limits— and then beyond. There are no perfect scores. "Everyone that comes through this course screws something up, makes some awful mistake, goes through something that they don't like," an army psychologist tells me. Or as Farris puts it, "Everybody cracks at the end of the day."

But there's no shame in that, he adds. Or there shouldn't be.

Failure is part of the process. It's how students learn what they need to work on.

Nobody wants an army full of Benny Kauffs.

THERE IS A minor phenomenon in sports in which practically every team tries to frame itself as some kind of underdog—as a group of scrappy upstarts out to prove their doubters wrong. "Nobody believes in us," they all say, even when such a statement is objectively false.

Put another way, everybody wants to be Rocky Balboa.

The reason for this is that, when the individuals on a team conceive of themselves in this way, they are effectively telling themselves they have nothing to lose. And when a player has nothing to lose, he's more likely to see the demands of a situation as pure challenge—not at all threatening—and to therefore perform aggressively: without hesitation or fear. Hell, no one believed in him anyway!

John Starks knew a lot about being an underdog. By almost any measure, the kid from Tulsa, Oklahoma, wasn't supposed to make it. Raised by a single mother (with help from his grandma), Starks was one of seven kids, and his road to the pros was almost comically winding: As a high school athlete, he played in only two varsity games. With no scholarship offers, he bounced between colleges a semester at a time, took a break to work a brief stint at Safeway, where he bagged groceries and stocked shelves, and attended two more junior colleges before earning a spot at Oklahoma State University, a Division I program. In the 1988 NBA Draft, there would be seventy-five players taken, but Starks wasn't one of them. He'd eventually sign with the Golden State Warriors, but they soon released him. From there, he caught on with the Continental Basketball Association and the World Basketball League. In 1990, he earned a tryout with the New York Knicks, and that audition could reasonably have been considered his last shot at an NBA career— and that's how he played: with something to prove, with a fearlessness that bordered on mania. How else to explain an undersized guard and roster aspirant trying to dunk on one of the league's most dominant defensive big men in an intrasquad scrimmage? Starks rose up against star center Patrick Ewing, who not only turned away the dunk attempt but also knocked Starks to the floor for good measure.*

He wasn't afraid to fail, that was for sure. But at times, Starks could play with so much fire on the court he'd lose control of what he was doing entirely. As far back as junior college, he would watch tapes of his performance after every game—and not just to review his form; he wanted to see how he had behaved. His goal was to identify

---

* Starks was injured on the play, which turned out to be a blessing, as it forced the Knicks—who had plans to cut him later that day—to keep him on their roster, due to NBA rules forbidding the release of injured players.

those moments when the mercury of his temper was rising and to consider how he might better handle such situations in the future. "You kind of assess when that is coming on, and you just have these self-conversations," he says. "You talk to yourself. You tell yourself, 'Just calm down, stay focused.'" Though Starks would be the first to admit it wasn't always so simple.

As he puts it, "Sometimes yourself don't want to listen."

Those who covered Starks in the NBA have described him as having "pure heart" (Ahmad Rashad) and being "a coiled spring" (Ira Berkow) with "a propensity for the absurd" (Peter Vecsey)—and yet, nobody tempted Starks to succumb to his emotional demons quite like Reggie Miller. Really, the two players were meant for each other—in a poetic, tragically flawed kind of way. The perfect foils. Reggie was a highly touted prospect from a family full of athletes with a penchant for getting under people's skin, and he looked at the Knicks guard—the series of early life rejections, the unlikely and overachieving career, the untamed and fiery temper, the desperate need to prove himself—and salivated at what he saw behind those doleful eyes: a target. "He knew John was a hothead," Cheryl Miller says of her little brother. "He knew exactly the buttons to push." And he attacked what many perceived to be Starks's insecurities.

"I was a nobody coming in this league," says Starks, "and Reggie was an established player. Basically, he treated me like the twelfth guy on the bench." During games, Miller would taunt Starks about his stats and question whether he belonged. He'd tell Starks, "You can't guard me. Why are you even trying?" Miller succeeded in making their rivalry feel personal. Per Starks, "He was trying to be nasty about it." He also never let up—neither during the games, nor after them. Cheryl Miller describes her brother as "cold-blooded," as she recalls the way he'd turn the knife on Starks, even in postgame press conferences. "He'd go, 'I don't know what was wrong with John Starks. Maybe he wasn't held enough as a kid. Maybe he had a bad breakfast. Maybe room service got messed up. I don't know. You'd have to ask him.' And he'd have that smirk on his face."

That smirk that so many wanted to wipe away.

Despite his winding road to the pros, Starks says he never doubted his ability as a player. Never questioned whether he belonged. But it's inarguable that Miller got to him. He could be "unraveled" by him, per veteran sportswriter Ian O'Connor. Starks has admitted to missing critical free throws at the end of a 1995 playoff game because he was thinking about Reggie, and he almost always responded to the pest's provocations, engaging with Miller in both on-court confrontations and via the press—occasionally expressing some truly weird sentiments, like when he said, "I'm gonna cut his dick off and make him eat it." According to Cheryl, Reggie didn't brag about many of his on-court altercations, but he made an exception in the case of Starks. She says, "He was like, 'I own him. Cheryl, I own him.'"

During the first round of the 1993 Eastern Conference playoffs, the whole world got to see just how deeply Miller had wormed his way inside the mind of John Starks. The Knicks were leading their series with the Pacers 2–0, when Miller entered the potential decid-ing Game 3 with a plan to mentally abuse Starks, to uncage his famous temper. He did so with both taunting words and his usual cheap-shot physicality. Starks maintains to this day that it wasn't the trash talk that irked him as much as Miller's elbows. But with Reggie, it was always a package deal. For two-plus quarters, Starks strained to not let Reggie's relentless antagonism bother him—to not react. But with New York up by two points early in the third quarter, he gave in to emotional impulse. It was only a momen-tary lapse, but that was more than enough. As the ball was being inbounded on the other end of the court—following a Starks basket, no less—the Knicks guard ran down the floor barking at Miller. Of course, Miller barked back. Their faces drew closer, and then it hap-pened. Starks leaned forward and snapped his forehead against his rival's. It was almost imperceptible, hardly a Zinedine Zidane–level, full-on-assault headbutt. But Miller, a notorious flopper, knew how to sell it. He fell back with his eyes wide and his arms raised, "like

I hit him with a tire iron," per Starks. The whistles blew, Starks was ejected, and his teammates were left reeling. The Knicks lost that game by twenty-three points.

Starks wasn't oblivious to the ways in which his emotions and rash behavior could occasionally betray him—that's why he watched all that game tape—and others made sure he knew about it, too. Knicks head coach Pat Riley often scolded the shooting guard for overheating on the court. The media talked openly about Starks's "fragile psyche" and volatility. (Phil Taylor says of the Knicks guard, "He was just boiling over. There was no method to his madness.") Courtside hecklers like Robin Ficker zeroed in on him whenever the Knicks were in town. "I was always able to distract Starks," he says. "He was always kind of nervously looking back at me." From newsrooms to locker rooms, this was the consensus. Opposing teams even wrote Starks into their scouting reports: rattle him with trash talk, they said. Press his big, red button. Looking back on his career, Starks concedes his emotions were not always applied in the most productive manner. "I know at times I did go overboard, and it cost me. It cost my team victories," he says. But as he saw it, his weakness was also his strength. His passion was his superpower. "I definitely needed to be on that edge."

It's hard to argue with him. As a twenty-year-old, Starks had a better shot of becoming a grocery-store manager than a professional athlete; a few years later, he was going toe-to-toe with the best players on the planet. And while he'd make perfunctory efforts to control his emotions during games—at times, you could see him on the sidelines with a towel draped over his head; underneath, he'd be repeating the same words, "Just calm down. Stay focused"—he also believed there was a competitive danger in turning the dial down too far: he didn't want to lose that edge. For better or for worse, Starks understood he was plagued and fueled by his emotions in equal parts, and he effectively decided not to pursue self-regulation strategies in response to trash talk and other personally upsetting on-court activities. He believed he needed to ride the waves of his emotions to perform at his best—and he'd accept boneheaded outbursts as an occasional cost. Sometimes, especially when he felt he wasn't playing well, Starks wouldn't even try to control the fire inside of him, he tells me. He'd just say to himself, "You know what? To hell with it. Don't even worry about it." On those nights, he says, "I don't even try to calm myself down. I'd just say, 'I'm going to be so engaged in the game, I'm just going to throw caution to the wind and just let it rip. Whatever happens, happens.'"

As Starks saw it, he had "nothing to lose."

And most nights, that might have been true. Against Reggie Miller, it was decidedly a miscalculation.

THE BEST WAY to win a debate, according to Sam Nelson, the director of speech and debate programs at Cornell University, is "Don't get into one."

That seemed to be the operating philosophy for players like John Stockton and Tim Duncan, who found themselves as regular foils for top NBA trash-talkers not named Reggie Miller. In Duncan's case, Kevin Garnett made it his personal mission to unsettle his even-keeled rival, who competed with such outward calm and boring efficiency he was nicknamed the Big Fundamental. In Garnett's first game after being traded to the Minnesota Timberwolves in 2002, in a matchup against Duncan and the Spurs, Marc Jackson remembers being awed by the single-minded vitriol with which Garnett attacked his opponent. "KG was excessively aggressive," says Jackson. "He put his hands in his face. He was like, 'I'm going to bust your ass!' I'll never forget that. KG was on a whole other level that day for his trash talking. Then I realized KG had something personal—with KG and Tim."

Duncan was Garnett's white whale, the one dude he couldn't crack.

"Several times I saw KG putting his finger in Tim's head and yelling right in his ear, and Tim didn't say a word back to him," says

Sean Elliott. Per Jackson, "Tim would just hum to himself." Which was surely infuriating. During the 1999 playoffs, Garnett's trash talk toward Duncan was so demonstrative that beat writers for the San Antonio papers felt compelled to report on his behavior, even as "Duncan just smiled at his adversary" in return. In the final game of that series, KG ditched all subtlety when he used the opportunity of an on-court skirmish between two other players to blatantly smack Duncan upside the head.

But nothing seemed to ruffle the Big Fundamental.

If anything, KG's obsessive efforts backfired, as Duncan maintained the forbearance of a parent while doubling down on his rock-solid, boring style. Garnett has admitted Duncan's equanimity "really, really, really pissed me off." Per KG, "I'd be spending all this energy trying to get him off his game, I wouldn't realize that he'd gotten me off mine." In other words, his unrequited trash talk became his liability.

It was much the same for Gary Payton versus Stockton. The snarling guard whose game was forged on the streets of Oakland tells me it felt like screaming into the abyss whenever he played against the Utah Jazz. "He would never say nothing to me," says Payton. "That would mess me up. That messes me up because I would say something to him, and he would act like I wasn't even there." Payton's description of Stockton reminds me of a linguistic concept called grounding or building common ground. "The idea behind grounding is that when we're trying to communicate with each other, we're trying to get on the same page," says Matthew Marge, a linguist and former senior computer scientist at the Army Research Laboratory where he worked on artificial intelligence communications programs. To build common ground, Marge adds, "we execute a variety of different behaviors to align with each other's information," like nodding or saying *OK* or *uh-huh*. "Those are the signals we use to give each other evidence that we're understanding the words we're saying to each other."

It was exactly those signals that Stockton withheld from Payton. He denied his opponent the evidence of even basic human understanding, like an elevator button that refused to light up no matter how many times you pressed it. For someone like Payton, who wasn't used to being ignored, he didn't know how to handle that lack of acknowledgment. He got mad, talked even more trash. He *smashed* that elevator button. But still, it didn't light up. "He was getting me out of my game," says Payton. "He flipped the script on me."

Whatever gears were turning beneath their stoic facades, Stockton and Duncan had obviously done the necessary mental work to resist these provocations. They controlled their emotions. The SERE instructors would be proud.

———

AS AN NBA player, Shane Battier always looked to work the angles, to tilt the odds in his team's favor—for instance, steering opponents toward areas of the court where they were less efficient scorers. "I knew players better than they knew themselves," says Battier, who'd go on to serve as vice president of basketball development and analytics for the Miami Heat. "I knew exactly what was good for them and what was bad for them. I was trying to find an edge."

But there was one area in which Battier knew the odds were against him: talking trash. As well studied as he was about the strengths and weaknesses of opposing players, he knew himself even better. He had no doubt it would be to his competitive detriment to respond to an opponent's verbal provocations. "The second you engage a guy like Gary Payton, you're toast," he says. "The guy is gonna wreck you psychologically." Which isn't to say he didn't believe there was an edge to be gained against a smack-talker. He explains, "If you take the complete opposite mind-set and don't give the guy anything, it can be a weapon. If a guy is yapping at me, I know it'll take him off his game if I don't react at all."

Battier's tight-lipped style was an extension of a lesson he learned while playing college ball at Duke, where Coach Mike Krzyzewski drummed a simple mantra into his team: "Never let your opponents see you sweat." Even when doing summer conditioning drills, like running sprints and ladders, Coach K forbade his players from showing any signs of fatigue. No bending over. No grabbing their shorts. "He said, 'Look, if your opponent sees you're tired, that's going to give him confidence,'" remembers Battier. "I took that to heart. I never wanted to allow my opponent to see me crying to the referee. I never wanted my opponent to see me dogging my teammate out. I never wanted my opponent to see me injured or fatigued. I wanted to give them absolutely nothing. I wanted them to think, 'Wow, this Battier guy is like a robot.' Trash talk was along those lines. I never wanted to show that a guy was impacting my game."

Battier was largely rewarded for this strategy of outward dispassion, as many would-be trash-talkers in the NBA simply turned their attention elsewhere. He says, "Most people just gave up, to be honest with you." But not everyone.

For all their on-court encounters, Battier and Kobe Bryant never actually spoke outside of an NBA arena, Battier tells me: "I never had a conversation with him." But when they were between the lines, the two players communicated constantly. "There was a psychological trash-talk battle without words," he says, describing a series of tactical mind games Kobe would deploy in an effort to unsettle and intimidate a player who received frequent accolades for his unusually effective defense against some of the game's best scorers. Bryant would be especially friendly toward Battier before tip-off in one game, "and next time we'd play, he'd be cold as ice. Not even acknowledge my existence." Meanwhile, if Battier found himself on the floor diving for a loose ball, Bryant would hover over his sprawled-out opponent "for a second longer than he should have." Other times, during stoppages in play, Bryant would deliver unnecessary physical contact after the whistle, bumping shoulders.

It was a whole lot of little things, all of which were designed to have an effect.

"I knew exactly what he was doing," says Battier.

Known as the Black Mamba—a nickname he bestowed on himself—Bryant was famously aloof, a loner who cultivated a no-nonsense, kill-or-be-killed persona. Even among teammates he was standoffish and subscribed to old-school ideas about dominance displays and the importance of machismo. As a leader, he modeled himself after Michael Jordan, whose aggressive, unrelenting, keep-up-or-go-home style probably discouraged as many players as it inspired. According to an NBA staffer who has worked with a number of Bryant's former teammates, behind closed doors players often describe Bryant as "a bully and an asshole." As one alleged story goes, Bryant's Laker teammates were lazing around watching a movie one day, when Kobe walked in, took the remote, and changed the channel. Just like that. "It was basically like, this is my house, motherfuckers. Deal with it," the staffer says.

Kobe could be harsh, edgy.

Looking back on it now, Battier admits Kobe's intimidation efforts were "a little unnerving." Still, he knew better than to be baited by pride and get into a "pissing contest with one of the greatest players of all time."* In the face of Bryant's ongoing provocations, Battier only increased his resolve to show no emotion, to have no reaction whatsoever. "I did what John Stockton did to Gary Payton," he says. "I gave Kobe nothing. I never talked to him. I never looked at him. If he made tough shots, if he missed tough shots—I never celebrated, I never looked down. I wanted to be an absolute robot because I knew that would infuriate him."

Bryant wanted to draw his opponent into a contest they both knew he couldn't win.

So Battier refused to play. He opted for a different game.

---

* Brian Scalabrine was similarly aware of the limitations in his game and knew he needed to resist the temptations of trash talk. "If you say something to me, and I start getting emotionally involved and deviate from the game plan, that is so detrimental for my career," he says. "I'm not good enough as a player."

IT'S NOT WHOLLY accurate to say guys like Stockton, Battier, and Duncan didn't respond to their antagonists: Their silence *was* a response, and an effective one. For one thing, it denied players like Garnett and Payton the chance to use their opponent's reactions as a tool to motivate, to dial in their focus, or to otherwise reach their zones of optimal functioning. Payton has always been fairly open about this particular vulnerability in his game. During his playing days, he'd tell anyone who asked that opponents would be wise to keep quiet against him, to stop taking the bait. "I'm always getting hyper when someone talks to me," he said after a March 1995 contest, in which he got into it with Detroit Pistons guard Lindsey Hunter. "It was the worst thing to start up with me because I'm good at it, very good. He should have shut his mouth and kept playing." Later that year, Payton told *Sports Illustrated*, "If you're playing against me, don't turn your back on me, don't pump-fake on me, and most of all, don't talk to me."

Silence disarmed the garrulous guard.

According to Bernard Ward, Payton's childhood friend who would go on to earn a master's in sports psychology, there was at least one other approach that would have worked against a player like Payton, too. "If you got a trash-talker talking crazy," he says, "all you got to say is, 'Man, you right. Please take it easy on me.' That's how you humble him. You agree with him. 'Yeah, Gary, my mama ain't no good.' You don't fight with him because he was groomed for that. People never figured that out."

Acceptance may seem like a weird strategy in the face of a face-threatening attack, but it has fairly sound psychological backing. Acceptance is at the heart of rational emotive behavior therapy (REBT), which was developed by the pioneering twentieth-century psychologist Albert Ellis, under whom Scott Goldman studied. Per Goldman, a person is almost always best served by accepting that a thing has happened—"that it is part of my reality"—and then choosing what to do with that information, like using it for motivation or letting it go, if it's not useful.* As the theory goes, a person doesn't have to be insulted just because someone insults them; they have more agency than that. It's like what Eleanor Roosevelt once reportedly said: "No one can make you feel inferior without your consent." Or in the words of Epictetus, the ancient Greek philosopher whose teachings informed both Ellis's work and the subsequent development of the field of cognitive psychotherapy: "If you are insulted, it is always your choice to view what is happening as insulting or not. . . . If someone irritates you, it is only your own response that is irritating you."

To put it another way: you can't control what other people say, but you can control your response to it**—and in so doing, you can deny your abuser not only the emotional leverage necessary for psychological manipulation, but also the basic satisfaction of a reaction. Per Ward, a controlled and unemotional response takes "all of the oomph up out" of a trash-talker. Izzy Kalman, the bullying expert, sees this kind of acceptance as an underutilized strategy in the battle against school-age bullying, too. "The solution to being a victim of verbal bullying is that you don't get upset," he says. You don't run and tell a teacher; you refuse to be a victim. "You have to learn not to get upset. If you kill me, of course, that's a crime, and you should be arrested. But if you insult me and I get upset, who's really hurting me? I'm hurting myself."

---

* Acceptance has also proven to be a surprisingly effective emotional regulation strategy, per Maya Tamir, a psychology professor at the Hebrew University of Jerusalem and director of the Emotion and Self-Regulation Laboratory. "It's almost a paradoxical effect," she says, "because what is acceptance if not telling yourself, 'I'm *not* going to regulate?'" One theory as to why this works is that acceptance short-circuits the self-immolating feedback loops in which we often find ourselves when we're not just upset or afraid, but we're also upset about being upset or fearful about being afraid—and this reaction to our reaction sustains and amplifies the negative emotions over time. "If we can just say, 'OK, so I feel fear. All right, got it. There's something that makes me scared, so I'm scared. I'm normal.' Then it just stops."

** Sometimes, as often is the case with SERE, that may be the only thing you have any control over.

This ability to control one's mental narrative—to refuse to be victimized or upset by what someone else is doing—is a good predictor of success not only on a schoolyard or ball field, but also within the high-pressure world of SERE. Indeed, those who are able to do this—to tell their own stories of what's happening around them and subsequently use that to inform their responses—are typically the ones who make it through the course best. That's how Sharon Engelmeier, the 7th PSYOP Battalion commander—and a former basketball player, who nearly set the California state high school record for consecutive free throws made—processed the abuses of her pretend captivity. When the American flag started to burn, for instance, she minimized the significance by telling herself, "That's just a five-dollar piece of cloth." And when her body screamed for relief while forced to hold an extended stress position, she said, "I'm doing the best that I can." There were a few moments early on when some things the instructors said made her slightly clench, she admits—things that were "a lot more provocative in nature"—but even those she quickly dismissed. "I'm just like, 'Dude, you're wasting your time.'"

At one point, Engelmeier even remembers thinking, "Sometimes life's a game." And so, like Battier, she played it her way.

THE MAKINGS OF MENTAL TOUGHNESS

A NORMAL PERSON would have simply panicked. Major Taylor Murphy was at the bottom of Mott Lake, outside Fort Bragg, when he realized he couldn't breathe. Along with seven other members of his A team, Murphy was trudging across the bottom of the lake as part of a nighttime infiltration dive, the first leg of a two-day training exercise. The divers moved in teams of two, with buddy lines tethered between them and a length of PVC pipe running front to back. That served as their main means of communication. (Five shakes meant "stop"; two meant "go.") Visibility-wise, no one could see shit, and not just because the sun was down. It was October 2016, right after Hurricane Matthew had torn up the Atlantic coast, and the water had been shaken like a muddy snow globe. "It was like chocolate milk," says Murphy. "Even to see the compass, you had to hold it against the glass on your mask. It was so bad." What's more, the lake floor had become a veritable junkyard with all the detritus blown in from the storm.

It was probably a tree stump that did it. That's what the lead team likely slammed into with the PVC pipe, which stopped so abruptly Murphy and his buddy crashed into the divers in front of them and were similarly rammed from behind. At that point, Murphy felt five shakes, but it was too late: they had a giant mess on their hands. In the collision, the buddy lines crossed and snarled, creating a Gordian tangle that also wrapped around the tree stump, or whatever it was. And if that weren't enough, a number of the divers discovered they suddenly couldn't breathe. Murphy was one of them; he took a pull from his inhalation hose and felt nothing but resistance. "It was a chaotic situation," says Murphy, who quickly identified what was causing the blockage: the tangled buddy lines were pinching off his air hose, too. "Someone could have easily died. It could have been really dangerous."

Especially if anyone had panicked. If one of the divers had started flailing, perhaps, and deepened the tangle of the lines. Or did something really stupid, like impulsively swiping at his mouthpiece—or his buddy's mouthpiece—and removed the air source entirely. (At that point, it'd be a race to the surface to survive: to successfully activate the quick release of your buddy line and pray none of your other equipment was caught up on anything along the murky bottom.) According to Murphy, it's not uncommon for divers to find themselves fouled up on something, or for it to take a while to get unfouled. As it happened, his dive detachment had encountered similar obstacles earlier that week. "But we'd never experienced buddy lines pinching off air sources before," he says. That was a frightening new wrinkle.

Still, nobody panicked.

For the next ten or so minutes, in total blackout conditions, Murphy worked slowly through the chaos of his tangled buddy line, while taking frequent breaks to reopen his air hose—to, you know, breathe.

In this way, he fell into a seemingly unending rhythm: *Work on the entanglement; unfoul the hose; breathe. Work on the entanglement; unfoul the hose; breathe.* "It felt like it took an eternity," he says. "But we were able to eventually work through it."

To keep their lizard brains at bay.

To breathe—at least every now and again.

I MEET MAJOR Murphy on a pool deck in Key West, mercifully far from Mott Lake—both geographically and spiritually.* The pool is located on the northwest section of the island, inside an annex of Naval Air Station Key West, which doubles as home to the Special Forces Underwater Operations School, aka dive school, of which Murphy is the commander.

I never imagined that reporting a book about trash talk would bring me here—to a naval air station at the southern tip of the United States. To be fair, I didn't expect to spend a week at Fort Bragg, either. But the more I learn about mental skills, in general, which are the raw ingredients of mental toughness, and the military's training method-ologies, specifically, which systematically teach soldiers to metabolize the anxiety of increasingly stressful situations via employing those mental skills, it starts to seem inevitable. Really, nearly everyone with whom I speak at Fort Bragg and Camp Mackall suggests that Key West needs to be my next stop, not because they talk so much shit at dive school—they don't, at least not officially—but because it may be one of the most pressurized mental-skills proving grounds on the planet, as they test each student's ability to perform under intensely

---

* At the time of my visit, Key West was hosting its annual Fantasy Fest, which is described on its website as a "10-day party in paradise for grown-ups," but struck me as a thinly veiled excuse (for mostly boomers) to drink without consequence amid a COVID-be-damned sex party. Along the city's main drags, men approaching retirement age hit the bars in tutus and thongs, while their female companions (wives?) favored mesh tops, body paint, and nipple stickers. Multiple people stopped me and asked for directions, mistaking my lack of thong and coconut bra for a sign of being a local.

stressful conditions. "It's the most physically demanding advanced skill that we do and requires a tremendous amount of resilience," Colonel Matthew Tucker says of combat diving.

Per Andy Morgan, "It'll make you anxious just watching."

This morning, the dive-school students—mostly Green Berets looking to learn an advanced skill—are scheduled to take an emergency-procedures test while using closed-circuit rebreathers, which differ from standard scuba setups—or open-circuit rigs—in that a diver's exhaled air (i.e., CO_2) isn't released from the system, but is instead cycled through and chemically scrubbed of carbon before being inhaled again as pure oxygen. Closed-circuit systems have obvious military appeal, since they can be used for more clandestine operations, like infiltrating an enemy port without detection (because no released air means no bubbles), but they are also significantly more technical and dangerous. Risks include passing out without warning (if divers fail to purge all trace nitrogen from their lungs), oxygen toxicity, and third-degree burns to a diver's mouth, esophagus, and lungs because of how the carbon-scrubbing chemicals react with salt water.

But all that is table stakes for using the closed-circuit rigs.

Today, the students also have to navigate an obstacle course of underwater hazards in the pool, while coolly and correctly solving each predicament with which they're presented. Essentially, this is a stress test. But it's hardly the first one the students have experienced here. By the time I get to Key West, the students are about halfway through the Combat Diver Qualification Course, which is designed almost entirely to identify and train soldiers who are able to remain unfailingly calm in even the most adverse and life-threatening situations—in those critical moments when every evolutionary fiber in their bodies is screaming out in primal panic: this training is a case study in stress inoculation. The students don't have to be unusually strong in the water, per Murphy. "We don't necessarily teach people to be Olympic swimmers," he says. "We teach them to be experts at not drowning." To that end, there's just one thing they can't be: a liability—to themselves or anyone else in the class.

Nothing is more dangerous than when someone starts to panic, when the stress of the situation overwhelms a person's attention and they enter fight-flight-freeze. In the water, the usual cause is hypoxia, which is the feeling of being out of oxygen.

"If you're underwater and you start feeling hypoxic, the immediate stressor is going to be, *I need to do everything I can to survive*," says Murphy. Plenty of students practice their breath holds before coming to Key West, and therefore assume they'll be spared these primal pangs of terror. The problem, per Sergeant First Class Nick Dolan, a dive-school supervisor with whom I walk along the topside of the pool while the emergency-procedures test is underway, is that even if the students have learned to hold their breaths for as long as three minutes underwater, it's usually a static breath hold, meaning they're keeping mostly still while doing it. "A static breath hold doesn't translate to that CO_2 drive," he says. "CO_2 makes us want to breathe in, and when you're working and your CO_2 is elevated and your lactic acid is elevated, all you want to do is breathe in, even if you have enough oxygen. The CO_2 is still telling you to breathe in." This urge to inhale is more than instinctual, adds Dolan. "It's biological. But you can train past those diaphragm spasms. You can train yourself to slightly ignore that signal. We find ways to train beyond that comfort zone."

Indeed, many of the course's earliest events are designed to increase the students' breath holds—and their CO_2 tolerance, specifically—to help them overcome the initial and evolutionary panic that comes from feeling hypoxic. The events are also meant to build a generalized sense of confidence for the students in the water, per Murphy. To show them they can succeed—that success is in fact possible—even as the tasks ramp up in complexity, and they're asked to demonstrate the same steady resolve under increasingly stressful conditions. For example, one of the course's highest-attrition tests is

known as the one-man confidence exam. For that test, which typically comes at the end of the second week, students are blindfolded,
with duct tape over their masks, and placed on their knees at the
bottom of the pool, while breathing on an open-circuit scuba rig.
What happens next is a series of underwater hazards and rapid-fire
air-source interruptions—a dislodged mouthpiece, a fouled air hose,
and so on—which are intended to create a prolonged sense of hypoxia
for the students, who may only get one or two breaths between inter-
ruptions. "What we're really looking for is someone who can remain
calm and work through a problem, like you're seeing all these guys
do right now," Murphy says, as I stick a five-gallon bucket that's been
jerry-rigged with a clear plastic bottom into the pool, like a personal
porthole into this underwater world. It's amazing how placid it all
seems. The divers look as relaxed and unbothered as otters, as they
glide along. From where I'm standing, there's no way to know what's
really happening beneath the surface—what thoughts might be racing through any of the divers' heads, or what kind of anxiety they
might be grappling with.

Murphy sees the ability to "break things down into manageable
pieces" as one of the keys to combat diving. That's what he and his
team did in Mott Lake. "Typically, when I'm under the water, I'm
just focusing on whatever the next task is going to be," he says. "You
can recognize, 'Yeah, this situation sucks, but here's what I need to
do to get through this.' You understand, 'I just need to get another
breath.' You do whatever it takes in order to follow the proper proce-
dures to get another breath." You don't worry about surviving. You
don't think about *anything* except what you need to do next, which
in his case was to work the tangled line, and then get another breath.

Just one more breath.

And then another. And another. And another.

It doesn't matter how long it takes. "You keep going," says
Murphy.

To hear him tell it, everything he and his dive team did on the
bottom of Mott Lake sounds so procedural, almost mechanical. And

yet, it's easy to imagine the kernels of negative thoughts creeping in—as the minutes added up; as the mess of the buddy lines remained unsolved, the air hoses pinched; as the divers maybe allowed them-selves to consider how badly any number of things could go wrong and how quickly. A stray thought catching in the brain, a pound-ing pulse, the urge to escape one's own skin. But he says no. There was never a point at which he was concerned because it was noth-ing they hadn't been trained to handle. "We'd all been through the training that you're getting to see a little bit of now," he says, as another diver pops his head above water, course complete. "That's the reason we were able to remain calm and execute. Because of the training."

Because they had been inured to performing under pressure.

———————

WHENEVER STEVE SMITH Sr. made a catch on the football field, he would end the play by spinning the ball on the turf. Always a voluble and erupting presence, Smith became known for this sig-nature act that pretty much everyone assumed to be a nonverbal but in-your-face celebration aimed at his defenders. The league certainly interpreted it that way in 2013, when NFL officials warned Smith before the season he could be flagged for his ball spinning, as part of an effort to enforce taunting rules more strictly. But just as his running monologues during games were meant primarily for himself as a form of self-talk,* the gesture had little to do with antagonizing opponents, Smith tells me. "It was all about routine. Me spinning the ball was my routine," he says, just as his routine after a dropped pass or missed block was to clap. "Once I clapped and got back to the huddle, play is over. When I used to spin the ball, that was me

---

* Of his on-field chatter, Smith says, "A lot of times, I wasn't talking to my opponent. The defender just gets to hear me talk to myself out loud. He gets to hear what I feel about him." Smith might say, *This guy. Why does he think he can cover you today?* "But I'm not really talking directly to him. He just gets the ear hustle."

psychologically getting out what happened and then resetting and moving on to the next play."

Smith developed these routines by working with a golf psychologist. The idea was for the gestures to serve as physical reminders—or cues, as they're called—to redirect his focus toward the only thing that mattered: the next play.

Many sports psychologists recommend cues as a way for athletes—or soldiers or performers of any kind—to reorient themselves in real time. To recognize if their anxiety levels have dipped below or, more likely, risen above their individual zones of optimal functioning. To avoid unhelpful thoughts or emotions, like dwelling on a past mistake, indulging a seed of self-doubt, or feeling angry over some perceived injustice (like a missed foul call or an opponent whispering some nasty noise in their ear). To stop worrying about the outcome of a competition or how long it's going to take to untangle that buddy line and focus ruthlessly—and exclusively—on the task at hand. In other words: to overcome distractions of every kind, anything that might steal even an ounce of your attention, and to remain intensely present.

For some athletes, trash talk can serve as this kind of cue to dial in. But on the flip side, it is also often used as a way to test if other players have the mental skills to do the same—to acknowledge and block distractions, whenever and however they happen, and then quickly refocus. "We are testing to see how mentally tough you are," Bernard Ward says of himself and fellow trash-talkers. "That's why we do it. It's a whole 'nother skill set. Are you going to stick your tail up under your butt, or are you going to play?" Luis Scola came to understand this was what was happening to him as a rookie in the NBA, when opposing teams ran their offenses directly at him and hooted taunting discouragements from the bench. He was being tested. As he describes it now, what first felt like demeaning and bullying attacks—*Why are you focusing on me?*—were in fact invitations to compete. "Eventually, you realize you have to go out there and play," he says. "You have to just compete and guard a guy like Kevin

Garnett. OK, he is going to talk, and you just have to guard him anyway."

One reasonable definition of mental toughness is the ability to do what you need to do (i.e., what the performance situation demands) when you need to do it, even in the face of all possible distractions or the perceived pressures of a given moment. What's more, applying the necessary mental skills to stay calm and focus on the task at hand is in fact the answer to trash talk because it's also the answer to performing well under any kind of pressure. Those who succumb to the psychological stresses and provocations of trash talk—who let opponents get underneath their skin and respond unthinkingly out of pride or emotion, who second-guess themselves or worry about how they're being perceived, who allow panic to sink in (which often takes the form of what we think of as choking in sports), or who otherwise shrink in the face of seemingly raised stakes and threatening situations—are often dismissed as mentally weak. "This guy is soft, this guy has a fragile psyche, this guy chokes under pressure," says Mark Aoyagi, listing the usual tropes of explanation. But the performance psychologist doesn't actually buy any of that.

As he sees it, there's no such thing as a fragile psyche, only an untrained mind.

ACCORDING TO AOYAGI and every other performance psychologist with whom I speak across the worlds of both military and sport, the foundational elements of mental-skills training come down to two things: self-awareness and self-regulation.

What is meant by awareness here is not just the acknowledgment of one's weaknesses, as discussed previously, but a kind of global finger on the pulse of everything that's happening in one's brain and body, from one's stress levels and emotions to one's thoughts and attention. It's about knowing things like, What's your ideal internal state in a performance situation (i.e., IZOF), and how does it change based on the specific demands of a given task? How does your body react to stress (both cognitively and physiologically), and how does that affect your performance? What tools can you use to get into the zone? Or to get back there? Or to toggle between different levels of activation? What's your heart rate now? Is it too high, too low? Are your muscles overly tense? How are you interpreting that stress in your body? As a challenge or as a threat? Do you question your ability to succeed? Are you scared? Excited? Angry? Is that how you want to feel?* And what about your focus? Are you distracted by your internal dialogue? Thinking about the play that just happened? A mistake you made? About what's at stake? Or what everyone will say about you after the game?

If so, admit it. Admit all of it. Because you need to be honest about where you are to get where you need to be. You also need to know how to self-regulate.

From a physiological perspective, self-regulation starts with one's breath. "The most basic piece is, as we inhale, our arousal level rises, and as we exhale it drops," says Aoyagi. That's why you'll often see a baseball pitcher take and release a deep breath before delivering a pitch, or a basketball player doing the same before shooting a free throw. In general, tasks that involve accuracy or fine-motor skills require lower levels of activation, he says, and "slow exhalations are a great way to start bringing your arousal level down."

With some athletes, Aoyagi will go beyond the basics of breathing and teach them additional relaxation techniques, like autogenic training and progressive muscle relaxation. Autogenic training, he explains, is a mind-to-body technique that involves repeating a phrase to oneself, almost like a mantra—*My right arm is heavy and warm. My right arm is heavy and warm*—while progressive muscle relaxation

---

* As I learn from Maya Tamir, people often want to feel certain emotions, based on whether or not they believe those emotions will be useful—for example, feeling angry in a situation that involves confrontation. What she has discovered, however, is that it's not the emotions themselves that provide utilitarian benefit, but our *beliefs* about those emotions. "When you expect an emotion to be useful, it's useful. When you don't expect an emotion to be useful, it isn't," she says. "Isn't that amazing?"

is a body-to-mind technique that involves alternately tensing and releasing various muscles in one's body as a way to better understand what true relaxation feels like, since so many people unconsciously hold tension in their bodies. "Ultimately, what you're trying to do is get to a level of skill where, through practicing these techniques and building off of them, you can toe the free-throw line or the service line and, in one breath, get to where you need to be," he says. "That's the skill they develop—the ability to get there quickly and on time."*

When Scott Goldman encounters athletes for whom distraction is an issue, he tries to impress upon them the importance of attentional control: of being deliberate about where they choose to place their focus and helping them understand that it is in fact a choice. Often, he uses the metaphor of talking to an attractive woman (or man) at a noisy party. His point being that the athlete would clearly be capable of suppressing ambient sound in such an environment to have that conversation. To accentuate this idea, Goldman will sometimes take his phone off the hook while they're talking and let the dial tone scream. *Ehhhhh! Ehhhhh! Ehhhhh!* "You are prioritizing," he'll tell the athlete. "So this thing that Gary Payton [or whoever] said to you, are you going to make it your primary signal, or can you let it serve as ambient sound? Are you going to let some of this

---

* Trash-talk provocateurs like Kevin Garnett and Gary Payton were masters of this kind of self-regulation. According to J.A. Adande, Payton had the ability to work himself—and his opponents—up and then calm down very quickly, because "it was a normal part of his routine." He says, "It was easy for him to do." Meanwhile, multiple referees tell me they "loved" Kevin Garnett, in particular, because (1) he was always polite and (2) they could rely on him to help lower the temperature of even the tensest contests, because he was similarly adept at bringing his aggressive ferocity into check when asked to by the refs—and because he often served as an intermediary between officials and his teammates. "He played with a lot of emotion, but there were a lot of times he was able to bring that emotion down in a heartbeat," says retired referee Joe Forte, who never believed KG's famous intensity was ever truly out of control. Unlike John Starks, the volatile guard who rode his emotions like a twenty-foot wave—and occasionally endured some violent wipeouts, as a result—Forte says Garnett "was well aware of what he was doing. He always had the ability to rein it in."

internal dialogue that you're having in your own head get loud, or can you disregard it?"

Can you dismiss it as just noise?

Jon Metzler, the mental-performance consultant, has a similar approach. He suggests imagining one's attention like a ticker tape or the scroll on the bottom of a TV sports channel, where they rotate through scores and statistics. "Let's say your alma mater comes up on the ticker, and they're beating Florida State or whatever, and it catches your attention," he says. "You can either grab onto that, or you can just kind of let it float off the screen. You gotta determine, Is that something that I want to grab my attention? What's the most important thing to focus on in this moment?"

If you were to ask Robin Ficker, the heckler would tell you he's never encountered someone with more unshakable concentration than a retired podiatrist—a man named Tom Amberry, who took up free-throw shooting as a late-in-life hobby. (In 1993, Amberry claimed the Guinness World Record for most consecutive free throws made with 2,750; it took him twelve hours, and he only stopped because the gym closed.) Ficker went head-to-head with the former foot doctor on a late-night program around that time. The gimmick ran the length of the show. Amberry put up foul shots, while Ficker tried to get under his skin. But even Ficker, arguably the most distracting man in recent sports history, was no match for the white-haired retiree. Says Ficker, "No matter what I said, no matter what I did, he didn't miss once. I thought of everything and threw it all at him. I couldn't make him miss."

According to Amberry, there was nothing special about his foul-line success. He simply tuned out potential distractions by narrowly focusing on the repetition of his shooting ritual. Nick Harris tried to achieve something similar in his NFL career by homing in on specific elements of his punts, he tells me. "All I had to do was drop the ball flat and kick it in the sweet spot," he says. "If I could do that, in the midst of whatever else is going on around me, whether there were people who were trash-talking, or the conditions were bad, the wind was in my face, the snap was bad, it all boiled down to that split second of dropping the ball flat, keeping my eye, and just crushing it right in the sweet spot."

He accepted what was beyond his control and focused only on those aspects of performance over which he could exert some measure of influence. Ken Ravizza, the sports psychology pioneer best known for his work in major-league baseball, had a catchphrase for this sort of thing. He'd say, "Control the controllables." That was his way of reminding players to sweat process, not outcomes;* to stay in the present; to be aware of themselves and focus on what was immediately in front of them: the next pitch, the next putt, the next play—and to let everything else fade away. In Spike Lee's 1998 film *He Got Game*, Denzel Washington's character conveys a similar message to his basketball-star son, Jesus Shuttlesworth, while talking shit to him during a pivotal game of one-on-one. He says, "No matter what I say to you, I ain't got nothing to do with your game."

Control the controllables.

Focus on what matters now.

Don't get upset.

But all that's easy to say, harder to do.

Especially when the stress starts to mount. When Bibles start to burn, or an air hose gets pinched. When someone starts turning the verbal screws on you.

———————

THE DAY AFTER the emergency-procedures test down in Key West, the dive-school supervisors—each of whom the students call dive sup, pronounced "soup"—invite me out for a ride in the Atlantic Ocean on a Zodiac-like soft boat, which the students have spent their postlunch hours learning to assemble. There are sixty-knot winds coming from the south, from Cuba, and three- to four-foot swells

———————

* Because when you're concerned about outcomes, like success or failure, you're not focused on what you're doing in the moment. As Brian Decker says, "We try to not ever talk about outcomes."

rippling across the water. "Nothing crazy, just kind of annoying," one of the supervisors says. At some point, they offer me the chance to pilot the watercraft. I open the throttle wide, and we tear across the small waves, which send each of us momentarily airborne, before crashing back on the thick plastic of the boat's inflatable tubes that have all the cushioning of asphalt. It hurts at first. But by the time we steer back to shore, I barely feel a thing.

The guiding philosophy of stress inoculation at dive school is no different than it is at SERE school—or pretty much anywhere else in the army, for that matter. It's also not so different than the training principles that inspire sports coaches to introduce possible threats and distractions—like hostile crowd noise, trash talk, the specter of punishment, or anything else that might disrupt players' concentration or detract from their performance—into their practice sessions.

The theory behind stress inoculation is that a person can be desensitized to—or otherwise trained to manage—an anxiety-inducing environment without having an overwhelming stress response via repeated exposure to just such an environment. In other words, if you want to perform under pressure, you need to train under pressure. You have to get used to it. A performance psychologist who has worked with professional sports organizations on both sides of the Atlantic, James Bell describes it as "the concept of exposing people to high levels of challenge, high levels of threat—the things that they are going to ultimately have to face." Or as Bangor University's Stuart Beattie puts it, "You've got to practice under the conditions that you're going to be competing in. If not, you're setting yourself up to fail under those conditions."

Former New York Knicks head coach Pat Riley cultivated famously intense and occasionally violent practice sessions in the early 1990s, which were awash with trash talk, even as he publicly admonished players like John Starks for getting caught up in verbal altercations during games. He did so because those were the bludgeoning, high-pressure conditions in which he wanted his team to be comfortable competing—and the ever-present trash talk contributed to that tense environment, in which emotions sometimes boiled over. "Riles, he promoted that, behind closed doors," says Starks.

Danny Manning, who joined the college coaching ranks after retiring from the NBA, likewise injects trash talk into practice, in part because he wants to prepare his players for the pressures of playing away games and wants to know how they will react when the taunting noise ratchets up. Specifically, he tells me about the hot-box drill, by way of example. As Manning explains it, the hot-box drill features one person playing defense, and that person doesn't get to stop until he prevents the designated offensive players from scoring. "When you get scored on five or six times in a row, then everybody's going to be talking to you," he says. *Keep him in the box! He's in there! We got one! We got one!* And when that happens, the coach wants to see "where that player is going to go mentally." Says Manning, "Is he going to just completely obliterate somebody with a foul, so you don't score, or is he going to try to stay locked in and play great defense?" When players struggle to deploy the proper mental skills in practice, Manning will expose them to more situations like that. "We continue to challenge them and try to help them get to that point," he says. "You have to know what type of result to expect when we go into a hostile environment and everybody's cheering against us. You don't want to experiment with that. You got to know."

Robin Ficker is of the opinion that he would not have been nearly as disruptive during NBA games if teams practiced with hecklers or other trash-talkers trying explicitly to distract players. "They needed to do some role-playing," he says. "These guys weren't prepared." As for what he'd recommend: "Call these guys every name in the book and see if they react."

Dan Weigand, a performance psychology professor and the former editor of the *Journal of Applied Sport Psychology*, would seem to agree with Ficker. He tells me that he doesn't see a lot of teams or even individual athletes practicing with trash talk as a form of distraction, and therefore a way of creating stress inoculations, but he thinks they probably should. When working with athletes himself, he'll start off by asking, "What kind of trash talk pisses you off?" And then he'll incorporate exactly those kinds of upsetting stressors into their practice sessions, much as SERE instructors explore student sensitivities during the POW exercise. As Weigand explains, athletes need to practice their responses to trash talk, as with any other potential distraction, until they're so used to doing it that "it becomes an automatic response." Says Weigand, "This should all be practiced."

In Special Forces, the stress inoculation is built into the program from day one, as soon as someone enters the assessment and selection process. For starters, physical and cognitive tasks are layered on top of one another—for example, candidates may be asked to do a twelve-mile ruck march, while remembering specific information they encounter along the way*—but the biggest stressor for most folks is the level of ambiguity in which they have to operate, which is designed to reflect the uncertainties of real-world environments. This element of ambiguity is so crucial to the process that some candidates have to sign nondisclosure agreements, per Captain Karl Hausfeld, who's in charge of assessment and selection for the Civil Affairs units, and whom I meet early one morning at Camp Mackall. We stand among the pine trees, as soldiers race past us, as part of some physical-training evaluations. As he explains, the candidates are kept almost completely in the dark throughout the ten-day course: they're given minimal direction, no feedback, and never know how long any task could last—or what's coming next. A grueling foot movement could be followed by a navigational exercise or an academic task or a panel interview, in which candidates are as likely to be asked why they want to join Civil Affairs as they are to name as many uses for a fork as they can in thirty seconds. Or they could be told to get some sleep.

More likely, they'll be told to keep going.

---

* According to Brian Decker, the best way to stress a person out physically is to stress them out mentally. He says, "When the mind is being burdened by some sort of stressor, it's going to increase the signals your body is sending that say, 'I'm fatigued. I'm tired.'"

That's specifically the case for one event in particular, Hausfeld tells me, moving farther away from the soldiers lest anyone overhear us, in which the candidates are led to believe—through sheer muscle memory and past training experiences—that they're approaching the end of a physical task. But when they slow down, the cadre say, "Hey, candidate, keep going. You weren't instructed to stop." The assessors do this because they want to see how the candidates react—not just in that moment when "we are seeing their hearts get crushed," as Hausfeld says, but also, more importantly, how they bounce back, like players in the hot-box drill. "If they crumble, they might not make time for the next event."

When Stuart Farris went through assessment and selection for Special Forces in 2000, he didn't have to wait for the training exercises to begin to see how heavy a toll the stress of ambiguity could take on some folks. For the first two days of the course, he and his fellow candidates received no instructions whatsoever, he tells me. They just sat in their huts, watching a whiteboard on which the cadre would eventually—or at least theoretically—write instructions for what to do next. "Every fifteen minutes, it was someone's turn to go check the whiteboard. We didn't know what was coming," he says. "Literally, for two days, we didn't do any testing or anything physical or anything like that." Five people quit from Farris's hut alone in that time. They just couldn't handle it. "They were on *edge*, man."

———————

DURING MY RESEARCH for this project, I came across a variety of potential factors that might help explain why some people are more resilient to stress than others. Some are biological, like the presence of certain hormones in a person's body and brain. For instance, studies have shown a correlation between low levels of neuropeptide Y (NPY) and the development of post-traumatic stress disorder, while high levels seem to be protective against acute stress. (Andy Morgan likewise found NPY to be predictive of stress hardiness in his lab tests at both SERE school and at dive school. He found the same for high levels of naturally occurring DHEA, an anabolic hormone.) Other potential factors are environmental, which could be as seemingly arbitrary as whether or not a person has older brothers or sisters. (In sports science, there's a phenomenon known as "the little sibling effect," which describes the finding that younger siblings are more likely to become elite athletes and also more willing to take risks.*)

At SERE, there were clearly some students who dealt with stress better than others, according to Morgan. He came to think of the soldiers as falling into one of three categories: those who were switched on and had a kind of meta-awareness of what was happening, even as their hormones revved into high gear; those who were angry, defensive, and arrogant and made things harder for themselves (and others) but didn't realize it; and finally, the "scared rabbits," who were in a complete threat state and doing all they could to avoid danger. "They're almost flinching backward," he says.** In the opinion of the SERE psychologists I meet at Camp Mackall (each of whom, along with the instructors, requests anonymity), those who do best with the stress of the POW-camp exercise often find ways to make the experience more digestible, just as Major Murphy suggests combat divers "break things down into manageable pieces." But ideally, students will learn to use their self-regulation skills to cope in one way or another. "A lot of that is just basic self-reflection," a SERE psych says. "I think it comes down to the basic understanding of who you are and what you need. It's all about utilizing what's effective for you to cope in stressful situations." For example, a Special Forces chief tells me how he learned he was far more claustrophobic than he'd ever imagined when he went through SERE and found himself in a confined space. "I was having difficulty breathing," he

---

* Brian Decker tells me he looks for risk tolerance when gauging the likely resiliency of NFL prospects, because it demonstrates a willingness to fail.
** When someone does suffer a panic attack or otherwise seems incapable of managing the stress of SERE, the psychologists will step in and try to reorient that student, coaching the student toward the resistance techniques, mental skills, and coping tools he or she has been taught.

says. "I remember it as clear as day." To get through that, the chief shifted his attention away from the collapsing walls of his external environment to the inside of his mind, where he imagined himself to be taking apart and reassembling a motorcycle engine—over and over again. "He knew to go there. That's awesome," the SERE psych says of the chief's coping strategy. "When some students get over-whelmed, we'll tell them, 'Go to your favorite vacation spot. Look at every detail you can find.'" Or sketch the blueprints for your future home—that's what one soldier did to make it through real-world captivity, the psych says. "It's stuff like that, where people find out these little vulnerabilities [about themselves], but they know, 'OK, I can cope with this.'"

Ultimately, that's what the stress inoculations of SERE are about, per Decker. "It's not just exposure to these very difficult situations," he says. "It's exposing you but also giving you the tools to manage that environment. Teaching you that you're capable of doing things that you never thought you could do." It's screwing up, and then pressing on. It's demonstrating resiliency in real time, and then filing that experience away for future reference, for whenever you need it again. The SERE psych says, "The more they go through stressful experiences and learn from those stressful experiences—that is what is going to help them in the future."

In the end, adds Decker, "You walk away with this global belief in yourself to handle adversity."

———

IN THE INSULAR world of SERE, there has been a long-running debate across the different branches of the military about how best to produce stress inoculations. Per Andy Morgan, there are clear divid-ing lines: The air force, which has the least stressful SERE school (and even allows its students to go home at night), believes in a series of mini-stress exposures, while the army and navy take more of a shock-and-awe approach. "It's sort of like teaching a kid to swim," says Morgan. "You can either wade in slowly, or you can drop them in the deep end. Both can work. They argue over which is better."

Everyone agrees SERE seems to be doing something good, though. For one thing, familiarity—not being caught totally off-guard by a situation—is thought to be an important mediator for stress. There's even some data from Norway to back this up, where researchers were allowed to unexpectedly capture cadets who'd been through a prisoner-of-war-like training and some cadets who hadn't. Initially, upon the point of capture, all the cadets had identical stress responses. But after a few hours, the stress levels for those who'd been through the training dropped to more normal levels, while the others remained distressingly high. "So novelty is doing a negative thing for some people," says Morgan.*

For the most part, Morgan tries to stay out of the wider debates about SERE. But he does have a perspective on this, which is you can't produce a stress inoculation without first causing distress. "If they're just stressed, but not distressed, it's very difficult to produce the stress inoculation, because the learning of safety is not the unlearning of fear," he says. "The learning of safety is a recovery assessment. That's where stress resilience comes from." From learning that you can survive. That you need not feel threatened.

To further explain what he means, Morgan tells me about an experiment that was conducted on rats, in which babies were separated from their mothers. As you can imagine, this was a highly stressful event for the rat pups, and scientists were trying to determine why some of the pups would suffer long-term trauma, while others had stress reactivities that would eventually return to normal. At first, the scientists theorized the determining factor was the

---

* According to B.J. Armstrong, novelty also did something negative for NBA players who hadn't grown up with trash talk and then encountered seasoned talkers like Gary Payton. "When you play in the playground, everyone knows a Gary Payton. I grew up with people like Gary," he says. "I understood him. For people who had never seen that before, they would respond to it."

duration of separation, or perhaps what sort of trauma the pups experienced while they were away. But neither was the case. "The variable that seems to account for whether the rat pup turns out to be OK is the amount of licking and grooming it gets from the mother when it's returned," says Morgan. In some cases, the mothers reject their pups, which is very bad. But when they accept their babies back and greet them with affection, he says, that elicits hormones like oxytocin, which counter the negative effects of the stress response. For this reason, Morgan sees the arguments over how much stress to induce in students at SERE as largely irrelevant: "I'm like, 'Guys, you're missing the point.'" As long as the training is causing distress, "it's really the recovery day that matters."

The recovery day or debrief day. That, you may recall, is when the students head back to the classroom and sit face-to-face with their tormentors to discuss what the hell just happened. This is the true learning portion of the course. According to a senior instructor, pretty much every student has the same question: "Why did this happen to me?" And the instructors will tell them, "You did this, we did this. You did this, we did this. For next time, don't do X, Y, and Z." But the instructors are doing more than alerting the students to their psychological vulnerabilities and proclivities under pressure, they're also giving the students context for their suffering—giving it meaning—and thereby helping the whole horrible event make tangible sense, instead of letting it linger as a purely emotional experience.* As a result, many students start to put a positive spin on their SERE school training during this time; they increasingly see the abuses and deprivations they endured not as evidence of their weakness, but of

---

* Scott Goldman tells me about a similar intervention developed by Canadian psychologist Hap Davis while working with elite-level swimmers who failed to qualify for the Olympics. To help the swimmers recover from that setback, he asked them to identify what key element was missing from their performance. In other words, why did they fail? Did they bungle a flip turn? Did they take an extra stroke? The specificity was important, as the idea was to be rational, not emotional.

their strength, their perseverance, their ability to survive—and thus the recovery process begins.

When I ask Brian Decker how he's imported the lessons of SERE to the NFL, he talks about creating practice environments that are harder than the actual game. "You put people under very stressful conditions," he says. "You place a premium on execution under increasingly difficult loads of stress." The idea is to make practice humbling, he says. Not humiliating, but humbling. "You want to see the limits of your ability. We need to be taking them to the point where they're failing on almost a routine basis. They're touching the edge, and then we help them interpret that in a positive manner. We create a narrative around that to help them see future struggles in a different way." To build resilience, to understand failure as survivable, and ultimately, to believe they have the resources to succeed in almost any situation.

This process isn't exclusive to SERE. It's hard to build mental resilience in any context without first experiencing some form of adversity—some failure, some trauma. For example, Stuart Beattie tells me about his experience working with the UK's Royal Air Force (RAF). As he explains, many of the RAF's pilots-in-training come from privileged backgrounds and have had almost everything in their lives come easily. "They breezed high school, they breezed university, they breezed their master's, and they normally breeze their flight training," he says. Right up until they get to fast-jet training, that is. "That's where they crumble because they don't know how to deal with failure." What happens is the trainees get into the jets for midair exercises, in which they have to chase down or alternately avoid another plane, but they become so overwhelmed by the demands and pressures of the situation (and so threatened by the possibility of failure) that they simply freeze. "The stories I've heard from the pilots is they've had to pull [the students] out of this dive because they're going to crash the plane, or they're going to collide with the other plane," says Beattie. "It takes them a long time to get over that because, in essence, that's the first time they've seen failure, and they don't know how to deal with it."

Stuart Farris has seen a similar phenomenon in Special Forces. "The dudes who had never failed before had the hardest time dealing with that," he says. "They would literally mentally disintegrate because they couldn't process the fact that, like, 'Oh, crap. I'm actually struggling. I'm not the best guy in the room.'" On the other hand, "the people who had challenged themselves through various phases of their life, who had fallen down and gotten back up and kept going, they could always deal with that really well."

Early-in-life adversity is a theme that comes up frequently for high-achieving athletes, too, and not just anecdotally. For example, as part of Bangor University's participation in UK Sport's Great British Medalists Project, a multidisciplinary study that compared elite athletes (those who made it to the highest levels of international competition) and superelite athletes (those who won medals), researchers found that superelite athletes were far more likely to have experienced "a foundational negative life event," such as an impoverished upbringing, a dysfunctional home life, or a history of abuse, and used sports as a way to positively cope with that stress. "They were really good at overcoming adversity because they'd experienced so much adversity in their personal lives," says Beattie. It's possible we can even see evidence of this neurochemically, too. At least that's my interpretation of an experiment that Lynn Dobrunz, a neurobiology professor at the University of Alabama at Birmingham, tells me about, in which she and two grad students gave the exact same traumatic experience to rodents of two different ages—adolescents and adults, essentially. What she found in the brains of the adult rodents was a decrease in NPY, the neurotransmitter believed to facilitate stress hardiness. In the young rodents, meanwhile, researchers found that the traumatic event generated an *increase* in NPY. "Maybe that's some of what fuels resilience is having adversity or trauma or failure early, and then that raises your NPY levels and makes you more resilient when you're older," Dobrunz says, caveating her comment as speculation.

Not everything has to be a big-T trauma. Sporting contests are often defined by their little failures—a missed shot, a dropped pass, a swing and a miss. Players who are trash-talked during a game and fail as a result—due to distraction, perhaps, or self-doubt, or panic-level anxiety, or whatever reason—would also qualify as having experienced a kind of trauma. But each of these events also gives players the chance to bounce back and see that traumatic event as survivable and thereby gain stress inoculation.

Or not.

Steve Smith Sr. has witnessed plenty of athletes suffer some small setback in competition and utterly collapse as a consequence. "I've seen guys fold and never get over it," he says. "I've watched a guy catch a pass, play well, drop a few passes, and that dude is done for the day." Chris Kluwe struggled to get over his on-field failures at first, he tells me. "I would get so wrapped up if I had a bad punt that it would affect my next two or three punts. The thing is, in sports, we're all going to screw up," he says. "Everyone screws up. It's impossible to be perfect. One of my coaches in college told me this: It doesn't matter if you screwed up. What matters is, Are you going to screw up again?"

WHEN BRIAN DECKER interviews college athletes before the NFL Draft, he mostly probes for just these sorts of stories. Specifically, he asks questions that get at notions of resilience and prompts the players to share examples from their past when they've experienced setbacks, and to describe how they worked through those difficulties. "It's really tough to measure what's going on in a person's mind, but to some degree, I can measure their reactions, their behaviors," he says. "Most people who are very, very resilient, you're going to see numerous positive coping strategies."

Because mentally tough people know how to cope.

And yet, a consideration that comes up frequently in my reporting is whether there are some things that we shouldn't even *try* to cope with, things that are better *not* to be inoculated against and instead remain sensitive to. Former NFL and NCAA basketball ref Gene Steratore thinks so, which is why he had certain red lines as an official. He says, "You should not prepare for things that are so egregious that they were not fathomable prior to the event." Scott Goldman has a similar view. As an example, he tells me about a sports psych consultant who used to conduct interviews on behalf of an NFL team at the predraft combine—a dude in a position of serious power, in other words—and would sit across the table from young football prospects, most of whom were no more than twenty years old, and ask them, "How would you react if I told you I fucked your mom?" And then he'd straight up tell them, "I fucked your mom last night."

The NFL has since instituted rules against asking certain types of questions during this intake process. But even if the league hadn't, Goldman questions the value proposition. "I'm just not so sure the data we gain in that moment is worth the potential cost," he says. After all, it's not like this is an opponent talking mess in a game situation; it's a man with a clipboard who controls these kids' future. "Are we devolving if we focus on the idea of making ourselves more robust to that behavior?"

Put another way, at what point do efforts to build resiliency cause more harm than good?

It's a question that cuts at the heart of trash talk: where to draw the line.

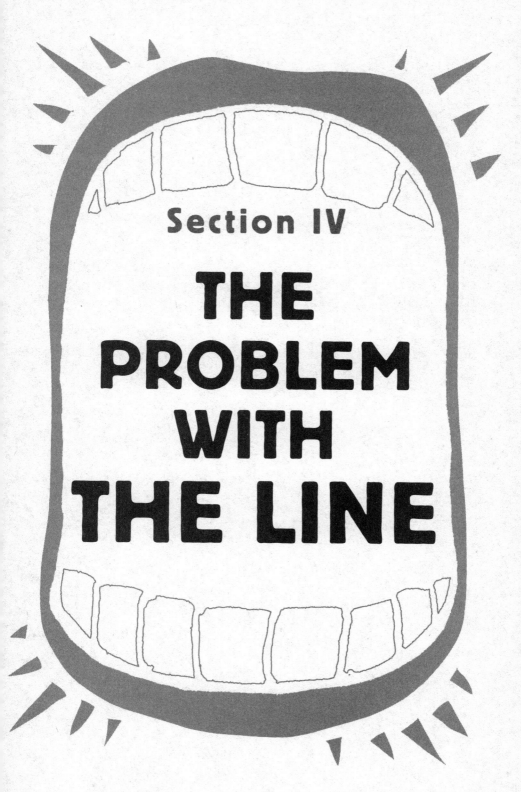

Section IV

THE PROBLEM WITH THE LINE

IT'S NOT COMPLIMENT BATTLE

THE FIRST TIME Earl Skakel heard a joke about his dead parents was on television. More specifically, it was 2016, and he was onstage at the Comedy Store, a legendary club on Los Angeles's Sunset Boulevard, in an upstairs dungeon of a space known as the Belly Room—and the cameras were rolling. Standing shirtless across from a professional joke writer and in front of a panel of celebrity judges, including Jeff Ross, Jimmy Kimmel, and Joe Rogan, Skakel was competing in the preliminary rounds for inclusion on a new cable show, which was to be aired on Comedy Central and which was being adapted from what had quickly become one of the Comedy Store's hottest weekly features: a show in which two comics are pitted against one another in a contest of brutal insults designed to deliver as many gut-punch moments as possible.

This wasn't just any show, in other words. This was *Roast Battle*.

Skakel was no stranger to the format. He was in the audience when the first-ever battle took place, during the summer of 2013, a happy accident of an idea that was intended simply to break up a parking-lot fight, when an off-duty doorman tried to make a young comic leave the club because he was underage. In the three years since, he'd become a Belly Room regular, both as a competitor or a battler and as a fixture of the show itself. When he wasn't onstage, Skakel performed in a role known as the House Racist, who would contribute short and cutting exchanges from the audience with the show's host and cofounder, Brian Moses. As a battler, too, Skakel imagined himself to be stepping into character. A pro-wrestling fan, he modeled his onstage demeanor after Rick Rude, a successful heel in the 1980s and early '90s who would torment audiences by calling them fat and ugly sweat hogs and admonish them to "keep the noise down while I take my robe off and show the ladies what a real sexy man looks like." Giving his opponents plenty to make fun of, Skakel would come onstage dressed in leather pants with a bare, oiled chest and fingerless biker gloves, ready to say some truly heinous shit.

You have to be, he explains. "It's not compliment battle."

He knew it'd happen eventually—that someone would make fun of his parents, with whom he'd been extremely close and had died months apart years earlier. Still, there's a difference between knowing a thing may happen and that thing actually happening. As it happened, Skakel admits, "It hurt, to be honest with you." He loved his parents, after all, and they were dead, never coming back. Now here he was, in the midst of a major career opportunity and being publicly reminded of one of his life's most painful memories. But don't feel too bad for the shirtless comedian. Skakel had come prepared with some monstrous material of his own, and from the second he stepped onstage, he'd known what he'd have to do: make a joke about his opponent's best friend, who had recently died by suicide.

THERE CAN BE a tendency among comedians, the LA based especially, toward cynicism. And yet, from the beginning, people seemed
to recognize that the weird verbal sparring matches happening up in
the Belly Room were far from the typical, jaded, two-drink-minimum
fare. Even though the very first battle was, by all accounts, pretty shitty
and uninspired—the would-be brawlers basically just screamed "fuck
you" back and forth, per Julie Seabaugh's *Ringside at Roast Battle*, a
history of the show—others immediately wanted to do it, too. They
understood the potential.

The early days of *Roast Battle* are described as a uniquely exciting time, as the fledgling show searched for its footing and groped
to figure out what it could become. "It has always been about the
fight-club element," says Brian Moses, referring to the show's implicit
edginess, underground cachet, and insinuations of illicit activity. As
comedians clamored to be next in line to dish out and absorb this verbal abuse, seemingly nothing was off-limits: rape-attempt jokes were
followed by dead-family-member jokes and by cheating-spouse jokes
and eating-disorder jokes and substance-abuse jokes and transgender
jokes and on and on. Per Moses, "The amount of miscarriage jokes I
have heard that are awesome is awful." Competitors were testing the
boundaries of not just decency, but also of offensiveness itself, as the
most sensitive and personal topics were trotted out for public ridicule.
Comics mercilessly attacked one another's defects, blemishes, and
deformities. At times, it could feel almost lawless. Comedian Dave
Attell has called it "this circus shit," while Jeff Ross, who is known as
the Roastmaster General for his star turns at celebrity roasts and who
eventually teamed up with Moses and *Roast Battle* cocreator Rell Battle to codify a few rules of engagement,* tells me, "It was like punk
rock. It was dangerous."

---

* The rules are as follows: (1) original material only, (2) no physical contact,
   and (3) battlers must hug at the end.

But that was part of the attraction.

In a town full of artifice, this felt real. To call it dark humor would be a disservice to Pantone charts everywhere; this humor was blacked out. But it was also unusually egalitarian: everyone and everything was a target. And the forbidden quality only increased the sense of belonging for the wildly diverse group who dared to attend. Says Moses, "This is the only place we can hear these things being said."

Adding to the atmosphere was the physical space itself. The Belly Room could hold 120 people, when all the tables were removed, and with its black mirrored walls and low ceilings, it fostered an explosive energy, with sound that ricocheted in every direction, with nowhere to escape. "When it's packed in the Belly Room, it's an energy I've never felt," says Skakel. "I've been to Kiss concerts. I've been to Metallica at the Coliseum. As weird as it is to say, nothing beats the energy of the Belly Room when it's fully rocking." Comic Nicole Becannon remembers her first time there. It was on a date. The romance sputtered, but she was immediately hooked on the powder-keg vibe. "It was electrifying," she says. "Like an underground boxing match."

Unlike pretty much every other comedy show in existence, there's an intentionally blurred line between audience member and performer during roast battles. It's not just the official hecklers, like Skakel's House Racist character or Sina Amedson's Saudi Prince (who rates the confrontations by giving "two towers down"), or even the silent sketch troupe known as the Wave, which bursts onto the stage, after good (or bad) jokes, and punctuates the proceedings with prop-heavy slapstick. The audience itself "is a character of the show," says Moses. Like the needling of the gathered crowd around a game of the dozens, he adds, "they are there to instigate."

In all, the energy could be intoxicating.

It didn't take many times onstage for Becannon to become the top-ranked battler, per an official ranking system, and she kept coming back to the Belly Room to do it again, despite her better judgment. "Every time, I was like, 'All right, no more. I'm never doing this again,'" she says. "And then two weeks later, I'd be like, 'All right, I'm ready.'" She isn't the only one to point to *Roast Battle* as providing a seductive, hard-to-quit thrill. According to veteran battler and actor Alex Duong, "It makes you feel alive."

WHEN I TRAVEL to Los Angeles, on Moses's invitation, to tag along with him and other members of the *Roast Battle* crew, I discover the show has graduated from its dingy upstairs digs to the neon lights of the Comedy Store's Main Room—for the time being, at least. Part of the reason for this relocation is that the club has struck a deal with a streaming service to broadcast some of its shows, and *Roast Battle* is meant to be a main attraction. This is just the latest commercialization of a product that started as little more than two seemingly inebriated dudes screaming "fuck you" at each other. In addition to the show on Comedy Central, which ran for three seasons, there have been international versions in Canada, Germany, Mexico, Spain, South Africa, and the United Kingdom, which is to say nothing of the untelevised copycat acts that have sprouted up across the comedy world.

In a lot of ways, Moses was the perfect progenitor for *Roast Battle*. For one, he grew up in a shit-talk tradition, as he and his dad regularly played the dozens. "Tagging on each other, we called it," he says. "That was schoolyard stuff. That was family stuff." What's more, he appreciated the sporting aspects of verbal competitions, like rap battles—which were emerging from the underground and into the mainstream as he was growing up—and he never understood why others didn't see the same potential. "I was always like, 'God, it'd be great if ESPN had something like a rap battle,' know what I mean?"

The sports network aired the National Spelling Bee. Why stop there?

Roast Battle didn't invent the modern genre of insult comedy. Comics like Lisa Lampanelli, aka the Queen of Mean, followed in the footsteps of expert ball busters like Don Rickles, who "a lot of people thought stole his act from Jack E. Leonard," per comedy historian Wayne Federman. Meanwhile, as far back as the 1930s, the prospect of "good-natured abuse," as the *New York Times* put it, attracted celebrities and other New York City luminaries to Club 18 on West 52nd Street in Manhattan, where comics like Jackie Gleason and Jack White, who also owned the place, would insult those in attendance.* Some might describe it as roasting, although technically the first roast, which magazine writer Jeff MacGregor has aptly described as "the grand American show-business tradition of pretending to honor a man by pretending to love him by pretending to hate him," wouldn't be held until 1949. (Before that, the Friars Club, which was formed under a different name by a group of Broadway press agents in 1904, held only testimonial dinners.)

Even offstage, comics have been cracking on one another long before the advent of *Roast Battle*. Comedian Luke Schwartz tells me he still prefers "the circle," which is shorthand for the impromptu and free-flowing gatherings on the Comedy Store patio, in which comics give each other shit. (He calls out Jesus Trejo as a master of the circle, for his ability to come up with put-downs that no one else would think of. "Like, he'd say, 'Your pants have been talking to your shirt too much,'" or some such, he tells me, because I'm wearing a blue shirt and blue jeans.) Spend enough time in the circle, Schwartz adds, and eventually attention will swing against you, as the other comics pin you at the bottom of an insult dogpile. It's happened to him a few times. "You just have to take it," he says.

Early on, it seemed possible that *Roast Battle* was just a fad. According to Moses, it wasn't long after the first verbal altercation that the midnight shows in the Belly Room hit a plateau. The insults

---

* In the 1980s, a similar scene emerged at a club called Comedy Act Theater in LA, where celebs like the Showtime Lakers would show up to be insulted by comedian Robin Harris. "He'd insult them all. He was famous for that," says Federman.

continued to fly, but the excitement dwindled. "It wasn't getting any better," he says.

Months passed.

Then, in the fall of 2013, Kim Congdon took on Sarah Afkami in the first-ever all-female battle and something clicked. "They were no-names," Moses says of the two comics. "But they are names to us because they finally showed us what the *Roast Battle* could be." That night represented an inflection point in the life of *Roast Battle*. What changed was this: the insults were not just objectively offensive; they were also profoundly personal. "They were friends!" says Moses. "It was because it was specific, and they knew each other so well. That's really what it was." The comics invested the audience by becoming vulnerable. By exposing themselves and one another. Because they were friends, Congdon and Afkami raised the stakes of their encounter, and in so doing—by risking something that went beyond the baseline indignity of being put down in public: the possibility of both deeply personal shame and damage to a real-life relationship—they laid out a blueprint for *Roast Battle*.

Skakel says the best battles he's seen are always between people who know each other. It could be roommates, former lovers, whomever. "But there needs to be some kind of preexisting relationship," he says, because there needs to be something on the line. Some possibility that the jokes will be so unexpected, so cutting, so mean, so viciously undeniable that it will momentarily stun a person. Moses says there can be a physical reaction when that happens. "You can see when a punch lands," he says. "You can see it literally hit that person."

It's that specter of verbal violence that pulses through the Comedy Store crowd each time Moses brings a new pair of comedians to the stage—two willing combatants, who have signed up to hurt and to be hurt, who are prepared to say unimaginably terrible things, knowing it's all on the table: your divorce, your dead kid, your DUI, all of it. And it's that same quiver of violent excitement that animates the chant that Moses uses to mark the start of each new confrontation and that fills the room like bloodthirsty cries from the cheap seats of the Roman Colosseum.

Ba-ttle! Ba-ttle! Ba-ttle! Ba-ttle!

The audience understands that lines are about to be crossed—that's a given. But in these moments, the room's frothing tension comes instead from one of the only remaining unknowns: just how far each comic will be willing to go.

ACCORDING TO DUTCH historian Johan Huizinga, all arenas of competition—and of human ritual, in general—exist within what he calls "play-grounds," which he defines as "temporary worlds within the ordinary world, dedicated to the performance of an act apart." In such a temporary world, which Huizinga also describes as a "magic circle," in reference to the carefully drawn boundaries before a game of dice in the *Mahābhārata*, an epic poem of ancient India, there are "special rules" that are enacted, which take precedence over the rules of the world beyond. The magic circle is fundamental to whatever endeavors take place therein—it's what separates a boxing match from an arrestable offense; what allows a football defensive lineman to viciously drag the quarterback to the turf; and, some would argue, what allows competitors to communicate with opponents in ways that might ordinarily be considered hostile, threatening, and offensive. As Chris Kluwe says of trash talk in the NFL, "This is an environment where it is accepted. Like, you are expected to engage in this behavior. Even if you don't say anything, you are expected to know this is part of the artificial universe you are inhabiting right now."

Former boxing champion James Toney was so convinced trash talk was an immutable feature of the combat-sports world that he earnestly denied having ever talked trash when author Todd D. Snyder asked him about his reputation as one of boxing's more ruthless talkers. "I didn't talk trash," Toney said flatly. Snyder pressed him: *James, come on, buddy. What about this fight? What about that fight?* But Toney was insistent. He said, "No, man. This is the fight game.

That's not trash talk." As he saw it, talking shit was just part of the mechanics of getting into a fight—like, "we've got to say not nice things about each other," per Snyder.

Roast Battle is another activity that very much depends on the existence of a magic circle. While many outside observers dismiss the comedy show as a nihilistic spectacle of bullying behavior, that attitude reduces the nuance of what's taking place. As Moses puts it, in parroting this gawking perspective of outraged disbelief, *"You're letting people talk trash to each other?!* Yeah, it's almost like the UFC. *You're going to let them punch each other in the face?!* Well, yeah. But everyone is consenting to it."

They're opting in.

Also like the UFC, *Roast Battle* establishes a framework wherein seemingly harmful attacks can appear awful on their face, while remaining fully sanctioned. Moses refers to the environment he has helped to create as "consensual chaos," as comics insult one another in violation of nearly every personal sensitivity and societal taboo, past and present. But he has also discovered there are limits, that in fact not everything goes. For a brief time, there was a rule that allowed white comics, when battling other white comics, to say the N-word once per show. "That was like their lifeline," he says. "We were just like, 'Why not? Let's hear it!' But there was an incident." Someone said something that felt genuinely racist—that breached an intangible but deeply felt divide. "We had to get rid of the rule."

A magic circle is not just defined by its official regulations, either. In *Roast Battle*, in addition to its three etched-in-stone statutes—original material only, no physical contact, hug at the end—there are also some widely adopted customs that add further dimension to the show's permissive structure. For example, before stepping onstage, many comics engage in information exchanges with their opponents, meeting up for get-to-know-you sessions over coffee or beer, or just trading questions via text message. As part of that exchange, the battlers often allow each other the opportunity to draw boundaries or otherwise designate specific areas of their lives as off-limits, as simply too sensitive. "We give each other permission," says comedian Sarah Fatemi. Retired battler Mike Lawrence—who won that first season of *Roast Battle*, is widely regarded as one of the top, if not *the* top, roast joke writers on the planet, and is described by comics in almost mythic terms for his ability to eviscerate others onstage—tells me he would always ask opponents what they considered to be out of bounds as part of his prebattle prep. "People always say, in roasting, nothing's off-limits," he says. "It is, and it should be."

Though not everyone agrees.

───────────

BELIEVE IT OR not, there may be no sport for which the debate over acceptable trash talk poses a greater existential dilemma than cricket: the sport was basically built for talking shit or sledging, as it's known. Despite the languid vibes, cricket—and especially red-ball cricket, which is the form of the game that lasts up to five days—requires of its participants intense and unrelenting focus: veritable ultramarathons of mental stamina. A batsman may be on the field for hours (if not days) at a time, and yet any single slipup—any momentary lapse in concentration or judgment—could spell the end of his turn and prove disastrous for his team. It makes strategic sense, then, that some teams would employ sledging as a tactic—that they'd want to give the opposing batsmen something to think about other than how best to attack the hard, small ball traveling toward them at speeds of up to one hundred miles per hour.

These days, many teams attempt to achieve this psychological edge through intimidation—by making a batsman feel as uncomfortable as possible, via a combination of off-putting physical tactics (like throwing bouncers, aka short-pitched bowling, which are balls that bounce close to a batsman before leaping up to head height, where they can do serious damage*) and verbal ones (like sledging). "Those two things definitely go hand in hand," says prominent

───────────

* "I've seen a guy's eye pop out," a cricket journalist tells me.

cricket writer and pundit Jarrod Kimber. "A lot of sledging comes around the short-pitched bowling because you want them to feel that fear. You want the batsmen to not be focusing on the next delivery."

Hit him in the throat.

He doesn't have what it takes.

Smash his face.

Over the past fifty-plus years, no group of cricketers has more enthusiastically embraced this menacing style of play—or more aggressively strained to discomfort their opponents—than the men's national team from Australia. By all accounts, the Aussie team, which is sometimes referred to as "the Baggy Green," was at its sledging best (or worst) from the mid-1990s through the early 2000s. That was when the team was led by Steve Waugh, a man who believed so deeply in the psychological unsettling of opponents he gave it a new name: "mental disintegration." Under Waugh's captaincy, the goal wasn't just to outscore their opponents, but also to leave them reduced, demoralized, and, yes, defeated. They played a hyperaggressive brand of cricket—always on the attack, always pressing for an advantage—and "sledging was almost an extension of their personality," says British sports journalist Tim Wigmore. In some ways, sledging became a matter of faith. As Kimber says of Waugh, "He sledged the way that a biblical literalist would. I'm talking about the Bible. He was that full-on into sledging."

For a time, the whole country seemed to be in on it. Opposing nations would arrive in Australia and be greeted with hostility from the moment they stepped off the plane. "It was quite something," says Mark Butcher, whose international cricket career for England coincided with the Waugh years. "Generally speaking, when you arrive anywhere as an England cricket team, they roll out the red carpet for you but not in Australia. They kind of make it as uncomfortable as they possibly can from minute one." Customs agents would tear their cricket cases apart, under the pretense of looking for alien plant life. Cab drivers, newspaper writers, civilians on the street—they'd all alert the foreign players to their uselessness.

Meanwhile, at the cricket grounds, the sledging would become surround sound, as the Aussie players kept up their steady patter of attack, which always bordered on brutish, if not brilliant, and rowdy fans did their share from the stands. It went beyond heckling. Spectators were known to hurl golf balls at visiting teams and throw containers of piss in the air while doing the Mexican wave. "Actual piss," says Kimber.

Much like the dozens, there is no agreed-upon explanation for the origin of the term *sledging*. While its etymology seems to come from *slaegen*, an Anglo-Saxon word that means "to strike violently," and former Australian captain Ian Chappell has pinned its earliest use to a cricket match in the mid-1960s, when a player was seen to be acting "like a sledgehammer," others say the term caught on after a cricketer taunted his opponent, whose wife was allegedly having an affair with a teammate, by singing "When a Man Loves a Woman," by Percy Sledge. Regardless of when it was first uttered, the term wouldn't fully take hold in the public consciousness until the 1970s with the rise of those Chappell-led teams, which seemed a little rougher around the edges than previous generations and greeted the world with an aggressive on-field swagger. According to Lawrence Booth, a writer for the *Daily Mail* and editor of the *Wisden Cricketers' Almanack*, those Australian teams in the 1970s "regarded themselves as men's men, and part of that was intimidating the opposition. It was almost a sign of their machismo that they could come up with the most vulgar insults." As cricketer-turned-writer Bill "Tiger" O'Reilly put it in a 1979 opinion column in the *Sydney Morning Herald*, "Sledging is the word minted to describe the modern practice of talking an opponent into error."

Such a practice was hardly new, of course—not even then, not even in cricket. But just as trash talk in basketball in the early 1990s was seen as a trend story–worthy phenomenon, Australia's sledging came as a whiz-bang shock to much of the cricketing world. "Cricket hadn't had that on that level before," says Kimber. The Aussie players simply removed all subtleties from their gamesmanship: their violence became more explicit; their threats unveiled; their insults less backhanded; their aggression unrelenting.

It was the ruffians versus the rest of the tea-sipping world.

In many ways, the Australians' aggressive verbal tactics—which would not only lay the foundation for the nation's future teams, including Waugh's squad of mental disintegrators, but also tilt cricket's competitive landscape toward a more confrontational style in general—were more of a change in degree than a change in kind. But that subtlety was perhaps lost to those on the outside, who suddenly had to contend with unprecedented levels of naked antagonism— or what has been called "premeditated toxic confrontation"—while trying to succeed at difficult and dangerous athletic tasks. To them, the Australians' antics were qualitatively different than anything that had come before. "In cricket, there's kind of an obsession with what is called the spirit of cricket, which is like, it's not within the rules, necessarily, but there is a spirit, which you are meant to adhere to," says Wigmore. "The argument about sledging is whether it contravenes this kind of fabled spirit of cricket." According to sledging critics in the 1970s and the half century since, there is no debate: the Australians—and all those who've followed in their foulmouthed wake—have violated that spirit.

They've crossed an invisible, unforgivable line.

IT'S TRUE: NOT everything can be trash talk.

For example, gossip is not trash talk. At least as I have come to think about it, trash talk is characterized by its presentation of a challenge, by its upping of the stakes, and almost always by the existence of a wider competitive context. (That context can be athletic, social, political, or otherwise. Even the battle for one's legacy, as was the case with the Greek invective poets. Doesn't matter.) But in this way, talking trash is fundamentally confrontational in nature. As Michael Gervais puts it, "You have to have some courage to do it." Gossip, on the other hand, exists in the shadows of social life. It has been argued that human language emerged from our ancestors' desire to gossip because it helped ensure social cooperation within a group. But even if that's true, gossip is never done face-to-face with one's target and is only intended to reach that person circumstantially: by affecting other people's opinions of them. It is talking shit about someone explicitly in that person's absence.

Bullying would also not qualify. It fails the trash-talk test because trash talk presumes antagonists and their targets to be on equal footing—to be two capable and willing competitors. Bullies, however, exploit uneven power dynamics to punch down and wage unfair fights. It's the difference between candidate Donald Trump disparaging his Republican opponents on the 2016 primary debate stage and Trump as president, with the force of his office and millions of Twitter followers, insulting individual citizens on social media. Put another way: trash-talkers invite a response, while bullies seek to silence.

There are countless definitional contortions we could put ourselves through—like trolling,* throwing shade,** and so on—but my intention here isn't to create an exhaustive taxonomy of rude behaviors. My point is merely that these distinctions exist, and they are important to acknowledge. Otherwise, there's a danger that every manner of impolite or potentially antisocial communication is simply lumped into the same bucket and labeled as "trash talk." But that'd

---

* Which is the (often online) practice of upsetting other people for one's own amusement. Not all trolling is trash talk, but a trash-talker can certainly troll. Just ask Philadelphia 76ers center Joel Embiid, aka "Troel" on Twitter, where he's constantly talking shit.

** Which is a more linguistically or gesturally coded way of disparaging a person publicly. According to drag performer and fashion designer Dorian Corey, who was featured in the 1990 documentary *Paris Is Burning*, about New York City's ballroom culture in the 1980s, shade evolved from what's known as "reading," which is a drag-specific insult tradition akin to the dozens. "You get in a smart crack, and everyone laughs," Corey says. "You found a flaw and exaggerated it, then you've got a good read going." I say shade qualifies.

be wrong. "It does a disservice to the concept," Jeremy Yip says of such sprawling categorizations.

There are degrees of difference within trash talk, too. In addition to its wide range of functionalities (many of which have already been discussed), there are also variations in tone—trash talk can be playful, strategic, or born of genuine enmity (which is rare, based on my conversations, but significantly more volatile). There may also be a point at which trash talk, regardless of its intended purpose, becomes something else entirely—something more sinister, something closer to pure abuse. To take an extreme example, think of the harassment Jackie Robinson endured when he broke into the major leagues, which not only leveraged racism as a vector for bench jockeying—or more likely, leveraged bench jockeying as a vector for racism—but also capitalized on Robinson's promise to not retaliate, and therefore the constraints that surrounded any possible response. In fact, for many of Robinson's contemporaries, that power imbalance may have been the more egregious transgression, since jockeys were known to hurl ethnic slurs at other players, too. As teammate Eddie Stanky once shouted at Robinson's tormentors, "Why don't you guys go to work on somebody who can fight back?"

But even with all that nuance, there is a problem with determining when exactly trash talk goes too far, or where exactly on the continuum of incivility it officially crosses the line. Here's the problem: short of outright racism (at least nowadays), no one can agree on where that line actually exists, or if it exists. For example, Warren Sapp had three things he wouldn't talk about on the football field: "Your wife, your money, and your kids, because I can't make your money, I'm not sleeping with your wife, and I don't want to raise your fucking kids." Oh, and no mommas. "I will fight you," he says. But such triggers reveal more about Sapp as an individual than they do about universal standards of acceptable trash talk. Any survey of athletes will uncover opinions about the line that are as varied as the players themselves. Some say not to invoke kids, or moms and wives (but have at those girlfriends!), or a person's off-field problems. Len Elmore puts it beautifully when he says it's beyond the pale to "exploit someone's sorrow."

But others feel differently. Those players—the violators—maintain that everything is fair game and nothing is out-of-bounds. For them, the *whole point* is to make someone mad.

"I mean, what line?" Bryan Cox once said.

"I don't know what too far is," per Basketball Hall of Famer Kevin McHale.

Kevin Garnett has become an almost apocryphal figure for his (allegedly) trailblazing trash talk, which, if you believe the stories, he'd take places no one else would go. Some of his greatest hits include calling Charlie Villanueva "a cancer patient," because he suffers from alopecia; telling Carmelo Anthony his wife "tastes like Honey Nut Cheerios," to imply he'd had sex with her; and wishing Tim Duncan a "Happy Mother's Day, motherfucker" during a playoff game on Mother's Day in 1999, when it was well known that Duncan's mom had died a day shy of his fourteenth birthday.* Whether or not these incidents happened as reported, there's no doubt Garnett was always looking to gain a competitive edge. In his words, he "played with no apologies," and if he'd let someone else tell him how far was too far, then he'd have been competing on someone else's terms—and that

---

* For the record, Garnett has denied saying these things and insists he's never talked about "a cat's mama or his girl. Not even once." And I'm happy to take his word for it. However, I'm also happy to take the word of Charlie Villanueva, who accused Garnett of making the cancer-patient statement. (Per Jackie MacMullan, "He definitely said it. Everybody knows he said it. He denies it, but he said it.") And the word of Duncan's former teammate Sean Elliott, who played in that Mother's Day game. Elliott says, "I wasn't on the court for that one, but I heard he said several things to Timmy." And seemingly the word of Garnett himself, who (at the time I begin my reporting) had yet to delete this May 2013 tweet from his official feed, which was posted amid a playoff matchup between KG's Celtics and Anthony's Knicks: "Me, Melo and Whoever Jordan Crawford's boy is are all Eskimo Brothers." (Update: the tweet seems to have been deleted sometime in late 2022, but I have a screenshot.)

doesn't work. As Phil Taylor puts it, in regard to the alleged Honey Nut Cheerios comment, after which Anthony tried to confront KG as the players were leaving the arena, it's all about saying something that "will make another guy come out to wait for you by the bus." Because that means you're in his head, or he's at least in his feelings.

UFC president Dana White has expressed the view that very little should be off-limits in the context of MMA, in particular: "This is not a nice sport. This is a very rough sport. We say a lot of mean things to each other." But in the press conference that follows UFC 264, when Dustin Poirier defeats Conor McGregor in their trilogy bout, White changes his tune slightly. Asked about a broken-legged McGregor chirping about Poirier's wife from the floor of the octagon, he says, "Ah, I don't like that. Yeah, that's not good. Leave people's family and wives and all that stuff out of it." And yet, Poirier himself is less bothered by the family stuff than by McGregor's prefight prediction of killing him—and he promises to hold McGregor to account for that. "We are going to fight again," he says, "whether it's in the octagon or on the sidewalk. You don't say the stuff he said." Poirier isn't alone in this opinion. In the media tent after the event, I chat with Chad "Ochocinco" Johnson, the former football star known for running his mouth, and he tells me he felt a dark energy coming from McGregor. "I'm the king of trash talk," he says. "But Conor. Conor, man. Conor crosses the line." Christy Martin would surely side with Poirier, too. In fact, it was a similar sort of deadly insinuation that caused her to explode during a press event before her 2005 boxing match against a then up-and-coming Holly Holm, whose friends showed up carrying a tombstone. According to Holm, it was just a joke meant to alleviate the young fighter's nerves, but Martin, who smashed the prop, wasn't amused. "I understand the dangers. I understand that when we go in, we're not guaranteed we're coming out," Martin says, adding that she has personally known at least four fighters who have died in the ring. "You don't cross that line—death. You can die in there. That's so classless. I will talk shit all day, love it. I'm never going to say anything like that."

By that logic, it would be more acceptable, then, to invoke death as a trash-talk tactic when competing in noncombat sports—and maybe it is. But tragedies can happen in any arena. In 2014, for example, an Australian cricketer named Phillip Hughes died after being hit in the neck on a bouncer during a domestic cricket match, and much was made in the aftermath of what his opponents were allegedly shouting at him just before it happened: death threats. Were they wrong to sledge him like that? To try to intimidate Hughes as a batsman and make him uncomfortable? Or was it only wrong in hindsight because of a tragic accident? (The coroner who conducted an inquest into Hughes's death found no one at fault but encouraged "those who claim to love the game to reflect upon whether the practice of sledging is worthy of its participants.")

Ultimately, it's all subjective, though—and that's the problem. Even if folks could agree in theory that some things ought to be off-limits—that it is in fact possible to go too far—it'd be impossible to agree on which things precisely; individual lines are fated to be in constant conflict. As Kimber aptly puts it, in regard to cricket, "One person's banter is another person's sledging." Which is to say nothing of the real differences in cultural sensitivity that might make something more upsetting to one group than another—like the word *bastard* in India (offensive) versus Australia (affectionate)—or the cultural relativity inherent to concepts like "sportsmanship" or the "spirit" of a game. "Where I grew up, the spirit of cricket *was* abusing everyone as long as you shook their hand at the end of the day's play," per Kimber, who tells me it wasn't uncommon to have grown men on opposing teams threatening to rape his mom by the time he was fifteen. These cultural deviations can not only lead to potentially biased in-game enforcement, based on rulemakers' interpretation of things like sportsmanship (more on that later), but also to on-field conflagrations, especially in international competition. When France's Zinedine Zidane, the son of Algerian immigrants, headbutted Marco Materazzi during the 2006 World Cup final, it was because the Italian player had called his sister a whore, and he felt duty bound to respond. Since, Zidane has doubled down on the righteousness of his actions. Saying he'd rather die than apologize to Materazzi. "It would dishonor me."

Or consider Sean Avery.

The renowned and widely reviled hockey pest insists he always stuck to a personal code of conduct. He says, "I never went after anyone's kids, I never went after anyone that had substance-abuse problems, and I never went after anyone's sexuality or race." But that didn't prevent him from earning a reputation as one of the league's most flagrant line crossers. Of those who hold such a view, Avery says, "They don't know what the fuck they're talking about. If I tell a guy that his wife's a whore, first of all, that's a subjective opinion." He adds, "I never crossed those boundaries." But of course, those were *his* boundaries, and there's no debate over whether he crossed other people's. In fact, like Garnett, Avery's whole goal was to say something that would explicitly strike another person's nerve; it was his *intention* to be upsetting. Even Avery concedes he competed with an emotional ruthlessness. As he tells me, "I never gave a shit how anyone felt on the opposing team."

———

BEFORE EVERY CELEBRITY roast that she did, Lisa Lampanelli would rate her jokes on a scale from C to A-plus—and discard anything that didn't make the grade. "A-minus at worst," she says. Lampanelli was merciless in her standards. For a month or more, she would work with a team of writers to fine-tune her material, finessing the setups and punch lines, writing and rewriting, striking and starting again. "I don't like a lazy joke," she says. "I would be obsessed with every single syllable."

You could see the evidence of this single-mindedness in the chaos of pen marks that decorate her old roast scripts. Lampanelli, who retired from comedy in 2018, tells me the only reason she agreed to speak is she recently rediscovered these old pages in a storage unit she keeps near where her mom lives. "I threw everything out," she says. "Actually, I recycled it because suddenly I decided to be an environmentalist at fifty-nine." But the pen marks brought her back: she could barely believe the mania that characterized her erstwhile writing process. She marveled at "all the little editing we would do."

She would rehearse, too. Lampanelli compares those practice sessions to political-debate prep. "If you ever saw that movie with Julianne Moore about Sarah Palin, how they'd coach her. It was like that," she says, referring to 2012's *Game Change*. "The guys and I would sit around, me and my team, and we'd be like, 'No, you go *up* on that syllable.' It was so specific."

Lampanelli would never actually stop preparing, though. Even when she was sitting onstage, on the night of the event, waiting her turn, she'd still be writing. If you pay close attention, you can see it. When the broadcast cuts to commercial, the cameras pull back for a wide shot of the dais—and there she is, head down, scribbling, defacing her ever-changing script. "I'm going, 'OK, make that better, make that different.'" If that sounds like a lot of work, that's because it is. "Roasts are not a lighthearted matter," she says. "They're fucking miserable." But the payoff could be equally immense. "It's so much fun when you know a joke is a fucking home run. And you know it in advance, by the way. You just know."

It's possible Lampanelli felt the need to outwork her peers because she came to comedy late. By the time she first picked up a microphone as a thirty-year-old, she'd given most comics her age at least a decade head start. But what she lacked in stage time, she made up for with a kind of wizened emotional intelligence. "I could always see when someone could take a joke," she says. It could be body language, the pitch of someone's laughter, or something as small as a shift in the mood of the room—she was sensitive to those things.

It was never Lampanelli's intention to become an insult comic, or as she puts it, "to go up and say cunt for a living." At first, the future Queen of Mean was just "a regular old comic, talking about my life or whatever." It wasn't until she got interested in crowd work that she started making fun of everyone. Weirdly, nobody seemed to mind; if anything, they seemed to like it. Why else would audience members reach out to her before shows to tell her where they'd be sitting and to provide short bios? "I think the art starts with not meaning it," Lampanelli says of her ability to push the envelope of insults so much further than most comics. "You don't really want to hurt people's feelings."

Or at least she didn't.

During the roast of *Baywatch* star Pamela Anderson, for instance, Lampanelli couldn't shake her sixth sense that the guest of honor was having a hard time being the punch line—that the jokes were maybe more cutting, more vicious, more personal than Anderson had thought possible when she'd first signed up. "I get choked up talking about it now," says Lampanelli, "because I could tell it was hurting her feelings in that way a woman has of just laughing when she's hurt." Worse, no one seemed to be letting up. For Lampanelli, the tipping point came during a commercial break, when Anderson looked across the dais to her ex-husband Tommy Lee. It was an intimate moment amid a true public spectacle, and for just a second, Anderson seemed to lower her guard, to drop "that fake fucking smile that women have to do," per Lampanelli. "They just looked at each other, and he mouths, 'Are you OK?'"

The moment didn't last long. Anderson shook herself out of her stupor, smiled, and braced for the next round of put-downs. But Lampanelli was haunted by the exchange, by the pleading in Anderson's eyes. She looked at her script—that collection of A-plus material she and her team had spent weeks working over—and decided to tear it all up. "They were so mean to her that I literally sat up there furious at what those guys were saying," she says. "I crossed out almost every joke I had about her boobs, the slutty stuff, or anything like that."

The Queen of Mean knew what she had to do.

She said to herself, "I'm getting these fuckers—for *her*."

BENEATH ALL TRASH talk there is an essential violation—an incitement, a provocation. As psychology and neuroscience professor Kristen Lindquist says, "If it's not a violation, then it's not arousing. It's not activating." And it's probably not trash talk. In comedy, every joke has to be a violation on some level, too, or else it won't be funny. Even so, Jeff Ross recoils at the idea that there's any cruelty in the work that he does. "It's not a word that enters my mind even a little bit when I'm working," he says. "It doesn't even compute as you say it now." The comedian knows he says mean things, of course, things that sting—that cut at people's insecurities and poke at their sensitive areas. His point is just that he's not doing it viciously. "I do it as their friend, not their enemy."

In fact, that's one of Ross's rules of roasting. Just as he won't make fun of people who aren't present or who have otherwise not volunteered,* he won't talk about people he dislikes. "I've tried it," he says. "It either backfires, or it's not funny." Lampanelli similarly conceived of her insult comedy as an exclusively prosocial activity. "The point wasn't to make people uncomfortable. It was to include them," she says.

Comedy can be slippery. It can disavow itself and claim an easy (if occasionally dubious) innocence. It can always say *Just kidding*. But that's not what Ross and Lampanelli are doing here. What they're driving at is a sentiment that's captured by the phrase that closes all Friars Club roasts—*We only roast the ones we love***—because such a sentiment suggests it's possible to buy some leeway with the sorts of things that are OK to say.

To gain some moral clearance and push back the line.

---

*   When I ask how he learned those lessons, Ross says, "Richard Branson poured a drink over my head. Penny Marshall almost beat me up. You learn the hard way."

** Ross even adopted a version of this phrase as the title for his 2009 book, *I Only Roast the Ones I Love*.

To get away with it.

On a basic level, they're absolutely right: when determining degrees of offensiveness, there can be mitigating factors, even beyond the existence of a magic circle. The poets who engaged in the insult battles of Scottish flyting, for example, were expected to enter the contests with a "mutual respect," if not a friendship, per scholar Kenneth Simpson, so as to avoid bloodshed. Or take the Talmud. The book of rabbinic arguments is riddled with insults and put-downs—but that combativeness is meant to be understood in service of constructive discussion. Likewise, the insults exchanged among Roman politicians were considered to be purpose driven, per historian Martin Jehne. "When they start to insult each other, they relate it in a way to the *res publica*, to the state, to the community," he says. "They claim they are working for the community, and this gives them the authority to insult."

Many comedians describe their experiences with *Roast Battle* to be similarly noble. They talk about things like catharsis, therapy, and self-improvement. Alex Duong is convinced roasting has made him a better person—not least because it forced him to get sober. He says, "All the shit that's wrong in your life, that sometimes you can't see, is put under a fucking magnifying glass. And you're like, 'Oh, yeah, that's where I'm fucking up.'" Kelsey Lane talks about roasting's healing effects. Specifically, she tells me about a *Roast Battle* joke in which her opponent made fun of her parents being, in her words, "heroin-addict musicians that would abuse me." She says, "I was grateful that he used my pain to make me laugh. I don't think there's anything more beautiful than that." As Lane sees it, roast comics have the potential to work toward a greater good, just like the Roman politicians, or like athletes pushing rivals to their limits.

But still, therein lies a measure of inescapable brutality, if not actual malice.

In *Black Planet*, David Shields observes there is a "necessary cruelty to be a great athlete." And athletes agree: WNBA great Diana

Taurasi has described herself as a "kindhearted asshole." Tiger Woods's longtime coach, the legendary Butch Harmon, has credited his former pupil's achievements, in part, to a similar edge. "You got to have a lot of prick in you," he's said. When the British government agency UK Sport commissioned its study of elite and super-elite athletes, meanwhile, researchers found that superelite athletes "were more likely to be selfish and ruthless when it was advantageous for achieving their desired success—i.e., their sport achievement was more important to them than being nice or liked." In other words, a willingness to discard the feelings and needs of other people—both on and off the field, in some cases—may be the price of success at the highest level.

In the comedy world, Earl Skakel believes he lost during the first season of *Roast Battle*, in part, because he wasn't cruel enough. "Because I'm friends with [opponent Sarah Tiana], there was a level I wasn't willing to go past," he says. "I didn't want to hurt her feelings." But that was a mistake. "If you want to win, you can't hesitate," he says. *Roast Battle*, in particular, tests a person's willingness to say potentially very hurtful things—things that would very clearly be unacceptable in other venues. According to veteran battler Alex Hooper, "You hit them where they don't want to be hit." But it's also more than that. As humor scholar Joanne Gilbert explains, laughing at someone, as the structure of roasting demands, is predicated upon what French philosopher Henri Bergson described as "a momentary anesthesia of the heart." What she means is, when we laugh, we stop caring about that person. "There's a moment of what I call dis-identification," says Gilbert. "You're looking at the person as a thing to be laughed at rather than a person in their full multidimensionality, you know? It's not that it's a conscious process, and it may only be momentary. But that's the only way the joke works."

You're laughing at their expense.

Or they're laughing at yours.

In either case, someone could get hurt.

MIKE LAWRENCE KILLED a man. That's a thing people say.

Sometimes they say it as a joke, though Lawrence doesn't find it particularly funny; other times they say it to get at the heart of a thing that happened—an onstage encounter between Lawrence and veteran stand-up comic Ralphie May during the first season of *Roast Battle* on Comedy Central, in which Lawrence destroyed May through a variety of raw nerve–exposing one-liners and in which he jokingly predicted his obese opponent would soon be dead. In fact, the forty-five-year-old May died of cardiac arrest about a year later. That's how Jeff Ross says it, somberly, pointing at the spirit of the thing: "He killed a man in the ring."

Brian Moses describes Lawrence as a "joke monster" and "legitimate surgeon" for his ability to see through people's superficialities (their looks, their weight, their race, their religion, etc.), which become primary targets for so many other comics, and diagnosing deeper insecurities: he's a master of saying the thing you didn't see coming, the thing you maybe can't even admit to yourself but will cut you to your core. After his battle against Ralphie May, there were a number of comics who were legitimately scared to share the stage with Lawrence, which I can understand. I was nervous just to speak with him on the phone. The idea of talking to comics—to insult comics, especially—feels dangerous at first because they have the power to hurt. But for the most part, these are not people who seek to cause needless harm. Instead, they are often self-effacing and quick to reveal their own vulnerabilities. For his part, Lawrence comes across as friendly, thoughtful, and self-aware. "I imagine people brought up the Ralphie May situation," he says, and I can practically hear him wince.

I reach out to Lawrence because I want to know more about what makes for a good joke—and the ingredients of an effective insult joke, specifically. How was he able to so regularly bloodhound his way into meaningful material? To begin with, Lawrence says, a roast joke—like any joke—has to be funny. "People are like, 'Oh, these jokes are mean.' But mean can come second," he says. "It's got to be funny because funny is your excuse." That may seem obvious, but not everything people say on the *Roast Battle* stage always seems like a joke. "I've seen roast battles that get ugly and personal and people are just saying what they think about each other, and you're like, 'Well, this is just uncomfortable.'"

As for his process, Lawrence starts, like most comics, by engaging in an information exchange and doing research about his opponent. But if there's a special sauce to his uniquely cutting lines of attack, it's less about any obscure bits of trivia he may uncover about a person (although those can come in handy, too) and more about the way he orients himself to consider those details. He wants to know what the information *says* about a person. He wants to know what makes that person tick. "I call myself an emotional roaster," says Lawrence. "I go through your feelings."

At times, this can be more of a code-breaking exercise than a discovery mission. Take social media. "Social media is the illusion you're putting out there," he says. "So it's like, 'What's missing? What don't you want people to see?'" If a person is presenting a life of achievements and luxury, for example, Lawrence would likely talk about their failures. Other times, the juicy bits are just buried. That happened against K. Trevor Wilson, when the comedians talked before their battle, and Wilson mostly rehashed the usual ways in which people insult him. "You know, 'I'm fat, I'm bearded, and my uncle was crazy,' or something," says Lawrence. But then, at the very end, almost as an afterthought, Wilson said, "Oh, yeah. I've also never been in a relationship." And Lawrence's eyes lit up.

He says, "I'm like, 'Boom! There we go.'"

The idea is to get at something real beneath the surface—something that resonates and isn't easily dismissed. "If I was them, what would I be afraid of being made fun of?" he says. Because everyone has something that bothers them, that just plain sticks in their craw. Lawrence mentions Michael Jordan and his seeming inability to let go of the fact that he didn't make the varsity basketball team as a sophomore in high school to prove his point. "Like, he brings that up at his Hall of Fame speech," he says. "We all still have that thing, so you just have to find it. What's the high school thing? What's the thing that bothers you?"

It's those kinds of personalized prompts that lead to emotional roasting, per Lawrence. Ultimately, the key is thinking so deeply about a person that you see the world through their eyes. "You're focusing on the individual," he says. "You're thinking about their childhood and their journey and all that dumb shit, and you're writing jokes, a lot of times, that you could only write about that person. You're *really* thinking about them—I think that's it. You're taking on what you think their mind-set is, what you think they're worried about. It's weird to say the word *empathy*, but . . ."

He trails off.

But there it is: empathy.

IT SEEMS INCONGRUOUS, on its face. But empathy is actually a key ingredient in cruelty, according to primatologist Frans de Waal. "Those capacities are related," he says. "In order to be cruel, you need to know what is hurtful to someone. People always think that empathy is 100 percent positive, but the capacity for empathy is that you understand the emotions and the situation of someone else, and you can also use them against somebody."

De Waal has witnessed this in the primate world. "Since primates are capable of empathy—they empathize with each other and reassure each other if they are upset—they can also be cruel." For example, he tells me about an experiment in which he and fellow researchers allowed a young chimpanzee to discover a box full of apples in an indoor space with a small window to the outside, where the rest of the group was gathered, apple-less. "I have seen young chimpanzees hold up an apple, right out of arm's reach of the guys on the outside, just to show them that he had an apple, but they were not going to get it."

Sociologists David G. LoConto and Tori J. Roth made a similar observation about athletes and empathy in a 2005 paper about trash talk published in the academic journal *Sociological Spectrum*. They write: "The same characteristics that make taking the role of the other effective in teaching, loving, or playing allows for the athlete to understand the other enough to understand what their weak points are." To understand, in other words, where an opponent might be vulnerable, and therefore, where best to attack.

Empathy didn't evolve for such nefarious purposes, in de Waal's opinion. "I think empathy evolved for positive reasons," he says. "But once you have empathy, you can use it, like a car salesman, to screw somebody."

Or to say the thing somebody doesn't want to hear.

Against Ralphie May, Lawrence knew he needed to call attention to his opponent's weight because it would be ridiculous to ignore it—and because the audience would demand it. But that was the obvious line of attack, and he didn't want to get onstage and just tell a series of fat jokes. The challenge was to acknowledge his opponent's extreme size without making it the focus of his joke list. "How do I elevate that?" he says. How could he, in other words, tell fat jokes that weren't just fat jokes? How could he make them emotionally piercing, too?

"Focus on the person."

With May, Lawrence homed in on the fact that his opponent was going through a divorce. "When we talk about emotional roasting—like, I am a child of divorce," he says. "When I saw he was going through a divorce, I was like, 'That's compelling to me. What if I can make divorce jokes that are also fat jokes?'"

Which is exactly what he did.

Said Lawrence, "Ralphie's going through a divorce. It says a lot that your wife would rather take half your money now, when she could just wait three months to get all of it."

And: "You know, the roughest part of Ralphie's divorce was getting the ring off his finger."

Lawrence made fun of May's weight—but not really. Instead, he used his weight as an excuse to make fun of other things, like his relationship and, ultimately, his career. That was the topic for Lawrence's closing joke: May's second-place finish to Dat Phan on the first season of *Last Comic Standing*. Lawrence had a feeling this was something that still irked his opponent, like Michael Jordan's high school disappointment. Says Lawrence, "I mentioned Dat Phan because I was like, 'You know what? I bet that actually bothers him. I bet that's annoying.' Even though he was a more successful comic—the guy sold out theaters and had a huge following and was so fucking funny—but I was like, 'I bet it still just pisses him off that he lost to that guy, who hasn't really done much.'"

And he made it a fat joke, to boot.

———

LISA LAMPANELLI WAS the final comedian to take the mic at the roast of Pamela Anderson. She was often asked to wait until the end of these Comedy Central productions to perform her material because she was such a fearsome presence on the dais. No one wanted to follow her. "Of course, there's some sense of pride in a woman being able to be like, 'You guys can suck my dick,'" she says. "But the thing is, that's harder!" As she explains, "Once you've heard fifty jokes about William Shatner and Priceline, it doesn't matter if my joke is five hundred times funnier, it's still been mentioned too many times. So I got to find other subjects."

In this case, going last also allowed Lampanelli the chance to unload on those who she'd felt had been unfairly cruel to Anderson, skewering roastmaster Jimmy Kimmel, in particular. "I'm gonna be honest," she said, not long after taking center stage, "I'm sitting up here tonight and I'm not comfortable with all these people taking shots at Pam Anderson. We on this dais are no one to make fun of this woman. I ask you, could any of you have done what she's done? No!

Would *Baywatch* have been number one if it were Jimmy Kimmel's boobs jiggling in slow motion? No. Jimmy can't get anyone to watch his show now and they jiggle at regular speed."

The biggest laugh of this portion of her set came at the expense of Kimmel's former cohost on *The Man Show*, Adam Carolla, as she wondered aloud if he could "have made David Hasselhoff rich just by wearing a bathing suit?" She went on, "Of course not. No one wants to see his furry nut sack in a Speedo. It would look like a squirrel fighting its way out of a Crown Royal bag."

Carolla shook his head, as the audience laughed and cringed at that mental image.

The comedian smirked, as if she knew she'd hit a dinger. But even if all her last-minute additions weren't home runs, Lampanelli made her point: the impromptu performance was an exhibition of real-time retribution—and a test of how well each of Anderson's abusers liked being on the receiving end.

After each of these televised roasts, Lampanelli would receive an influx of emails from fans complimenting her on how well she took the jokes aimed in her direction—of which there were plenty—and on her seemingly thick skin. But the former insult comic tells me there's no such thing. "I think people who say they have it are liars," she says. "I think we're all sensitive, and we all get our feelings hurt." Hers certainly were at all those roasts, wherein a few jokes inevitably made her squirm. That's why she'd keep one eye on the teleprompter—to know what insults were ahead and to force herself to laugh. *Get ready, bitch*, she'd say. *You're a good actor*. But there's no way to truly prepare oneself to be insulted, she says. "It's like saying, 'Can you prepare yourself for when your parents die?' No. You just fucking hurt."

Lampanelli has always known that comedy is, as she puts it, an "emotionally violent occupation," using a phrase she credits to Dana Carvey. But for years she was willing to absorb those blows. For one, the money was good. But also, she says, "The pleasure of killing outweighed the pain of the work that had to go into it, and the possible shrapnel that I took on the roasts."

Until it didn't.

In her final years as a comedian, Lampanelli no longer wanted to have her feelings hurt—and she didn't want to hurt anyone else's either, not even on someone else's behalf. Increasingly, she worried the inclusive intentions of her insult act were being misunderstood. Crowds were becoming combative. One particularly hostile interaction with an audience member went viral. There was less pleasure, more pain. From the beginning Lampanelli pushed the limits with her fans, but as is the case with *Roast Battle*, her transgressive humor, which always resided on a razor's edge, could easily fail. That's part of what makes line-crossing material so exciting—like a high-wire act—and what makes the laughter, when it comes, so redemptive, so hard to quit. A fellow comic once marveled at the inherent riskiness of Lampanelli's work by saying to her, "You're juggling knives and even the handles are sharp." In time, she came to understand that even the handles were dripping red. After an almost three-decade career in which many were regularly shocked at how far she was willing to go, Lampanelli decided she'd gone far enough.

Chapter 10

WHEN TO BLOW THE WHISTLE

SHEP MESSING WOKE UP on a soccer field in Boston. It was in the middle of an NASL game between the Portland Timbers and his team, the Boston Minutemen, and it took him a foggy minute to realize what had happened. The Minutemen coach pulled Messing from the game as it slowly came back to him. There had been a corner kick, and the goalie was making an effort to defend against the incoming ball, when a six-foot, two-inch opposing striker named Peter Withe caught him with a leaping elbow to the back of the head. He was knocked out cold before he hit the grass. After the game, Withe approached Messing. He said, "That's for all your bullshit talking."

According to Dan Weigand, former editor of the *Journal of Applied Sport Psychology*, physical retaliation during the course of competition is often a sign of poor mental preparation. "You can clearly see when a player has no established strategy for dealing with that other than retaliation," he says. But savvy athletes can also deploy more subtle means. In the days of bench jockeying, retributive violence typically took the form of beanballs, which are when a baseball pitcher intentionally throws at a hitter. (This still happens, of course, but it used to happen more.) In football, it's often the "frontier justice" at the bottom of a pile, per Mark Schlereth.* On the basketball court, recourse can come via especially hard fouls, or cheap shots to the kidneys when the refs aren't looking.

Research has shown that targets of trash talk are more willing to behave unethically because they are more motivated by pettiness and the desire to see their tormentors lose. Anecdotal evidence backs this up, too. Sean Avery says opponents "absolutely" played dirtier against him (which is partly how he'd know his on-ice pestering was having an effect). More than once, Canadian Football League defensive standout Charleston Hughes found himself on the business end of an offensive scheme that he believed was designed explicitly to cause him damage—like when a fullback came from his blind side on a pull play, launched helmet-first into his earhole, and started celebrating as Hughes lay concussed on the turf: "I got him! I got him!"

In recreational settings, things can escalate even further. In the brief time I set a news alert for the term *trash talk*, I come across multiple deadly incidents that stemmed from amateur athletic jabbering, including reports of a murder at a flag football game on DC's Capitol Hill and of a fourteen-year-old allegedly stabbing her opponent during a game of pickup basketball in Mississippi. Those may be extreme cases, but make no mistake: trash talk is inherently, linguistically violent, and sometimes it is met with physical violence.

It's not that those who talk trash are necessarily *looking* to fight. In fact, scholars often point out that, in many insult traditions,

---

* In *NFL Unplugged*, former defensive end Simeon Rice describes a matchup against the Eagles, in which Warren Sapp absorbed so many late hits, kicks, and eye gouges that he couldn't see after the game. Per Rice, "Those players were definitely harboring some ill will towards Warren due to the things he was saying."

talking shit serves as easily as a proxy for violence as it does a precursor to it. Or as Todd Boyd, the USC professor, puts it, "If you really want to throw hands, you don't need to talk shit. If you really want to fight, there's nothing to talk about. You talk, in a lot of ways, to keep from fighting." Earl Skakel learned a similar lesson inside a hockey rink, where he honed his trash-talking skills years before stepping on the *Roast Battle* stage. "Hockey players talk a lot of shit," says Skakel, who noticed something peculiar: his verbal altercations almost never turned into on-ice fights. "If you can win the fight verbally, you don't even have to fight physically."

Nevertheless, those who choose to talk shit should understand its violent possibility—that it is a live wire—and be prepared for the potential consequences, whether you're playing pickup hoops or hosting the Oscars. That's the lesson former NBA player and top trash-talker Marc Jackson imparts to his teenage sons, when warning them off reckless chatter. He says, "Sometimes trash talking might come to the point where you got to throw hands." Boxing announcer David Diamante compares the endemic volatility of trash talk—in which the line is always up for negotiation—to the aggressive form of play that comprises slap-boxing. He says, "You're supposed to just spar, but then someone goes a little bit harder. And you're like, 'All right. Fuck you, fucker.' And then you hit them harder, and all of a sudden, you guys are in a full-out war."

———————

THE HAPPIEST MOMENTS on an NFL field are about an hour before kickoff. Warm-up balls sail through the air, everyone is smiling, the game still nothing but pure possibility. As a ref, Gene Steratore used that happy time to his advantage. He'd seek out each team's emotional leaders—guys like Ray Lewis and Richard Sherman—and make conversation. Ask about their wives and kids or compliment some recent achievement. He wasn't just looking to make small talk; he was cultivating an in-game ally, someone to turn to who held sway with his teammates, who could rein them in when the passions of play threatened to burst into open combat. "Listen," he'd say, "while I got you here . . ."

Regardless of the sport, Steratore, who also worked as a college basketball official, never saw his job as prescribing athlete behavior, but instead managing the emotions of the game. As such, trash talk was one of those things he always needed to be keenly aware of. He wanted to know who promised to be in whose shorts all night, who informed whom they were playing like shit, and who just told a crossed-over defender, "That looked a lot worse than you think it did." It wasn't just verbal. In his opinion, "there's a lot of trash talk" in someone like Aaron Rodgers smiling at a lineman after taking a big hit, or in a mobile quarterback like Cam Newton posturing above a defender for even half a beat after running him over. "You have no idea about the amount of intensity that creates," he says.

Going into a game, Steratore would want to understand any wider context that could inform competitive tensions, too: like the presence of a known agitator, the records of each team,[*] a personal beef, or even an ill-advised Tweet. Once the clock was ticking, the ref would keep his finger on the pulse of things by making himself as present as possible—and especially in between plays, which both he and former NBA ref Bennett Salvatore describe to me as "dead-ball officiating." (Says Salvatore, "Most of your taunting comes during dead balls.") Steratore would put himself in position to overhear whatever was being said—not to extinguish the chatter, but to take its temperature. At times he'd remark on a particularly witty zinger. "Did you really just say that?" he'd ask. "You've got to be shitting me."

And then he'd hurry the teams toward the start of the next play.

---

[*] Forget the Super Bowl. Steratore says the most difficult games to officiate are late-season matchups between clubs with terrible records. That's when guys are playing for their jobs. "When you are one and nine in football, that means you've been a loser for two and a half months," he says. "That's the harder game. That's where more of the bullshit happens."

In our conversation, Steratore toggles seamlessly between his normal speaking voice, which he punctuates frequently with a great giggling laugh, and his sonorous Ref Voice, which, despite his Pennsylvania upbringing, is somehow inflected by an unmistakable country twang. (He sounds like a stern Johnny Cash.) It's easy to imagine the authority he commanded on the court or field. But Steratore didn't want to be feared, he tells me, or, worse, seen as a traffic cop. In fact, he tried not to penalize players, if he could avoid it, if he could give a look instead of a flag. His intention wasn't to stamp emotion out of the game, but to create a competitive space with clear expectations and boundaries. The measure by which he judged all contact and conversation was a simple one. "I allowed things to occur, so long as I felt they were good for the game," he says. "You allow them to do what they do, and then you let them know where the boundaries are."

According to Steratore, these boundaries offered players a channel for their emotions, their intensity, and their competitive hostilities, while mitigating the chance for violent explosion. "That allows everyone to breathe," he says. "It allows *more* shit to be talked."

THESE DAYS, THERE'S nowhere more shit is talked—and more lines are crossed—than on the internet. It wasn't always like that. In the earliest days of the internet, when things were almost entirely text based, there was a relatively limited number of users and the guiding social norms of online behavior were fairly easy to maintain. Every now and then, there would be an influx of new users who would do "dumb shit," as Jeremy Blackburn, an assistant professor of computer science at Binghamton University, who studies what he refers to as "jerks on the internet," puts it. But for the most part, that was because they didn't know the norms. Meanwhile, their transgressions were largely contained: they happened in September, when new classes of college freshmen gained internet access for the first time. For years, it happened like clockwork: new students log on, do dumb shit, are scolded, stop doing dumb shit.

Around 1993, something changed. Thanks to services like America Online, the internet picked up steam and more users started joining all the time, year-round. The "dumb shit" was no longer limited to orientation week or even the fall semester, and it soon became clear: the existing norms couldn't hold. This is an inflection point now known as Eternal September, and it put us on a crash course with today's often-toxic online environments, in which shitty behavior can become its own arena of competition. What at first was largely an unintentional breaking of norms morphed over the years into much more deliberate offenses—and as that toxic behavior increased so did the need for somebody to more officially draw the line.

Though there are clear differences between real-world trash talk and the incivilities that have exploded across digital spaces over the past three decades—for example, the former takes place in person, while the latter happens at a great distance, if not completely anonymously; the former also typically occurs because something is at stake, while the latter can often embrace a kind of fuck-it-all nihilism because nothing matters, lol, and so on—what Steratore describes as his officiating philosophy is not so different than the precepts of content moderation. Content moderation is the online practice of screening and potentially removing user-generated material that is deemed to violate a particular community's rules or standards, and it's important—as reams of research and countless real-life examples (most notably, websites like 4chan and 8chan) have shown—because without it, there is invariably a race to the bottom, as the toxic behavior of bad actors (or even those who aren't necessarily trying to be malicious but nonetheless cross the line, in other people's minds) goes unchecked and good actors either feel justified to engage in retributive toxicity or simply opt out of the environment entirely. "It's like the anti-entropy principle," says Eric Goldman, a professor at Santa Clara University School of Law, who has written about the challenges of content moderation. "Communities need active management.

That's the number one thing you can't miss. You can't just expect people to do the right thing, collectively."

I reach out to Goldman and Blackburn, among other content-moderation scholars, because of how much attention the topic of online toxicity has rightly earned in recent years—not least because it has spilled so far beyond its virtual borders, as the digital and analog worlds grow increasingly indistinguishable—and because I wonder if any of their hard-earned insights could be instructive in how we think about managing the competitive incivilities of trash talk, or vice versa.

One thing to keep in mind, especially in competitive settings, per Blackburn, is that losers are more likely to be line-crossers. That's at least what he surmised from his findings of a linguistic analysis of toxic behavior in *League of Legends*, an ultrapopular online game. In a paper based on those findings, Blackburn describes players "transitioning" toward toxicity during the course of competition. "Most verbal abuse of toxic players occurs in the late stage of the game," he and his coauthor write. "We believe the most likely explanation for this is that verbal abuse is most likely a response to losing a game." This insight echoes Steratore's description of late-season NFL games between teams with terrible records as being the most difficult to manage, and it likewise puts me in mind of the new levels of noxious incivility Donald Trump unlocked when he lost the 2020 presidential election—when he was, effectively, enshrined as a loser for all to see.

Another thing that sticks out to me is the degree to which online moderators have to assume that every interaction is now loaded with volatility, as even the smallest differences of opinion seem to escalate quickly into the harshest blood feuds. A particularly hilarious example of this comes from a subreddit community dedicated to the Paleo diet—which is a nutrition regimen meant to mimic the foods that hunter-gatherers would eat during the Paleolithic period—when members viciously turned on one another based on their ever-so-slightly differing perceptions of what that really means. "It was a really big fight," says computational social scientist Aaron Jiang. The problem, according to Cornell Law School professor James Grimmelmann, isn't just that we're in a period of hyperpolarization, but also that we're almost always having "the wrong kind of contact" with those with whom we may disagree. "You basically just encounter them in the context of arguments where everybody is trying to dunk on the other side all the time," he says. As a result, the discourse becomes less of a discussion than a battleground in which everyone is on a war footing.

In other words, we have a problem of bad faith. Online and off, many of us feel instantly threatened nowadays by those with whom we disagree because we believe they are trying to harm us—to make us look bad, to score points—and so we do the same in return, even preemptively. We've stopped giving one another the benefit of the doubt because we don't trust that we're safe. And so we overreact. But without that assumption of good faith—without at least a modicum of trust—trash talk is just abuse, or worse: fighting words. Brian Moses and I talk about the importance of trust in *Roast Battle*: how it's essential for comics to not only trust that an opponent is not actively trying to harm them (or at least not in a gratuitous way), but also that their insults will be received in the spirit with which they are intended. Steratore is getting at something similar when he describes his desire to establish competitive environments with dependable boundaries. It's the idea of creating a safe space to do unsafe things.* A space you can trust.

For their part, the moderators of the Paleo subreddit found a way to reel in the growing acrimony of their community with a single rule, per Jiang: they instructed members to not act as though their interpretation of the Paleo diet was the only acceptable version. Essentially, they were asking for good faith—and so far, it's worked.

---

* Which also speaks to "the necessity of applying strict formal structure to highly volatile matters," as American folklorist Roger D. Abrahams once wrote about the dozens.

ACCORDING TO JIANG, whose moderation-related research is geared toward minimizing online harms, it's increasingly important for platforms of all sizes to proactively determine what kinds of communities they want to be—to decide, for example, if they want to be places for trash talk and confrontation (like in, say, a first-person shooter game), or something else entirely (like a virtual knitting circle)—and establish rules to make that clear. "You have to take a stance of what are acceptable values here and what is not acceptable," he says. Which is no less true in trash-talk communities than it is in knitting circles. "Where do you draw the line between shit talking and actual hate speech? Because I don't think it's completely fair, especially for competitive gaming platforms or communities, to say, 'From this point on, you cannot insult other people.'" Enforcing such an edict would not only be unrealistic, but also undesirable: nobody wants a ref who can't stop blowing the whistle. And yet, each platform must decide: "Where is the point where the insult stops?"

And then: what to do about it when such an infraction inevitably occurs.

In the online gaming world, content moderators have developed any number of ways to combat what they deem to be line-crossing behavior. To name just a few, they can find ways to tie people's identity to their account to lower the toxic disinhibition that may come from anonymity; punish particularly bad actors via social sanctions; create opt-in and opt-out features, like mute buttons; or incentivize good behavior by creating prosocial reward systems. Regardless of which tools (or which rules) are put into place, though, moderators—like most humans—are very bad at predicting the unintended consequences of their actions. Even expressing a norm can backfire in some cases, per Grimmelmann, as moderators run the risk of inciting "exactly the opposite response." *Oh, I can't do that? Cool. Watch this.* In-game tools can also be abused. For example, game developers introduced a new reporting system for the popular online game

Dota 2 several years ago, in which the communication channels of a reported abuser would be automatically muted. The idea for this safety feature was to muzzle toxic players. The issue was, toxic players started reporting (and thus muting) everybody else. Says Grimmelmann, "The number one mistake of moderation is underestimating the determinedness and the creativity of trolls."

We have proven to be equally shortsighted about the potential damages of our theoretically corrective actions in the real world. As curator of political history at the Smithsonian Jon Grinspan tells me, "One thing I have noticed about past reformers is that those who organize around ending an existing evil, as they see it, often can't anticipate the next evil because they're so backwards looking: they fix one thing and break another, basically." When American sports leagues started policing trash talk in the early 1990s, almost immediately on the heels of the popularization of the term itself, they did something similar: they "abnormalized" the behavior, as sociologist Herbert D. Simons has put it. In college basketball, athletes could suddenly be called for personal fouls just for running their mouths, while major sports leagues like the NBA and NFL adopted new rules against taunting. Jalen Rose was once scolded for merely smiling at an opponent, when he was still a member of Michigan's Fab Five basketball team. "No smiling! Smiling and laughing will not be tolerated on this court tonight," referee Ed Hightower barked during the game.

Trash talk became punishment-worthy in the eyes of league administrators—and by extension, in the eye of the public, too. From a wider cultural perspective, these conversations often took on an explicitly moral (and implicitly racial) dimension, framed around the idea of sportsmanship. The same media outlets that helped create the trash-talk phenomenon mere months earlier now debated whether all this jabbering was symptomatic of coarsening on-court decorum—if sports were becoming "too street-oriented," which everyone understood as a euphemism for "too Black"—and if it wasn't time for a return to more sporting behavior.

The problem with sportsmanship is that it has always been an imperfect concept. Much like "the spirit of cricket," it lacks true objective measures. Instead, many of the professed values of sportsmanship—things like humility—are often vague, discretionary, and "culturally relative," as Simons argues in his 2003 paper "Race and Penalized Sports Behaviors." The tenets of sportsmanship are far from fixed: leagues will often redefine what qualifies as unsportsmanlike—such as touching a referee—based on how they want to change player behavior at any given time. But even more than that, just as one person's banter can be another person's sledging, one person's cultural expressions—such as talking trash or celebrating after an on-field success—can be another person's taunting or showboating. The poet and essayist Hanif Abdurraqib has written about trash talk as a kind of historical imperative for Black Americans. In his words, "Few things become more urgent and necessary than reminding the world when you're at your best." Or as David J. Leonard, professor at Washington State University, Pullman, says, "Trash talking becomes a way of celebrating one's self, celebrating one's voice, celebrating one's power in a world that does none of those things."

But sportsmanship doesn't account for any of that.

OSTENSIBLY, THE NBA'S earliest efforts to regulate trash talk in the 1990s—in combination with its stricter penalties and heftier fines for in-game fights—were meant to ward off the high-profile brawls and lower-profile "scuffles," as Bennett Salvatore puts it, that seemed to increasingly interrupt the course of competition. But really, it was about business as much as anything. As a more demonstrative brand of trash talk emerged from the playgrounds, and out of the fledgling culture of hip-hop, the sports world's rule makers fretted more than ever about what might look bad for their widening (and predominantly white) television audiences. Then NBA vice president of operations Rod Thorn explained, "It used to be that two players would be talking, and you might be able to hear it in the first row. Now, guys are jumping up in people's faces, and you can see what they're getting at in the top row of the building." What forced the league's hand from a disciplinary perspective, in Thorn's telling, was less the trash talk itself than the fact it was becoming more visible and more enduring.

Sociologist and Yale University professor Elijah Anderson has made a comparison between the early concern over trash talk and the panic that swept the American South in the 1950s "when black soul singers were singing all these rock and roll songs." Per Anderson, "A lot of white church-going types were really threatened by this. They thought somehow they were going to lose control of young people, that young whites would get turned on to black music." In this sense, the penalization of trash talk was always about control, too, even if only on a subliminal level. According to American University professor Theresa Runstedtler, trash talk "gets linked into this whole racialized discussion about the changing face of basketball," as Black athletes, starting in the 1960s and '70s, introduced new styles of play that were seen as foreign and threats to the game. Phil Taylor says, "I'm old enough to remember when coaches got upset when guys would dribble between their legs or throw a skip pass." He further suggests that old-school college coaches like Bobby Knight, in particular, felt "threatened by that sort of creativity and individuality that trash talk embodies," because it was beyond their control.

From a league perspective, the business concern—consciously or not—was whether audiences would be turned off by the rise of "Blackness that's uncontained," as Runstedtler puts it. She adds, assuming the attitude of league executives at the time, "What's the future of basketball if it's so infiltrated with Black hip-hop culture? Are fans still going to want to watch it?" The remedy to this presumed problem was to make the game "more respectable for fans," she says. "And usually, part of that, the cleaning up of the sport, has to do with cutting down on the appearance of overzealous celebrations or open trash talking."

But this impulse to muzzle Black athletes for commercial purposes had competitive consequences, too. Players like Gary Payton, who grew up in trash-talk traditions, had spent years cultivating their verbal abilities, along with their physical skills, in an effort to gain actual psychological advantages on the court. The rules against trash talk threatened to strip them of these aspects of their games by legislating in favor of cultural conformation—by demanding a little less noise.

There has long been a racial double standard when it comes to trash talk. Black athletes who talk during games are often cast as loudmouths, volatile, and showy, while vocal white players are lionized as leaders or scrappy hardworkers who leave it all on the floor. "It becomes a sign of his love of the game, and not, 'Oh, he's talking trash and gets angry,'" says Leonard. Before his exhibition bout against Conor McGregor, boxer Floyd Mayweather Jr.—whose public image is complicated by the fact that, in real life, he has done some genuinely villainous things—called out the sports media for criticizing his use of trash-talk tactics as "arrogant" and "cocky" and "unappreciative," while Conor McGregor—also maybe not a candidate for the World's Best Person Award—was lauded for doing the exact same things. But critiques of trash talk are almost always as much of a code as the trash talk itself. "What makes the conversation about the NBA particularly interesting," adds Leonard, "is it becomes a way to dismiss and deny the artistry and athleticism and the intelligence of players, when it should be, in fact, evidence of all those things."

For many players, there were also reputational concerns. In a 1994 piece in *Sports Illustrated*, Chuck Person suggested his notoriety as a trash-talker may have prevented him from making an All-Star team.* A reputation for trash talk similarly dogged Payton for much of his early career, as the Sonics wouldn't draft the talented guard

---

* More recently, it's Person's guilty plea in a college basketball bribery scandal that's likely hurting his image.

without first hiring a private detective to dig into his background; refs issued him regular technical fouls; the media cast him as angry and troubled, a double-edged sword of a player; and USA Basketball initially left him off its 1996 Olympic roster. "Payton's talkativeness made him less attractive to the selection committee, which generally picked the stars least likely to cause an international incident," wrote *Sports Illustrated*. But Payton refused to change his style of play— to compete as anyone other than his authentic, unapologetic self. It wasn't always easy: Payton heard the criticism but dismissed the fallout as irrelevant—the foul calls, the bad press, the missed opportunities. "If it would have bothered me, it would have made me change my game, and I wasn't going to change my game for nothing," he says. Payton understood and embraced the centrality of trash talking to his identity as both a player and a person. He knew who he was and knew what he needed to perform at the peak of his abilities. "I'm doing something right," he says. "So don't worry about what I'm saying on the court. I took a lot of criticism. I couldn't care less."

In time, this uncompromising approach paid off. As his career wore on and his stature grew, Payton helped shift the cultural conversation about what it means to be a trash-talker: he made it more cool, less deviant, and laid the groundwork for a whole generation of shit-talkers to follow openly in his wake. Even referees eventually became conditioned to the point guard's verbosity and eased up on their whistles. "They didn't really get it at first, and they were giving me a lot of techs," Payton says of the refs. "But I started talking to them and telling them, 'This is my game. I just talk. That's just me.' And a lot of the referees, they started leaving me alone."

Still, damage had been done. For a time, the term *trash talk* became so potent—so toxic—that it's still capable of putting some people off. When I reach out to Rick Fox to see if he'd be open to an interview for this book, for instance, his rep replies, "Were [*sic*] not interested in anything to do with trash talking." The stigma runs deep.

ROD THORN WAS telling the truth: the NBA's regulations on
player behavior have always had as much to do with optics as anything. Over the years, the league has continued to legislate against
visible acts of disrespect, like pointing, stepping over opponents, or
dismissively waving off officials. By the time Eli Roe refed his first
NBA game in the 2005–2006 season, the league really wasn't even
interested in anything the players were saying, as long as the cameras
weren't catching it. "The NBA generally didn't address verbal stuff
with us because they're more concerned about how it looks on TV,"
he says. Even without official mandates to this end, Steratore tells me
he felt compelled to send a message when he sensed the optics of a
game might be deteriorating. "If players are talking shit every time
we have a whistle, that doesn't look good," he says. "That doesn't look
good for anyone in the arena, and I'm sure it doesn't look good on
television. You feel that." (In such moments on the basketball court,
Steratore would issue a generalized warning by yelling to his fellow
refs during a dead ball, like before a free-throw attempt. He'd say
something like, "Hey, Joe, Bill! The next person to talk shit, T their
ass up.")

Steratore didn't like giving technical fouls or otherwise flag-
ging what he perceived to be natural reactions, like staring at or
chest-bumping a defender after a slam dunk. "That was always hard
for me," he says. But those were also often the things leagues wanted
to eliminate from the game—"zero tolerance"—and that occasionally forced his hand. Some players can be victims of their own body
language, too. A former NBA ref who asks to speak anonymously
brings up Draymond Green. "He gets very worked up, so it shows
up on camera," he says. "That puts you in a tough spot. Sometimes
you're just like, 'Damn, I have to tech him because this is looking bad
in front of the whole stadium and on TV." On the flip side are guys
like future Hall of Famer Chris Paul. The same former ref describes
Paul to me as deeply dismissive and disrespectful of referees, but also

incredibly subdued in his communication methods. "He knows to keep it under the radar," he says. "You hate him for it, but you can't really give techs."

I confess that I find this puzzling. Why would Paul want to annoy the refs? I wonder. How is that to his advantage? "To me, it's baffling," says the former ref, who is careful to add that professional referees would never compromise their integrity in an important game or even an important moment, but nevertheless suggests Paul's sour relationship with officials has otherwise cost him, like on fifty-fifty calls in the first quarters of midseason games. "It has to affect his stats," he says. And not just that. The former ref adds that officials can easily tune him out, too. "Maybe he wants to come up and talk about the clock or whatever," he says. "You want to be able to have conversations with refs. It just gets to the point where refs don't even really listen to you. They're just like, 'Ah, it's Chris Paul. Fuck him.'"*

MORE SO THAN anyone else on the field, including the players, referees are in a unique position to concretize the abstractions of these conversations—how far is too far and what is whistle-worthy behavior—because they're the ones who've been empowered to actually blow the whistle. Herb Dean tells me he rarely enforces the UFC's prohibition against abusive language ("I mean, we're punching each other in the face"), but the MMA ref has come to believe there's a point at which verbal abuse nevertheless reaches its limit. There's one fight that sticks out in his mind, when one guy had his opponent in a bad position and taunted him viciously as he tried to pummel him into submission. Saying things like, "Show me your face, bitch.

---

*   No other refs are willing to comment on the record about this alleged hatred of Chris Paul, although one former NBA official who asks not to be quoted by name on this point says it's not true that Paul is universally despised and that he's disturbed by the idea that any ref would treat one player differently than another. Though he adds somewhat cryptically, "Talk to me in another ten years."

Show me your face." Dean felt his stomach turn. "It's a hard thing to describe, but that was too far," he says.* "I did draw a line in my mind. It was horrible. It was demeaning. I felt bad. You know what I mean? This guy, he probably needed therapy after that."

Steratore has a similar philosophy. He believes trash talk is an expected and essential part of competitive sports—that everyone has opted in—and therefore athletes shouldn't be overly sensitive about what's said on the field. But he rejects the idea that athletes must absorb every insult and personal attack without flinching. "You can't become demeaning. You can't become degrading," he says. "We stay away from the things that we should stay away from in life. We stay away from ethnic slurs. Now, I can tell you you're playing like shit, and *you're* dog shit. But that's not demeaning. That's healthy."

Those kinds of red lines can get complicated in practice, even if they're relatively straightforward on paper. In 2014, for instance, the NFL adopted a zero-tolerance policy for racial and homophobic slurs. But I've yet to meet a ref in the NFL (or in the NBA, for that matter) who'll tell me they automatically penalize a (Black) player for saying something like the N-word, though most acknowledge hearing it plenty. More likely, a ref will issue a warning—*That shit is over today!*—or simply let it pass. "I don't remember ever addressing the N-word," says Roe. "Obviously, if a white person uses it toward a Black person, we would have to step up and address that. But I never had that happen." As with most trash talk, context is king.

---

*   A feeling of one's stomach turning is probably as good a line as any. In fact, as Valerie Curtis writes in *Don't Look, Don't Touch, Don't Eat*, there are biological roots for the human disgust response (it helped us avoid parasites), and she theorizes that the feeling of disgust has evolved over time from being purely physical (i.e., reacting to things that could make us sick) to also having social and moral components, which help preserve societal bonds and promote adaptive behaviors within groups. That is to say, something we see as antisocial or immoral can trigger basically the same feeling of revulsion as looking at a puddle of someone else's puke. Therefore, if we feel morally disgusted by something someone says, perhaps we should trust our guts.

SEVERAL YEARS AGO, Mark Zuckerberg posted a story about Facebook's moderation struggles and how they'd inevitably see a spike in behavior *juuuust* this side of wherever they happened to draw the line for what wouldn't be considered acceptable on the platform. "They could never get rid of the spike," says Eric Goldman. "No matter where they shifted the line, the same phenomenon occurred." Of course it did: it's human nature to test the limits—to push and push and push, until you're met with resistance. Until someone pushes back, or otherwise calls foul. ("Usually when someone throws a chair at you or a punch, that is generally an indication that you have crossed the line," at least in a football locker room, says Chris Kluwe.)

Goldman shares this story with me as part of a discussion about his 2021 paper, "Content Moderation Remedies," in which he argues that moderators should stop thinking in purely binary terms about objectionable content—that violations have only two possible responses (remove or don't remove)—and to adopt instead a more nuanced approach. When I ask why such an approach is necessary, Goldman tells me it's all about the gray space, of which trash talk offers a perfect case study. On the one hand, you have trash talk that is clearly prosocial, he says: "We'd want to make sure that content isn't removed." On the other hand, you have trash-talk-like behavior that can cause real-world harms, which I'd posit stops being trash talk at some point and starts becoming something else: abuse, bullying, trolling, harassment. "I'm not going to argue with that," says Goldman. "The point is that it's not a binary: trash talk or not. It's more of a continuum, and things will come up close to whatever line you draw." When it's less clear if something is or isn't part of the game: "What are we going to do about those?" he says.

From Goldman's perspective, a more nuanced approach might allow for better outcomes—for consequences that are both more accurately calibrated to the degree of each violation (like when a ref can give a look instead of a flag) and infused by the values and needs of individual communities. "Consequences should be whatever is necessary and proportionate to the harm," he says. "You want to redress the harm."

But such gray space can also necessitate judgment calls, almost definitionally.

"The really interesting question, I think, is whether a given decision is spelled out by a rule or committed to the discretion of the moderator," says Grimmelmann. "In law, this is the rules versus standards debate. When you have a vaguer standard, like unnecessary roughness, it gives the official on the field some discretion to decide what's over the line." The penalties for trash talk are almost always discretionary. The NBA gives no definition of taunting in its official rules, for example, but grants referees "elastic power." Meanwhile, the NFL lists "abusive, threatening, or insulting language or gestures to opponents" and "baiting or taunting acts or words that may engender ill will between teams" as unsportsmanlike acts but gives no specific examples as guidance beyond those descriptions. When I ask Roe how he'd decide within an NBA game what was fair and what was over the line, he's sort of taken aback by the question. "You'd think that all refs were taught something specific regarding trash talk and how to handle it and when to call a technical and when to warn players, but it's just so natural. I don't really remember too many bosses ever going over specific criteria, or specific things that are said and how to respond. Like you said, everybody's perspective is different, so from ref to ref, it's a little different." In this sense, it's clear the league is comfortable with a certain amount of gray space around the regulation of trash talk, which is how most players would prefer it, too. "Let us do what we do," says Gilbert Arenas. "Don't interrupt this shit right here. We're playing who's-got-the-biggest-balls game right now."

B.J. Armstrong tells me something similar. "I think it's important that the players who are competing and playing draw the line. When people outside start telling you what's acceptable or not, that's where it goes haywire. The players have to regulate themselves. Not the referees, not the coaches, not the executives. The players."

By and large, players do a valiant job of creating and enforcing their own norms, per Steratore. "It's not the wild, wild west," he says. "They police themselves, in most cases," even if the motivation to rein in one's teammates is often more about avoiding costly penalties than caring whether one's opponent may suffer physical, mental, or emotional damage. As Scott Goldman, the performance psychologist, says, "Another tribe calls foul? Fuck them." Still, Goldman tells me he sees lots of "behavioral shaping" happening in subtle ways behind the scenes, as young players learn the ropes of what is and isn't cool in a professional setting, like incoming freshmen in the days of the old internet. Shane Battier says, "There's a code of the locker room." In this sense, athletic trash talk seems to be in a decidedly healthier space than the discourse that screams out for moderation on the internet. Really, on-court trash talk may be as tame today as it's ever been: in many leagues, would-be rivalries and interpersonal animosities have been largely neutered by the increasing likelihood that opponents have preexisting relationships, thanks to more active free-agency periods and amateur circuits like AAU (Amateur Athletic Union) basketball. (In baseball, the decline of bench jockeying is likewise tied to the advent of free agency in the 1970s, which also corresponded to a rise in player salaries.*) Increasingly, players have reason to see themselves as part of the same fraternity, even if they're not always wearing the same uniform.

If there's any lesson in the trials and tribulations of contemporary content moderation, though, it's not to take any of this for granted. As we've seen in the years since the dawn of Eternal September, norms can erode quickly, and it only takes one person who's willing to test those lines for sparks to potentially fly. (We see you, Dillon Brooks.) Inevitably there are times when every ref feels compelled to blow the whistle.

---

*   With more money at stake, players felt they had more to lose, too.

MORE THAN ANYTHING, refs are consequentialists. They think about repercussions and where things might lead. Steratore always tried to reserve his flags and technical fouls for those moments when players were on edge, when he needed to lower the temperature—and quickly. Many refs talk about techs in this way—as tools of moderation, as a cooling mechanism. This approach is also why some bemoan the NBA's decision to start suspending players after receiving sixteen in a season, which has had the unintended effect of making each call that much more significant. "All that did was fuck us," says Roe. "As a ref, you just want to call a tech to keep the game under control. But now every technical is super analyzed, and you have to worry about, well, is this player going to get suspended again? We hated that rule."

There are times when no number of technical fouls would do any good, though. When tempers simply erupt. When a player is overwhelmed by emotions like anger or frustration and maybe throws a punch. It can happen in a blink, seemingly out of nowhere. Like "an IED went off," per Steratore. But those incidents are relatively rare. Far more often, refs can gauge the emotional explosiveness of a game by watching player interactions. "You have to monitor it very closely," says Salvatore, the longtime NBA official. "You monitor what happened after the statements were said to see if there would be a retaliation, whether it be a physical retaliation or a verbal retaliation. That's really the difference. That's where we got involved." Remember: as psychiatrists William H. Grier and Price M. Cobbs write of the dozens, "the essence . . . lies not in the insults but in the response of the victim." Referees understand the true meaning of trash talk can be similarly constructed in real time. In fact, athletes, refs, and sports psychologists all agree that the biggest determinant of trash talk—and where it leads—is not actually what is said, but how it is received. "Linguists tend to call this uptake," says Jonathan Culpeper.

According to athletes, one of the biggest mistakes a referee can make is failing to take in-game protestations seriously when players appeal to them for help, when they claim an opponent is going too far. More than that even, many athletes say violence is often deployed as a measure of last resort—that most competitors will only lash out when they feel they are being treated unfairly and have no choice but to take matters into their own hands because the refs are letting their opponents get away with something they shouldn't. Even John Starks has claimed vigilante justice as an excuse for his headbutt of Reggie Miller. Per Starks, he had been appealing to a ref about Reggie's antics, but the ref just said, "Shut up and play."

When Starks decided to draw his own line, the refs had no problem calling foul. But by that time—and by Steratore's standard of officiating, which demands that a game be proactively managed rather than reactively policed—they had already lost control.

Chapter 11

A LEGIT SOCIETAL CONVERSATION

IN THE MOMENTS before halftime in an early November game in 2017, Jacksonville Jaguars punter Brad Nortman was headed to the locker room and found himself about a step behind teammate Jalen Ramsey, who had just been ejected from the game along with Cincinnati Bengals wide receiver A.J. Green. At TIAA Bank Field, where the Jaguars play, the home and visiting locker rooms are connected underneath the stands by a long corridor; you can see clear from one end to the other. On this day, Green was still visible at the far end of the hallway: "a little speck," per Nortman. "Jalen was still shouting to A.J.," he says, "still talking about how he shut him down and how he's all talk, he's soft as can be. Like, that wasn't even a challenge, and I was just like, *Dude*! It was relentless." But more than anything, Nortman remembers thinking, "I am just thankful that guy is on our team."

Not everyone on a team needs to talk trash, but every team needs a trash-talker. It wasn't just Jalen Ramsey. Throughout Nortman's career, he was grateful for the emotional leadership provided by guys who talked mess. For one thing, it helped raise the energy and confidence levels of the locker room. (As former defensive end Antwan Applewhite used to say to Steve Smith Sr. before games, "Set the tone.") Beyond that, trash-talkers essentially volunteer themselves as psychic centers of attention—and as the main targets of whatever abuse may come from both opposing teams and fans, as a result. This matters because it absolves less sure-footed teammates from needing to engage in this way and allows them to focus more explicitly on their performance-related responsibilities. When Cheryl Miller entered visiting arenas, especially raucous environments like the University of Tennessee, she'd go out of her way to incite the booing crowds and attract their ire. She'd even get into it with opposing coaches. It was an effort to alleviate pressure on her teammates. "I thought I was taking the heat off them," she says.

Trash talk is important within a team for other reasons, too, and not just because it ramps up practice intensity. When Sam Cassell came into the NBA in 1993, the young point guard didn't hesitate to talk smack or otherwise announce his presence on the court— and no one gave the brash rookie more shit than the guys on his own roster. Former Houston Rockets swingman Mario Elie put it this way: "You know, you get a skinny little kid in camp, especially one who talks, and you want to see what he's made of. So we talked a lot of trash at him in practice, tried to rattle him. We dared him, bumped him, hacked him. But he didn't break. He'd come back talking just as much as us." More than hazing, it was a way to test his mettle.

According to Dacher Keltner, a professor of psychology at the University of California, Berkeley, these sorts of verbal altercations can be foundational for teammate relationships, as they help define otherwise fluid social situations and delineate roles on the roster. He says, "In a funny way, it could be a way of provoking the person to say, 'Look, you got to counter so that we can collaborate.'" Former Lakers trainer Marco Nuñez tells me Kobe Bryant often used verbal and physical challenges to feel out guys in his own locker room—and to determine which ones he could depend on. Says Nuñez, "Kobe obviously wanted athletes that had skills and could compete, but at the end of the day, there was always this term. He was like, 'Who do you want in the trenches with you when you are going to war? Who do you want in your trenches? Who is going to fight with you to the very end?'"

Equally fundamental, trash talk can at times play a necessary linguistic role, especially in professional football locker rooms, wherein many teammates are effectively strangers, thanks to free agency, short careers, and frequent player turnover. As Chris Kluwe describes it, trash talk serves as a common language—a way for athletes who otherwise don't really know each other to make a connection. "It doesn't matter your background. It doesn't matter what school you came from—everyone has trash-talked others. Everyone has experience with trash talk," he says. What's more, trash talk is basically a universal sign of a healthy locker room. Western Carolina University psychology professor Thomas Ford studies what is known as disparagement humor, and as he explains, trash talk within a group setting very often serves as a mechanism of bonding. This happens both when in-group members put down outsiders—which increases the social identities and sense of belonging of those on the inside*—and when they talk shit among themselves, as if playing the dozens. Says Ford, "Those are uses of humor to increase cohesion in groups and to strengthen bonds of friendship."

Impoliteness scholar Jonathan Culpeper similarly sees in-group razzing as having a prosocial possibility. As an example, he tells me about an adult woman who used to curse at her mother when leaving

---

* Ford describes this aspect through the lens of superiority theory—a theory of humor that goes back to Plato and Aristotle and has been more recently associated with French philosopher Henri Bergson—which suggests we find levity in the misfortune of others. "We enjoy humorous disparagement of people that we dislike or people that we don't affiliate with," he says, "because it serves as a basic motivation of enhancing self-esteem."

the house. Culpeper explains, "It's a case where it's superficially impolite, but they do not intend to cause offense." Rather, it's a demonstration of solidarity. "By saying these things, it actually reinforces the strength of their relationship, and their love for each other." Nortman says the best football teams he's been a part of had exactly that kind of unforced intimacy. "I mean, I talk trash to my best friends. There is a comfort level with people that you talk trash to," he says. Or as Hanif Abdurraqib writes in an essay about playing spades, "I meet my enemies with silence and my friends with a symphony of insults."

On the flip side, a lack of trash talk might indicate a more hostile and edgier environment. An associate professor of philosophy at Ritsumeikan University in Japan, Christopher Johnson tells me a story from when he was in grad school and shared a pint with a student from the former Yugoslavia. "He had been there when the war was kicking off," says Johnson. "I remember him saying, 'You began to worry when people wouldn't make fun of each other anymore. When people were afraid to do that, you began to sense the tensions building up.'" Lisa Lampanelli expresses a similar idea when she tells me, "The ones you feel safe with are the ones you can joke with." Performance psychologist Michael Gervais always listens for trash talk when he walks into a new team setting. He says, "It's not until there is trash-talking banter taking place that everybody goes, 'Oh, he is part of it.' As an external consultant that comes in and out of many places, it's noticeable." In this way, trash talk can also serve as a rite of passage, per Mark Aoyagi. "I would say it goes beyond prosocial bonding," he says. "It's a signal that we recognize that you can take this." That you belong.

—————————

FROM A MORAL philosophy perspective, one of the main points of contention about the permissibility of trash talk revolves around its perceived relevance (or irrelevance) to the competition in which it occurs. Is it essential or extraneous?

For athletes, the answer is obvious. Essential, they invariably say, part of the game. "Like the ball is part of the game," per B.J. Armstrong. For philosophers, however, the answer often depends on one's ideas about what exactly sport is meant to test. Many agree that competitive sports should be a gauge of "sporting excellence," as they put it. But while some conceive of this as being a demonstration of pure athletic skill, others also see things like mental toughness, resilience, and strategic thinking as both important and relevant challenges, especially at higher levels of sport. That's the perspective Australian philosopher Chuck Summers espoused when he became one of the first to write about the morality of trash talk in 2007. Such nonathletic but competitive skills, he writes, "cannot be extricated from our modern sports without gutting much of what is so fascinating about them." He adds, trash talk "should be understood as a test of the opponent's mental commitment to the contest at hand" and as a way "to make sure that one is getting the challenge one deserves." In other words, Summers was suggesting, as Armstrong has likewise suggested, that trash talk, by its very nature, invites one's opponents to bring out their best: to raise their game by rising to the challenge. And if they fall apart instead—if they wilt under the additional pressure—so be it. An athlete wouldn't want to lose to a mentally inferior player just because that aspect of his or her game wasn't tested. Per Summers, "For this reason, I feel no regret if I have reduced her standard of play through sledging."

But others disagree.

Nicholas Dixon is an ethicist, professor of philosophy at Alma College, and perhaps the most prominent figure of the anti-trash-talk faction. As he sees it, the philosophical argument against trash talk, which he has called both "extraneous" and "morally indefensible," is straightforward. "It's the same argument that criticizes insulting people in everyday life," he says. People simply have a right to not be insulted or degraded. This view is steeped in the work of ethical philosopher Immanuel Kant, who likewise believed it wrong to demean people or treat them as means to an end. "If I trash-talk you in order to make you play worse, I'm not treating you as a person who has rights, who has moral standing," says Dixon. "I'm treating you as an object to be overcome, and that's exactly what Kant's philosophy implored you not to do."

Dixon knows he runs the risk of coming off as a cartoonish prude with his anti-trash-talk views, or of seeming hopelessly disconnected from the realities of elite competition. He swears he's not trying to turn sports into "a Victorian tea party, where everybody is being overly polite." He's even happy to concede that many things, like tackling, are morally acceptable within the magic circle of a sport—and by virtue of competitors opting in. "I just think trash talking is not one of those things," he says.

To him, trash talk, when used strategically, is demeaning and gratuitous, plain and simple—as irrelevant of a challenge as kid-napping the child of a star player before a big game. "You could say, 'What a challenge that would be!'" he says. "But we would consider that reprehensible."*

Part of the problem, as Dixon sees it, is how many pro-trash-talk arguments don't stand up to scrutiny. He's highly dubious about the idea that trash talk is designed to bring out the best in one's opponents. "It seems to me that there's something a bit disingenuous about saying that," he says. "The raison d'être of trash talking is to make someone play worse." He's similarly skeptical that it's somehow fine to demean some things about a person (like his athletic abilities) but not others (like her dead parents)—that there is a line. "That's very revealing," he says, "because if trash talking really doesn't mean anything, if everybody knows that you don't mean the stuff, then why wouldn't it be OK to talk about someone's mother or father who has just gone through a tragedy?"

When I mention my theory that trash talk is a way to endow an event or encounter with deeper meaning—to make it matter—Dixon

---

* We would also consider it a terrible premise for a sports movie, judging from the Rotten Tomatoes ratings of 1996's *Celtic Pride*.

remains unmoved. "It seems to me there are ways of achieving meaning in your life that don't involve harming other people. It seems to me that an equally important part of meaning is having moral integrity."

Dixon may conclude that athletes talking trash are harming each other, but I think a more relevant concern is whether the players themselves feel that way. As I've come to learn, verbal antagonism isn't always what it seems.

IN NEW ZEALAND, there is a funeral rite within Māori culture called *tangihanga*. The body of the deceased is prepared and displayed, as loved ones come to pay their respects. But those respects are paid in an unusual way: mourners tell jokes and off-color stories. They dish out insults.

They talk shit.

This is considered a tribute to the dead. As Māori musician Tuari Dawson explains in an interview on the Janks Archive podcast, "The greater the man, the bigger the insult." The tangihanga is germane to our discussion because it gets at a basic truth of trash talk that's often overlooked, or even goes unseen: to be trash-talked is flattering.

Many athletes understand this implicitly: it's a competitive compliment for one's opponent to talk smack, even if it doesn't always feel that way in real time. "This is one area in which, in some perverse way, to be disrespectful is a sign of respect," says Phil Taylor, the sportswriter. On a basic level, it means your opponent is taking you seriously as a competitor and as a person of consequence—as someone to whom it's *worth* talking shit. It's like Warren Sapp's habit of only talking to quarterbacks, "because that's who the girls come to see," he tells me. Or the noticeable uptick in antagonism that greeted Seattle Seahawks wide receiver DK Metcalf on the field in the season after he made his first Pro Bowl. "They can't stop me any other way," he said then.

Taylor still remembers the look on some NBA players' faces when the great Gary Payton would start barking at them on the court: they basically flushed with pride. "They were almost honored," he says. "You know, 'I'm getting the Gary Payton treatment.'" Some of Muhammad Ali's opponents have admitted to feeling similarly tickled by the bluster directed at them in the lead-up to their fights, while former major leaguer Bill Wambsganss was shocked by the bench jockeying he received from the already legendary Ty Cobb during one of his first games as a pro. "Gee," Wambsganss marveled to himself, per Lawrence Ritter's classic oral history, *The Glory of Their Times*. "A star like Cobb picking on a raw rookie like me."

It was an honor, indeed.

Comedians likewise understand the inherent compliment of giving another person their attention, which is why so many regard the time they spend obsessing over someone before a roast as a deeply flattering activity. "You've taken the time to figure out who your opponent is, or who your honoree is," says Jeff Ross. In the case of *Roast Battle*, this can create a real sense of intimacy. According to Brian Moses, the comedy show has laid the foundation for a number of serious relationships. He says, "People become best friends after they roast each other. We have had people date, get married. It's nuts. They get to know everything about each other just from talking trash."

And yet, there is a quiet conversation taking place in some corners of the comedy community about the various tolls (moral, emotional, and otherwise) that insult humor can exact, not unlike the late-stage considerations that led Lisa Lampanelli to call it a career. As the host and cofounder of *Roast Battle*, Moses may seem an unlikely person to be at the center of these discussions, but he has always been thoughtful about what his show means—what it allows, what it unleashes, and why it (usually, seemingly) gets away with it—and he has emerged as a de facto nexus for these spiritual reckonings, as someone in whom other comics confide, whom they trust.

The topic comes up as part of a barstool talk that is at first about the baseline cost of delivering and accepting insults onstage: how words really do hurt.* Days earlier, Kelsey Lane had told me she can only battle once a month, for mental-health reasons. She's not alone. A growing number of comics, including Nicole Becannon and Sarah Silverman, have privately confessed to Moses they've had a hard time recovering from roasts or roast battles. "Sarah said it takes a month after a roast to get over what people said about her," he says. It could be a single joke that feels a little too personal—that has "that edge of, *ooooh, they mean it*," as Lampanelli puts it—or the generalized humiliation of realizing a roomful of people recognize your flaws.

That's what most bothered Becannon, the former *Roast Battle* champion. She didn't mind when people made fun of the tragedies in her life, as she calls them: her suicide attempts, the rape attempts. It was the surface stuff that cut deeper. "When I did my first battle, I never thought I would get ugly jokes," she tells me. "I didn't think I was ugly. I just thought I wasn't pretty."**

But when her opponent made a joke about her looks—and it killed?

Oof. That was a gut punch.

"That's the thing that hurts more," she says. "That can fuck you up."

Alex Hooper talks about this, too: the intense shame that arrives "when one hundred strangers see something in you, and they start laughing at you." He says, "Make no mistake, they are laughing *at* you." But for Becannon, who has long struggled with depression and self-esteem issues, those jokes did more than make her briefly blush; they tore at the scabs of a lifetime of mental anguish. In the aftermath of those battles, the comic would retreat home and lock herself

---

* Like, they are physically distressing and painful. Per Jonathan Culpeper, research has shown that emotional attacks are "potentially more hurtful and damaging than physical violence."

** For the record, Nicole is not ugly. She is beautiful and funny and kind.

inside. At her lowest point, she lay in bed for two weeks. "I didn't think I should go outside and see people because I was too ugly," she says. "It's ridiculous."

Mike Lawrence continues to pay the price for his battle against Ralphie May—and he's not even sure he did anything wrong. For one thing, May was a professional comic who was voluntarily participating in a televised comedy tournament (and in fact had hosted a dozens-style TV competition years earlier called *Baggin'*). Plus, the only real personal information Lawrence brought into play—May's divorce—was public knowledge. Still, he is weighed down not just by the fact that he joked about May's death shortly before he passed away, but also by the possibility that he injured a man who was suffering from private pain. "I carry a lot of guilt about the Ralphie thing because I never got to talk to him again," he says. "I think he really was upset about it, and that was not my intention."

Not helping Lawrence reconcile those feelings of remorse were the joking text messages he received from friends upon May's death. Messages like, *Hey, you did this.*

And: *You started it and he finished it.*

"I hated that," he says. "He was a guy with kids, and he was a really funny comic. I felt gross with myself because people would send stuff like that." Because they obviously thought he would laugh about it, too, and maybe even claim May as a pelt. "It's weird because I feel like, even in bringing it up, am I bragging about this? I'm not trying to."

It wasn't long after May's death that Lawrence retired as a battler. When I ask if that Comedy Central matchup contributed to his decision, he acknowledges it did. On some level, he just couldn't shake that gross feeling that crept up his spine every time someone made a crack about how he was a killer. The last thing he wanted was to put himself in a position to say more things he might come to regret. Of that fateful battle with May, he now says, "If I could take things back, maybe I would've just done more fat jokes."

We both chuckle, but I can tell from his tone that he also means it. Mike Lawrence knows he did not kill Ralphie May. But the dead man will always be his burden.

MY DISCUSSION WITH Moses turns to the topic of the Belly Room itself: how what happens inside its walls is always in conversation with the world beyond. The consensual chaos can never be fully contained. That's part of what happened when they ditched the N-word rule. It wasn't just that the word was misused, but also that a blogger wrote about the incident, other outlets picked it up, and the whole thing turned into a minor scandal. (D. L. Hughley talked about it on the radio; Moses found himself with folks like Joe Torry, an actor and former host of *Def Comedy Jam*, trying to fight him.) "At the end of the day," says Moses, "we're playing with language, and language is always changing."

As are the norms by which that language is judged.

The emergence of cancel culture, for instance, comes up constantly in my conversations with comedians. Depending on your view (or more likely, your political affiliation), the term can either capture the idea that people have become overly sensitive and wield outrage as a virtue-signaling cudgel, or that people in positions of power are finally being held accountable for things they do and say. For many of the comedians I speak with, the term is simply descriptive of a landscape they see as littered with newfound land mines on which they may step, or on which they've already stepped and are just waiting for the explosion.

Moses feels the outside world horning in on the Belly Room. Even though the core rules of *Roast Battle* have not been amended, and the Overton window of what's acceptable discourse within that space has never meaningfully budged, the behavior of comics therein has unmistakably changed, he says. They've witnessed other comedians being tied to cancel culture's pyres (some fairly, some maybe less so), and they are increasingly aware of potential repercussions, of the internet's eager outrage. That has shifted the calculus on what comics are willing to say or are even willing to have said. Moses fields calls from folks like Earl Skakel who'd like for online videos of their old battles to come down. Skakel confirms he worries about how those clips might be seen years later, in a different cultural context. When I ask if it ever felt weird to play a character called the House Racist, he says, "Back then, no. Now, yes."

Though Moses often indulges such requests, he's less sympathetic than you might think. "Some of this stuff has *never* been acceptable," he says of the line-crossing humor that represents the crux of *Roast Battle*—and that was (and is!) the point. From the minute he brought those first two dudes onstage, the show has been at least one thing: honest. There's never been any false advertising. As Moses sees it, *Roast Battle* is grounded in the thrill of transgression and the follow-up question: Can we get away with this?

"Can we get away with saying this about your dead dad? Or your dead brother? Or your brother who has cystic fibrosis?" says Moses. "Can we get away with this?"

———

ONE OF THE so-called unwritten rules of trash talk is the idea that "what happens on the field stays on the field." This is often meant to be understood in one of two ways. The first is as a caution against taking things personally—whatever is said during the course of competition is a function of that competitive environment, that magic circle, and if you get your feelings hurt, well, that's on you. The second is a little more foreboding, as a warning against discussing the particulars of in-game communication with outsiders, like an *omertà*, the mafia's code of silence and honor. When Charlie Villanueva accused Kevin Garnett on Twitter of having called him "a cancer patient," many in the NBA were more scandalized by Villanueva exposing a fellow player than by KG's alleged comment.

There are some who would additionally defend Garnett by categorizing his maniacal on-court behavior as a function of the competition itself, and KG as one of those guys who essentially inhabited a character during games. But philosophers resist this idea: that a person's actions in one arena can be roped off and quarantined from his life beyond and therefore escape moral judgment. Even if we were to accept the most extreme position that all is fair when it comes to trash talk—and especially at the highest levels of sport, where the most is on the line—a person's behavior will still reflect her true nature, they say. Christopher Johnson explains this position through an Aristotelian framework, in which we assess what it means to perform well "not just in terms of person playing game, but athlete as person." He says, "There is an integrity to my person that goes beyond who I am on this court or this pitch. And if you're prepared to say these quite vile things, there's going to be some sort of compromise with that integrity when you step off the pitch."

Johnson is asking: What kind of person do you want to be?

Are you willing to be the kind of person who would make fun of someone's family tragedies? Or imply you've fucked his wife? Or call someone a cancer patient? (Allegedly.) Are you willing to make another person feel physically unsafe?* Or leverage wider systems of power and oppression in an attempt to cause psychological pain?

In the days when Jackie Robinson first broke into the major leagues, plenty of opponents—most infamously, Philadelphia Phillies manager Ben Chapman—defended their racist jeering of Robinson by claiming they were simply trying to throw the rookie off his game.

---

* Cheryl Miller dealt with some scary stuff along these lines from opposing male fans. "To this day, it still baffles me why guys feel the need to trash-talk me," she says. Miller would try to defuse such situations, say something like, "Man, you're tripping." But at times, it could get dark. The men's faces would harden. "Just wait," they'd say. "There's going to be a time when you're not around anybody and I'm going to hurt you. I'm physically going to hurt you." Per Miller, "That's when I needed to make sure I was in a group. I never did anything alone. Never."

"We'll ride anybody if it'll help us win," said Chapman, who tried to further justify this position (and rehabilitate his reputation) in his later years by rattling off all the bigoted things he'd say to Jewish and Italian ballplayers, too. "It was all part of the game back then." But someone like Johnson would argue Chapman didn't understand—or simply refused to accept—that the things he said were ultimately, inescapably, a part of who he was. And even if Chapman truly believed he had a competitive excuse for racist abuse—and even if he didn't mean a word of it—he nonetheless revealed himself, fundamentally, to be the kind of person who says racist things.

That was the moral cost, and that's how history remembers him: as a racist.

On some level, these are ethical and competitive calculations that everyone must make—what one is willing to sacrifice in service of a cause—and trash talk happens to be an arena in which such calculations must be made. In which someone must decide what kind of person they want to be.

Johnson would take it even further. From his perspective, he'd caution that there ought to be limits not just on what individuals are willing to accept of themselves, but also, and perhaps more importantly, on what we, as a society, are willing to accept from one another. After all, as so many *Roast Battle* comics have discovered, even a magic circle isn't a vacuum. Says Johnson, "There is a genuine social and political interest in not allowing [a situation where there are no restrictions]." Just as athletes who subject themselves to possible harms by playing sports like football can place wider burdens on a community by, for example, requiring medical care when injured, athletes who endure psychological and emotional abuse can similarly take their wounds off the field with them. "That is going to have bearing on the way you interact immediately with your family, in terms of the attitudes you take to the rest of society, and so on," says Johnson. "The rest of society has an interest in that. It doesn't just affect you."

Plenty of athletes may welcome such consideration. But they'd also be right to point out that it'd be a mistake—if not outright disingenuous—to talk about sports (and the trash talk of sports) in isolation, as an exception to supposedly polite society. If anything, as they perhaps know better than most, trash talk is nothing if not a reflection of our broader world, from its occasionally objectionable themes (like sexism and homophobia) to its eye-gouging ruthlessness. As David J. Leonard puts it, the idea of winning at all costs is basically "capitalism personified." Chris Kluwe agrees and wonders how anyone can credibly reprimand a player like KG, while simultaneously lauding billionaire captains of industry for accumulating wealth by crushing competitors and running up profits at the expense of precious planetary resources, or while our elected leaders govern with petty cruelty and cling to the levers of power, even at the expense of democracy itself. "I definitely think there needs to be a conversation about that," he says of what behavior we collectively condone or condemn, and therefore what kind of people we collectively want to be. "But it's not just a sports conversation. It's a legit societal conversation."

IN THE YEAR before Donald Trump took office, one of the more headline-grabbing pieces of political trash talk involved a man wearing a pasta strainer on his head. As the vice president of American Bridge 21st Century, a Democratic super PAC, Eddie Vale was in New Hampshire ahead of the 2016 Republican primary. American Bridge is an organization that largely focuses on what's known as political tracking,* but Vale had no agenda. "We were there just to

---

* The practice of political tracking—in which a staffer tails and videotapes an opposing party's candidate at all times—has been around for decades. At first it was mostly about awareness: to better understand what was being said on the campaign trail. That changed in 2006, when longtime Virginia politician George Allen was caught using the racist term *macaca*, which means monkey, to describe his tracker, which helped sink his campaign for reelection to the Senate. Since then, trackers have grown increasingly aggressive in their tactics, asking hostile questions and generally baiting candidates like hockey pests, trying to catch them in a gaffe.

keep an eye on stuff," he says. It was mostly out of boredom—if also the influence of a six-pack—that he and a colleague decided to make a late-night Lowe's run after watching the GOP debate, in which Chris Christie called out Marco Rubio for repeating the same canned lines over and over and over, like a robot on the fritz.

They purchased supplies to make cardboard costumes and showed up to the Florida senator's next campaign event, introducing themselves with names like "RUBIO TALKING POINT 3000" and "MARCO ROBOTO." According to Vale, the plan was to make a quick scene and leave "because we had other stuff to do," but they couldn't believe how mad everyone was getting. "If they had just ignored us, we literally would have been done in ten minutes," he says. Instead, the pro-Rubio crowd surrounded the robots, shouted them down. One supporter tried to wrestle an automaton to the dirt. Staffers got involved. The media took notice. Says Vale, "We were like, 'Oh, this is annoying his staff. Let's keep doing it.'"

For two days, the "Marcobots" dogged Rubio across the Granite State (and even, as a coup de grâce, flew to South Carolina to book rooms at a hotel where they knew he'd be holding his next private event). The senator started altering his routines to avoid the robots, even pulling his bus to backdoor entrances at campaign stops. It became obvious they were under his apparently paper-thin skin. "This is not the single thing that's going to defeat any campaign," says Vale. "But when the New Hampshire election is two days away, and instead of focusing on their campaign, they have a ton of people trying to figure out how to avoid two people with metal colanders on their head, you're really fucking with their game plan."

Given what's happened to political discourse in the time since Rubio glitched onstage—the rise of violent rhetoric and innuendo, the demonization of those with opposing views, the naked insults and personal attacks in lieu of talking points—it's easy to look back on Vale's shenanigans as almost quaint gamesmanship, a feature of a time before the veneer of decency shattered completely beneath the unbearable weight of Donald Trump.

More so perhaps than any public figure in recent memory, Trump has strategically leveraged what Jonathan Culpeper would call "impoliteness strategies"—insults, boasts, threats, and so forth— to further his politics of tribalism and grievance, while ditching even the pretense of decorum. (It's for a reason his behavior and bombastic, trash-talking style has been deemed, on many occasions, "unprecedented.") In a lot of ways, Trump took advantage of our country's preexisting conditions, according to Vale: he saw the direction in which politics was already trending—not just the deepening polarization, but also an uptick in racially coded and misogynistic language, as well as a relaxation of standards around acceptable lines of attack (which Vale describes as an increasing disregard for questions of propriety in favor of pure calculations of what one can get away with*)—and then simply "smashed the gas."

When he did, many of us got whiplash.

FROM THE BEGINNING, American politics has been basted in incivility. Attacks came via partisan newspapers and pamphlets, or what were known as public toasts. According to Jon Grinspan, the historian, toasts were exactly what they sound like: formalized one-liners at public gatherings meant to capture a person's political views by celebrating one's supporters and putting down one's rivals— and followed by a collective shot of booze. "They're almost like tweets

---

* As an example, Vale compares his and his colleagues' decision in 2012 to not run ads against Mitt Romney for owning dressage horses—even though it would help paint him as an elitist—because Romney's wife, Ann, had talked about using them as part of her therapy for multiple sclerosis, to Trump's willingness to attack Ted Cruz's wife because he found her unattractive. "Our thing, we could justify its connection to politics: he's rich. But we didn't attack Romney's horses because of a two-degree tangential connection to his wife," says Vale. "Trump was just like, 'Your wife is ugly.'"

of the day," says Grinspan. "They're really carefully crafted. They're really cutting." The language could be superficially artful and refined, he adds, "but the implication is brutal and violent."

Things weren't much better on the campaign trail. While it was seen as poor form for candidates themselves to level insults at the opposition, or even to appeal for votes, their supporters held no such reservations. During the bitter campaign of 1800, surrogates for Thomas Jefferson attacked the incumbent, John Adams, by basically accusing him of being a hermaphrodite. In turn, Adams's camp called Jefferson a lowlife, "the son of a half-breed," and worse. The 1828 election may have been even more vicious, as President John Quincy Adams's supporters went after not just his opponent, Andrew Jackson, but also Jackson's wife, Rachel, whom they made fun of for being short and fat and smeared as "a convicted adulteress." Inside the walls of Congress, meanwhile, words often had bloody consequence. In the march to Civil War, things boiled over constantly in the form of fistfights, canings, and duels. As historian Joanne B. Freeman writes in *The Field of Blood: Violence in Congress and the Road to Civil War*, which traces the congressional violence of that era, a British foreign minister once warned folks back home to avoid the floor of the House of Representatives because the "congressmen were too dangerous."

But even the end of the Civil War couldn't bring peace to politics, per Grinspan, whose book *The Age of Acrimony: How Americans Fought to Fix Their Democracy, 1865–1915* details the "bare-knuckle" tactics that defined the second half of the nineteenth century. He says, "The heckling and the threatening and the political violence lasts another forty years." It wouldn't be until the early 1900s that a reform movement emerged to restrain this rowdy body politic. "There's this deliberate change in what's acceptable, what's civil, what's statesmanlike," Grinspan says of this effort, which put limits on things like public demonstrations and transformed election-day voting practices from communal revelries to private affairs. "They build a new culture with these new expectations. They dial down the mudslinging, and the political violence along with it." Before long, American democracy took on the quieter, more subdued tones that most folks spent the last hundred-plus years assuming have always been the status quo.

There's nothing inherently civil about politics. Especially in the United States, political civility is almost entirely a modern invention. It's tempting, therefore, to think about a norm-destroying figure like Donald Trump as less of a break from political tradition than a return to form—and in many ways, that's true: he is. But what's also true is that his transgressions have not been harmless, and there's a reason this modern moment of incivility feels different than those that have come before. It's not just that Trump coarsened civic discourse and hastened the shattering of century-old norms—which would be meaningful on its own, regardless of past precedent—but also that he did so in an era in which the widespread ramifications of incivility, from general rudeness to outright dickishness, in politics and well beyond, have likely never been so significant.

WHEN VIDEO-GAME COMPANIES introduced voice-chat capabilities in the early 2000s, any eavesdropper would have likely been shocked. "I can't even tell you the stuff you would hear," says Ryan Polidan, a longtime gamer who worked for years in the world of e-sports. Those early communication lines were choked with vulgarity and slurs. At times, they seemed to serve as little more than crowd-sourced thesauruses for the world's most offensive terms. "Everyone was dropping the hard 'r,'" says Ovilee May, a content creator and media personality, who wasn't yet a teenager when she first plugged in a headset. As many people describe it, there was a glee to this linguistic anarchy. Players were struck by the novelty of the technology—their sudden ability to talk to strangers and to do so with relative anonymity and seemingly no repercussions (both of which are key criteria for the online disinhibition effect*)—and started saying naughty things for the sheer thrill, like schoolkids drawing dicks in a bathroom stall. They just wanted to hear themselves speak.

But of course, others could hear them, too.

That matters because, as anyone who has spent any time on the internet knows, incivility is contagious, and the effects are not restricted to the digital world. Research has shown that when we are subjected to incivility, an overwhelming majority of us not only will respond in kind—that is, retaliate—but also will likely pass it on, by being rude, threatening, or deploying other forms of assholery upon other people, who may have had nothing to do with the initial act of incivility.** What's even more concerning, from a societal standpoint, is a person need not be the target of incivility to experience these effects; they just need to witness it. Incivility quickly becomes self-perpetuating. Just as the amygdala hunts for dangers in the world and goes into overdrive when we feel threatened, we become sensitized to incivility when we are subjected to (or again, merely witness) it and soon start to see it everywhere. We become less inclined to help others and more inclined to contribute to toxic environments. (A recent study of trolling behavior showed users were more likely to leave negative comments online when a forum was perceived already to be toxic.)

---

*   Something similar can happen among sports fans when they become part of a crowd, thanks to what's known as deindividuation, which is the loss of self-awareness (and therefore personal accountability) in a group. For example, a recent study of college basketball fans out of the University of Kansas and University of Wisconsin–La Crosse found many were willing to shout objectively horrible things, like homophobic slurs at opposing fans or "I hope you die" to a referee, and rationalized their behavior by claiming either they didn't really mean it or it was excused as part of the fan experience.

**   The reason this happens is the same reason insulting trash talk can be so effective. As organizational scientist Christopher Rosen has put it, "When someone is uncivil to you, it forces you to spend a lot of mental energy trying to figure out what's going on, what caused the rudeness, what it means," and that "lessens your capacity for impulse control."

What makes incivility such a uniquely modern concern is that it's everywhere, all the time. In 1800, someone may have accused John Adams of being a hermaphrodite, but how many people would have actually been exposed to that language? And how many times? And across how many mediums? Today, with the instantaneousness and scale of information technology, incivility not only travels at the speed of clicks, but it is also amplified by a fractured media ecosystem designed on all levels—from mainstream cable-news channels to online platforms like Twitter and Facebook to everything in between (podcasts, YouTube shows, etc.)—to magnify conflict and highlight extreme positions. In this environment, negativity is not only rewarded—on social media, in particular, angry posts receive more engagement than their more positively minded counterparts—but its attendant content is also more likely to be seen as truthful and absorbed into the belief systems of its consumers, whether or not that information is based in actual fact, thanks to repeated exposure (this is known as the illusory truth effect).

Modern technology is changing the way we experience the incivilities of sports, too, as the outside world presses ever closer to the action: broadcast partners plant more powerful cameras and microphones around the arenas (or on players themselves), and fans wield smartphone cameras like amateur paparazzi, capturing and disseminating small moments on social media that in previous eras would have passed without a second thought. J.A. Adande points out how Kevin Garnett largely escaped detection as a trash-talker in the early years of his career, before the rise of social media. "He didn't say it with the cameras on him," says Adande. "We became more aware of KG, but he'd been doing stuff like that all the time." In this sense, what happens on the field is decidedly *not* staying on the field anymore, if it ever actually did. The privacy of the game has been pierced.

Defenders of trash talk—and even those who believe strongly that there is a line, a moral boundary that must not be crossed—would argue this is unfair: that the language of competition is being plucked from the playing field, stripped of relevant and necessary context, and then held up for public ridicule. It is being removed from the magic circle. And they're not wrong. Trash talk can have very different meaning in different places.* But with regard to politics, in particular, the recent uptick in boorish behavior seems designed for public consumption. And it's not just that we have more exposure to these incidents of incivility; there also seem to be fewer constraints around them than in previous eras. In ancient Rome, politicians talked all kinds of shit but were not permitted to insult the public. In the British House of Commons, too, which has a well-earned and centuries-old reputation for creative impoliteness and snarky inter-ruptions, there are rules. Even in the uncivil days of early America, it wasn't the actual individuals in power (or aspiring to power) who did the shit-talking—they had people for that—because it was seen as beneath them.

Whereas nothing seems to be beneath a politician like Donald Trump.

———————

IN 2010, GORDON Hodson introduced a concept called cavalier humor beliefs, or CHBs. Hodson is a psychology professor at Can-ada's Brock University, about twenty minutes east of Niagara Falls, and among his research interests he counts things like intergroup relations, prejudice, and dehumanization. The idea behind CHBs, as he explains to me, is that some people are more easygoing around humor than others and are therefore "unconcerned about the social consequences of joke telling, believing instead that people should lighten up."

Those with higher levels of CHBs are dismissive of potential harms and try to absolve themselves of any moral responsibility when

---

* Brian Scalabrine learned that lesson when he retired from the NBA and started working as a sportscaster. "I got called into human resources," he says of his tendency to razz his colleagues. "I go, you know if I'm doing that it means I like you, right?" Scalabrine has since stopped talking shit at work.

making offensive or disparaging remarks. To them, comedy itself is the magic circle: it gives them clearance to say anything they want. You know, *Lighten up! It's just a joke!* There's a similar phenomenon among folks who talk toxic trash while playing online video games. They justify their abusive language by labeling racist, homophobic, and sexist slurs as "gamer words." This is meant to imply the words have been effectively divorced from their true meaning and should instead be understood as generalized attacks.* But to accept this claim would be dangerous.

As Hodson and his colleagues discovered, people with CHBs can unintentionally give cover to others who'd use derogatory humor strategically: to express actual prejudice and "to serve intergroup goals (such as keeping a disadvantaged group in a low status position)."** In European soccer, right-wing nationalists have long viewed the chants and trash talk of the fan experience as a perfect vehicle to both broadcast racism and recruit new members. In recent years, such tactics have also been infiltrating stands in the United States—as skinheads and Proud Boys attach themselves to Major League Soccer—and the digital world, where the toxic spaces of online games are seen as fertile recruiting grounds for extremist hate groups. These trends are complicated by the fact that some still see racial abuse as pure tactics of distraction.*** But the ability to use transgressive humor and

---

* That was NBA player Meyers Leonard's excuse, at least, when he said, "Don't fucking snipe me, you fucking kike bitch," while live streaming on Twitch. After the incident, he defended himself by claiming he didn't actually know what kike meant, just that it was a thing you could say to insult someone online.

** Comedian Sarah Silverman has used the phrase "mouthful of blood laughs" to describe the unsettling feeling she gets when it seems an audience member is misunderstanding the irony of her offensive humor and taking it instead at face value.

*** As a group of Inter Milan supporters said in a statement, defending the practice after one of their own players, Romelu Lukaku, who is Black, was subjected to monkey chants by opposing fans: "Please consider this attitude of Italian fans as a form of respect for the fact they are afraid of you for the goals you might score against their teams and not because they hate you or they are racist."

language to woo impressionable youth to violent causes is as clear an example as it gets that these are never "just jokes."

In any forum, the things we say matter. Even when disparaging political rhetoric is used for cynical and strategic means—or for drummed-up TV drama (as is often the case on cable news)—there can be real-world fallout. Take the Trump administration's so-called Muslim ban. That policy, which made good on an inflammatory campaign promise to restrict travel from a variety of Muslim-majority nations, ensured that actual human beings living in the United States (husbands, wives, parents, children) would be unable to reunite with loved ones overseas—and their lives were made manifestly worse because of a society that now treated them in a hostile way. Or more recently, consider the uproar over critical race theory, which is little more than the academic idea that it's worth exploring the ways in which racism has been baked into the system over hundreds of years of American history, but has been willfully mischaracterized by many of its opponents as anti-white and anti-American indoctrination. Trump himself has said, "Getting critical race theory out of our schools is not just a matter of values, it's also a matter of national survival," and it wouldn't be long before school libraries in Florida were emptying their shelves and covering books in literal caution tape. The point is, what starts as "just talk" rarely stays that way for long.

But not everyone is so concerned with the consequences of his words.

Part of the reason Trump has been able to use trash-talk tactics and incivility as effective tools of political messaging is that he isn't actually trying to broaden his appeal or to have substantive discussions. Instead, he disparages his rivals (and anyone else who doesn't pledge fealty) like existential enemies (the stakes couldn't be higher, folks!) and often with winking bigotries. This has served to both attract attention—like a carnival barker or promo-cutting wrestler—and reinforce the in-group identity for his core supporters: those who already see themselves as part of his tribe. Really, the trash talk *is* his message, and his willingness to say absolutely anything without regard for whom it might offend on the outside has become a value unto itself. Trump's rallies are case studies in superiority theory; it's all about who belongs, us versus them. Into this mix he sprinkles incendiary language like an aphrodisiac—little professions of love and loyalty to the men and women who buy his merch. According to Harvard psychologist Joshua D. Greene, who focuses in his research on moral judgment and decision-making, Trump's extreme rhetoric is no accident: it's a blinking neon sign to his base that he'll never betray them because he's made himself so morally repulsive to literally everyone else. (It's the verbal equivalent of getting a gang tattoo, per Greene.)

This is known as costly signal deployment.

But Trump's norm-breaking signals have been costly in other ways, too. According to statistics from the Department of Justice, hate crimes ticked up sharply in the year after Trump took office and have stayed high. It's probably not a coincidence that a 2019 analysis from the *Washington Post* showed such incidents more than tripled in counties where Trump held a rally in 2016. Meanwhile, a 2022 report in the *New York Times* found a startling spike in the number of threats to sitting members of Congress (of both political parties) since 2016, a phenomenon they attribute to a "mainstreaming of violent political speech," driven largely by Trump himself. In October 2022, Paul Pelosi, spouse of the right's favorite bogeyperson, two-time Speaker of the House Nancy Pelosi, was attacked with a hammer in his own home.*

Call it the Trump disinhibition effect.

---

* It's worth noting that derogatory language can likewise lead to violence in the world of sports, says University of Memphis professor Cody T. Havard. Per Havard's rivalry research, there are 1 to 2 percent of fans who report a willingness to "commit the most heinous act of aggression" against members of rival teams, including physical harm or even murder. He advises organizations against using words like *hate* in their promotional messaging, even if it's meant playfully. He says, "That could give those people that push they need to say, 'Oh, you hate them, too? Well, then I'm justified in my behavior.' And that could lead to some very bad things."

It's not just that he's functionally given license to some of humanity's lesser angels. Over and over, Trump tells his supporters how unjustly they've all been treated—like a coach frothing his team with bulletin-board material—and how the other side is the one that's crossing the line, if not outright cheating. (Keep in mind, targets of trash talk not only become more motivated to see their opponents lose, but are also more likely to act unethically to ensure that result.)

You can imagine the mentality: *If they're not playing by the rules, then why should we?!*

These effects help explain the petty vengeance that animates Trump's political energy. (The first 2020 campaign sticker I saw out in the wild read: "Make Liberals Cry Again.") It's nothing short of schadenfreude—taking pleasure from another person's pain—and that more than anything, this organized and self-righteous cruelty, this willingness to be straight-up mean and purposefully hurtful, makes me concerned about where this all leads.*

Fundamentally, trash talk is a neutral tool. It takes on the values of those who use it and the ways they apply it. Trump has deployed trash-talk tactics to drive emotional responses and inflame his base. He has looked to isolate elements of the population and then riven people into ever-deeper factions, while exploiting any perceived difference as a wedge. In so doing, he has tapped into the same ancient strains of human communication that provide the principles for activities like the dozens, major fight promotion, mental gamesmanship in sports, and even military training. But while trash talk is so effective in each of these venues, among many others, it should be clear from the example of the Trump years that, while it's understandably tempting to talk some shit on the campaign trail, the practice does not contribute to a very successful (or even moderately

---

* As Harvard psychologist Mina Cikara and her collaborators put it in a 2011 paper that explored the biological responses of schadenfreude: "If one attaches positive value to outgroup members' suffering, then one may be motivated to inflict suffering—in extreme cases leading to atrocities including genocide, and in more quotidian cases brawls among rival sports fans."

healthy) strategy of governance and especially not when done without restraints of any kind. Perhaps more so now than ever, the stakes of American politics do not need to be artificially raised.

LANDON DONOVAN COULDN'T believe what he was hearing. It was halftime during a late-season game in 2020, and the former US men's national team star, now head coach of the USL Championship's San Diego Loyal, was listening to Rick Schantz, coach for the Phoenix Rising, explain why homophobia is actually fine.

OK, maybe that's not wholly accurate. Let's rewind.

In its previous match, one week earlier, Donovan's team earned a draw against the LA Galaxy II. They should have probably gotten the win but gave up an equalizing goal in extra time while playing short-handed. It was a heartbreaker, as they badly needed the points in their fight for a final playoff spot. But the day's biggest excitement wouldn't come until after the match. Donovan and his staff were in the coaches' room, dissecting those critical closing moments and wondering what the heck had happened with defensive player Elijah Martin. Normally even-keeled, he had been sent off the field with two yellow cards, with the second one coming only minutes after the first. That's when they heard a commotion from the locker room—*Fuck that! He said that? He said that to you?!*—and it quickly became clear there was indeed a reason for Martin's uncharacteristic play: Galaxy II defenseman Omar Ontiveros had called him the N-word.

The part that Donovan found most disturbing was that when he walked down the hall to alert the opposing coaching staff, they already knew. They had been within earshot of the slur, apparently, and just shrugged it off.* If anything, he says, they "sort of reveled" in the fact that they were able to steal a point by getting that last-minute

---

* Ontiveros claimed the word wasn't meant maliciously, but more so as it's sometimes used as a substitute for words like *man* or *dude*, though Ontiveros is American and should have known better.

goal. "I don't think they realized the severity of what had happened," he says. (Two days after the match, the league suspended Ontiveros, and soon thereafter the Galaxy II let him go.)

The Loyal locker room was shaken up—not just by the incident, but also by their response, or lack thereof. In an official team statement, the players expressed disappointment in themselves for not walking off the field in a show of solidarity with their teammate when the slur wasn't met with immediate disciplinary action. They also announced they'd be retroactively forfeiting the game, even though it would hurt their playoff chances. "We don't even want to recognize being a part of a match where these types of actions take place," the team's chairman said. To further protest, the players planned an on-field demonstration for the following game. In the seventy-first minute, which was when Martin had been abused, they would stop play, stand together, and hold up a sign that read, "I will speak. I will act."

As it happened, they never got the chance.

Just before halftime, with the Loyal up three goals to one and the playoffs within reach, Phoenix forward Junior Flemmings got into a verbal altercation with San Diego midfielder Collin Martin,* who is openly gay, in which he allegedly (and repeatedly) called Martin a "batty boy," which is a Jamaican homophobic slur. According to Donovan, it was obvious from where he stood something had happened: Martin's demeanor visibly changed, like a *Roast Battle* comic who absorbs a much-too-personal blow onstage. "You could see there was a moment where it does cross the line," he says.

On the field, Martin appealed for support, first from one of Flemmings's teammates—saying something to the effect of, "What's wrong with this guy? He needs to stop"—and then from a referee, to whom he said of Flemmings, "He called me a f-g." But that only led to more confusion, as the ref issued Martin a red card, under the

---

* No relation to teammate Elijah.

mistaken impression that he was the one hurling abuse. "That's when all hell broke loose," says Donovan.

It was in an effort to sort out this mess that Donovan found himself huddling on the field with Schantz and two of the referees. As Donovan explains to me, Schantz was at first concerned one of his players had said something racist—he knew what had happened the previous week—and seemed almost relieved when he learned of the actual allegation. Donovan implored his counterpart to bench Flemmings for the second half as a disciplinary measure—to show that words have consequence—but Schantz all but rolled his eyes at that request. It wasn't just that he was dismissive of Martin's claim; it's that he was basically blessing antigay slurs as part of the game.

To Donovan, he said, "How long have you been playing soccer?"

In the moment, Donovan didn't know how to react. The Loyal coach stepped back from the huddle, sunk his head into hands. *Twice in two weeks*, he thought. *Is this really happening?*

INDIVIDUAL SOCCER PLAYERS, like Cristiano Ronaldo, are repeatedly subjected to homophobic abuse on the pitch, while whole fan bases, like Mexico's, are known to chant *puto* and *maricón*, both homophobic slurs, during national team games. For his part, Donovan says he's likely heard the term *batty boy* thousands of times over the years—though almost always as a generalized insult, like the way American schoolkids used to (or maybe still do) call something gay. He'd never given it much thought, if he's being honest. It wasn't until the previous week's incident with Elijah that he considered that teams and players might have an obligation to call out bad behavior as it happens—as a way to make clear when something should *not* be part of the game. "As I thought it through more and more, I was thinking about all the players I had watched in Europe or in other parts of the world get racially abused," he says. "You would see images of these players wanting to walk off the field, and all their teammates were like, 'No, no, no. It's OK. Stay. You're giving in. You'll let them win.'"

But by doing nothing, the abuse becomes normalized, accepted. According to Thomas Ford, the humor scholar, this is precisely how norms can change as a result of disparagement humor, too: when something crosses a line with racist, sexist, or homophobic humor, people have a choice whether to push back or to let it pass. If they let it pass, then that norm is relaxed. If they push back, they're essentially saying, "Hey, guys. Let's not accept this kind of stuff," he says. (What's more, Ford has found in his research that people who are exposed to racist and sexist jokes are subsequently more tolerant of racism and sexism and especially so when they already harbor—but repress—such beliefs. "The jokes give them permission to let down their guard and express their true selves," he says.) That more than anything had been what was eating at Donovan and his team: they'd had a chance to take an in-game stand—to push back—and they'd let it pass.

In his career, Donovan endured plenty of jeering himself—though it was never anything bigoted and typically from fans. They'd get on him for his receding hairline. Call him bald and whatnot. Maybe scream, "Rogaine," if they were feeling especially creative. There were only ever two or three on-field incidents that he felt crossed a line, the worst of which came during the 2002 World Cup in a game against Mexico. He was jawing in Spanish with veteran striker Luis Hernández, who then said, "I'm going to find your mom and I'm going to kill her." At which point, the twenty-year-old Donovan just went silent. "I didn't truly believe that was going to happen, but you never know," he says. "Like, I don't know the guy."

He does know one thing, though: abuse doesn't stop on its own.

In his experience, that was the case whether it was cursing fans or opposing players grabbing his jersey. In response to the fans, Donovan developed a habit of walking toward the offending section of the stands. It was a way to strip hecklers of their perceived anonymity. "As you get closer and closer, people just calm down and relax," he says. As for the garment grabbers, he'd try to shade them out of the behavior by saying something like, "Listen, man, if you want to trade jerseys with me, wait until after the game."

Back in the locker room, Donovan gathered his team and told them they had a decision to make—to play or not to play—and that whatever they decided, they'd have the full support of management. There was no easy or obvious answer. On the one hand, a competitive imperative compelled them to complete the game and earn a play-off spot—to not allow verbal abuse to distract them from the task at hand. And then there were the moral considerations: the chance to confront homophobia and reject the norm that such attitudes might be considered part of the game. According to Joshua Leota, who has written in defense of gamesmanship from a philosophical perspective, athletes need to weigh these competing imperatives carefully. "An athlete's behavior is not exempt from general moral considerations," he says over email. "Just as we should not fiddle while Rome burns (however excellently we are fiddling) nor should we imagine that the pursuit of athletic excellence excuses us from more general moral duties." Leota brings up Zidane's headbutt in the World Cup final as an example of a player deciding, rightly or wrongly, that his moral obligations (to defend his sister's honor) outweighed his competitive ones (to not get thrown out of soccer's most important game).

Donovan tells me he'd always considered Zidane's outburst a competitive failure, on some level. "It's your job not to respond," he says. But his experience with the Loyal has complicated his thinking about an athlete's responsibilities. In the waning moments of half-time of the game against Phoenix, Donovan reminded his players about their planned demonstration for the seventy-first minute and confessed that he personally was not comfortable continuing the match unless the offending player was off the field. (He was being diplomatic. Here's what he was thinking but kept to himself: "What a fucking bunch of hypocrites we are if we play this game right now.")

Ultimately, the players felt the same as their coach, and Donovan relayed their position to the referee. They would play, but only if

Flemmings were out of the game. The ref insisted his hands were tied, since he wasn't familiar with the term *batty boy* and couldn't in good conscience send him off. Next, he approached Schantz. But the Phoenix coach likewise wouldn't remove his player. Flemmings denied the allegation, and Schantz was taking him at his word.*

So that was that.

The whistle blew for the second half. The Loyal players took a knee and walked off.

SAN DIEGO MISSED the playoffs. But in the days that followed, the team received its laurels in the form of an overwhelmingly positive response from the public—from fans and nonfans alike, from folks who'd never before heard of the USL Championship—thanking them for taking a stand. It came as a surprise to Donovan, who normally stays off social media but in the aftermath indulged in an unusual amount of scrolling, curious to see the fallout. "I thought there were going to be severely negative repercussions," he says. "People were so appreciative. Not just people who might be gay or have been called homophobic slurs. Anybody who's been discriminated against and felt like they just had to deal with it forever." The most pointed criticism came not online, but from Donovan's inner circle, from his friends. They pressed him: Did the Loyal really have to walk off the field? Wasn't this all a bit . . . dramatic?

Donovan took their questions seriously. He replayed the incident in his head again and again. He asked himself: *Was there another way we could have solved the issue and still felt true to ourselves?* In the end, he decided: probably not. By handling themselves as they did, they not only left the field with totally clear consciences, but also created the conditions for accountability—and, perhaps, behavioral change.

---

* Donovan knows Schantz comes off as a villain in all of this and wants to give him some credit, too. He says, "He and I had long conversations since, and he's been very gracious, very apologetic, very contrite. It's been a good healing process for everybody."

"People react to consequences. They don't react to conversations," he says. "If you know you're going to get punished because you're behaving a certain way, you're not going to behave a certain way. That's just reality."

It's also how lines are ultimately drawn, and redrawn, and how new rules and norms can be put in place. When trash talk happens in a context in which people can face repercussions, it offers the potential of shifting our cultural and behavioral standards in a positive way. A good example of this comes from the Australian Football League. In 1993, an Aboriginal player named Nicky Winmar responded to racist taunts by lifting his shirt, pointing to his bare skin, and shouting, "I'm black and I'm proud to be black."* It was considered a landmark moment, "the first time an Indigenous footballer had really taken a stand," says Sam Duncan, who is the course leader for the sports media and sports business degrees at Australia's Holmesglen Institute and has argued against sledging in sport. Winmar's actions were not just symbolic; they also set the stage for change. Two years later, when another Aboriginal footballer named Michael Long lodged an official complaint after being racially abused by a fellow player, it resulted in the Australian Football League's adoption of a racial antivilification policy—and that provided, for the first time, formal mechanisms of recourse.

In any arena, it'd be hard to argue against the moderating effect of potential consequences. In the time before the Civil War, Southern politicians "softened" their tone when Northerners began to meet insults with violence, per Freeman's *The Field of Blood*. Likewise, she writes, once the threat of duels and other physical combat fell off in Congress, "verbal abuse soared." It's not unlike the explosion of trash talk in the NBA, as the league cracked down on physical altercations during the 1990s. Bennett Salvatore tells me he noticed an unsettling rise in "derogatory comments" by the end of that decade and into the early 2000s. "I would agree with that," says Joe Forte, who worked

---

* In 2019, a statue of Winmar was unveiled at Optus Stadium in Perth to commemorate this act of defiance.

twenty-two years as an NBA referee, starting with the 1988–1989 season. B.J. Armstrong was a rookie the following year, and he remembers players being more careful with their words than they were at the end of his career, and not just because they worried about someone punching them in the face, but also because "somebody could foul you—like, really, really hard." (For his part, Armstrong was never one to talk recklessly. He says, "Where I grew up, you didn't fight because you didn't know what was in that guy's bag.")

Physical violence isn't the only way to hold people accountable, though. Increasingly, leagues of all levels are trying to root out abusive behavior from fans by instituting bans and other harsh penalties. In 2021, a Pennsylvania high school's entire student body was forbidden from attending its varsity hockey games because of sexually explicit taunts directed at an opposing team's female goalie. In 2022, the Mexican Football Federation announced fans who participate in antigay chants at soccer games would receive five-year stadium bans. Shame can be another powerful motivator for behavioral change—and for the same primal reason social rejection is such a potent threat: it implies possible ostracization from the tribe. Professional lacrosse player Callum Crawford tells me he spent the early part of his career talking all kinds of crap—and getting very personal at times—only to spend the rest of his playing days trying to rehab his image with fellow laxers once he discovered everyone in the league thought he was a total asshole. "I didn't realize the reputation I was creating," he says.*

———————

PEOPLE ARE NEVER going to stop talking shit. This we know. Long before we had the term for it, trash talk was an irrepressible,

---

* Shame has its limitations. Perhaps unsurprisingly, it's less effective in cultures that embrace shamelessness—or against individuals who do so (like Trump, who seems to view the existence of shame in others as a weakness)—because it's decoupled from social consequence, if not actually rewarded as a social value.

inescapable feature of our competitive nature—an enduring human behavioral impulse to raise the stakes of confrontation; to play mental games as well as physical ones; to prove you belong or suggest someone else might not. Modern athletes who offer up verbal challenges in attempts to intimidate, distract, or manufacture motivation are leveraging the same competitive incivilities that gave the poets of antiquity an outlet for their artistic feuds; that gave carnival-barking wrestlers a means of talking customers into their tents; and still give rise every day to countless battles of verbal one-upmanship (of both the rap and roast variety), as well as more informal exchanges of insults in bars, barbershops, and schoolyards across the globe.

There is and has always been a complex and significant linguistic current that runs beneath trash talk's openly combative and occasionally offensive surface. Language can often be deployed in sophisticated and coded ways, and we run the risk of misunderstanding what's really being said—or saying something we don't mean—when we simply take trash talk at its word or dismiss it as a cultural curio. By its boundary-pushing nature, trash talk is a gauge. It tests one's ability to understand how a challenge is *really* being presented—what's really being suggested—and then respond in the appropriate way. The true meaning of trash talk is decided not just by what is said, after all, but also by what comes next. We construct that meaning collectively, one response at a time.

It's fair to wonder how much a small gesture from a borderline playoff team in a second-tier American soccer league was really going to move the cultural needle. But to diminish the actions of the San Diego Loyal would be to miss the point. For individual players and our wider society alike, morality is always borne out in the smallest moments. It matters who we are, even—or maybe especially—when we have an excuse to be somebody else. Trash talk is both a barometer for and mover of our personal and cultural lines. At any given moment, it tells us not only who and where we are, but also, unmistakably, who we're willing to be and where we're willing to go. When Donovan and his team walked off the soccer field, they inverted the typical calculus of competition. Instead of asking themselves what they were willing to sacrifice to win the game, they asked what they were willing to give up competitively to be the kinds of people they aspired to be.

During that halftime against Phoenix Rising, it wasn't immediately clear what course of action the Loyal players were going to take. As the victim of the abuse, Collin Martin was initially insistent the team continue with the game—that they not abandon their playoff chances on his account. "I'm fine. Let's just go play. It's not a big deal," he said. And yet, when Martin learned what the opposing coach had said to Donovan and the referees during their on-field huddle—his dismissive defense of homophobia as part of the game—he deflated. Per Donovan, "He was like, 'Really? He said that?' And then he sat down, and he was really dejected." Shortly thereafter, Donovan spoke to his players, leaving the decision in their hands.

It was one player who spoke up at first, a fullback named Tarek Morad, who had joined the team only a few weeks earlier. If anyone had reason to keep a low profile—or to want the season to continue—it was probably him. But Morad didn't mince words.

"No, fuck that. We're not playing, we're not playing."

The rest of the team chimed in, and a single voice became a chorus: there was no dissent.

When the San Diego players walked out of the locker room for the game's second half, they did so without yet knowing whether they'd be playing another forty-five minutes, or if they'd be leaving the pitch almost as soon as they arrived. Whichever way things went, though, they were prepared to accept the outcome. They wouldn't argue. They wouldn't cry foul. They would protest with their actions only. There was nothing left to say.

ACKNOWLEDGMENTS

Warren Sapp caught me off guard. Part of the problem was that the Football Hall of Famer called me from a blocked number. But more than that, we hadn't actually scheduled a time to speak. A week had passed since Sapp initially agreed to an interview and then—nothing. Silence. Until this out-of-the-blue phone call. It only took a few seconds for him to put me on my heels. "I already said this is Warren," he snapped, when I asked with whom I was speaking.

It was clear from the beginning this wasn't going to be a regular conversation; it had the potential for confrontation. When Sapp asked how long I wanted to talk, for instance, I clumsily evaded the question. I played coy. *You know, uh, just depends.* On the one hand, I didn't want to undershoot my request, if he was down for a long and sprawling call—some of my interviews for this book stretched across four or more hours and multiple days—but I also didn't want to ask for *too much* time, to appear greedy, because that might have put him off and given him an excuse to back out. *Nah, forget it.*

Sapp could smell I was giving him some bullshit, though.

He said, "I don't like it when people don't answer my questions."

Quickly, I apologized—*sorry, sorry*—but that only made things worse.

"Don't apologize. It's patronizing."

Sitting alone at my desk, I could feel my cheeks flush, my heart pound. There were other signs of panic. I felt like I was spinning. Like I had lunged in one direction, and now he was charging hard the other way, swimming past me, like he did so many offensive linemen. Of course, I should have expected nothing less. On the football field, it was Warren Sapp's job to unsettle opposing players, to make them uncomfortable. He was a master antagonist, as adept with his words—when he chose to use them—as he was with his physical style. Even across our wireless connection, Sapp lost little of this aggressive, attacking energy. I felt his presence, his spiritual imposition. I heard his footsteps. He was dictating the terms.

Thankfully, Sapp has grown more merciful in his postplaying days, though. The former defensive lineman threw me a lifeline and steered our conversation back to the task at hand. He told me he'd been given the impression this would be a ten- or fifteen-minute call. Was that right? I exhaled. Said, yeah, that's about right. Maybe twenty or thirty minutes, if he was willing to spare the time. He agreed, said we could talk. But not yet. First, he wanted to shower. Then we could start again.

When Sapp called back, I was ready. I told myself I could do this. I could go toe-to-toe with Warren Sapp—at least on the phone. In the end, Sapp was not at all stingy with his time. We spoke for more than an hour.

Thank you to Warren Sapp and to everyone who agreed to speak with me, for however long. This book would have been impossible without the unnecessary generosity of so many people across so many domains of expertise. Thanks in particular to Cheryl Miller, Steve Smith Sr., Sean Elliott, Danny Manning, B.J. Armstrong, Marc Jackson, Jason Bryant, Scott Goldman, Mark Aoyagi, Andy Morgan, Brian Decker, Eric Goldman, David Diamante, Jarrod Kimber, Howard Beck, Jason Turbow, Cody Havard, Joe Franklin, Ashley Merryman, John Raglin, Todd Boyd, Brian Moses, and Jeff Ross for going above and beyond in one way or another. I'd also like to shout-out those folks whose names may not have appeared in the preceding pages but were no less generous with their time and whose insights were no less instrumental in informing my thinking as I navigated the world of trash talk. Thank you to Dan Buccino, Howard Eskin, Bob Ryan, Stephen Kershnar, Jason Taylor, Peter McGraw, Michael G. Long, Bob Wallace, Rick Robey, Tom McMillen, Riley

Gibbs, Tony Ramos, Jordan Burroughs, Chael Sonnen, Valentina Shevchenko, Rosemarie Ostler, Valerie Rice, Barry Dougherty, Graham Betchart, Jamie Kennedy, Kim Congdon, Eric DiMichele, Stephen Llano, James Thomas, Tony Dunst, Darren Elias, Jamie Gold, Ben Kinsley, Rayford Young, Charles Oakley, Royce White, Eno Sarris, Davyeon Ross, Jeff Burmeister, Jim Arp, Brea Hapken, Rick Dietrich, Mike Fields, and Bryant Brown. Thank you as well to Rick Barry, who spent precisely thirty-four minutes on the phone with me. I know this because, when I thanked Barry for his time, he said, "So that's thirty-four minutes at one hundred dollars per minute, which comes to . . ." I laughed as he trailed off and told him to send me an invoice.

Turns out, everyone's a shit-talker.

In addition to the original interviews conducted while reporting and researching this book, I relied on a huge variety of additional sources, including many dozens of print and online publications like *Sports Illustrated*, the *New York Times*, the *Wall Street Journal*, the *Washington Post*, the *Los Angeles Times*, the *Boston Globe*, the *Chicago Tribune*, the *Seattle Times*, the *Pittsburgh Post-Gazette*, the *Baltimore Sun*, the *Dallas Morning News*, *USA Today*, the *New Yorker*, the *Paris Review*, *Smithsonian*, *Scientific American*, *Esquire*, the *Sydney Morning Herald*, the *Guardian*, BBC, the Independent, ESPN, Bleacher Report, Deadspin, The Players' Tribune, Quartz, Atlas Obscura, SABR, Yahoo Sports, CBS Sports, The Athletic, SB Nation, Complex, The Ringer, Hannibal Boxing, and a whole galaxy of MMA sites, among others. I also frequently turned to more than fifty book sources, many of which have been cited along the way. Most notable among them are Johan Huizinga, *Homo Ludens* (London: Routledge & Kegan Paul, 1949); Elijah Wald, *Talking 'Bout Your Mama* (New York: Oxford University Press, 2012); Alan Dundes, ed., *Mother Wit from the Laughing Barrel* (Jackson, MS: University Press of Mississippi, 1990); Jonathan Eig, *Ali: A Life* (London: Simon & Schuster, 2017); Todd D. Snyder, *Bundini: Don't Believe the Hype* (Boston: Hamilcar Publications, 2020); John Capouya, *Gorgeous George* (New

York: HarperCollins Publishers, 2008); Penelope Brown and Stephen C. Levinson, *Politeness: Some Universals in Language Usage*, rev. ed. (Cambridge: Cambridge University Press, 1987); Julie Seabaugh, *Ringside at Roast Battle* (Independently published, 2018); Jonathan Abrams, *Boys Among Men* (New York: Crown Archetype, 2016); and Kevin Garnett with David Ritz, *KG A to Z* (New York: Simon & Schuster, 2021).

Thank you to David Hollander, Dave Lockett, Rick Wolff, Ramsey Chamie, Ike Richman, Jason Rosenfeld, Sammy Steinlight, Brian Fisher, Dave Sholler, Rich Desrosiers, and Nick LoPinto, among others, who seemed as excited about this project as I was and offered to help make critical connections. Thank you to Fran Judkins, Robert Redd, Danny Cage, Peter Nelson, Kirk Berger, Raymond Doswell, Patrick Stiegman, Jenna Wolfe, Jacob Pomrenke, Janice Burton, Jenna Brady, Berta Recinos, Kate Kelly, Maggie Houlehan, Alicia Berber, Joe Favorito, Michael Marquart, Marc Laitin, Tracey Snyder, Jim LaBumbard, Raj Sharan, Matt Conti, and Andrew Howard, who also fielded queries, offered contacts, or otherwise helped open doors I never could have on my own. And thank you to Stephen Lai, who assisted with early research and transcription efforts.

The idea for this book was hatched on a playground court in Brooklyn, New York, sometime in 2019. I was playing one-on-one with my close friend and then neighbor Jim Strouse. Neither of us are shit-talkers, really, but Jim seems to be something of a magnet for trash talk. He was telling me about some recent smack he'd received from a very intense female pickup player at the Pier 2 courts, which jut out into the East River. She'd said things like, "It's going to be so embarrassing when you miss." And: "Your family is going to be so ashamed of you." Which is pretty good trash talk! (Jim admitted that it worked; he started to get inside his own head.) As we played, our discussion turned to some of the guys who sometimes showed up at the YMCA and how certain trash-talkers there regularly inspired friendly competition, while others—well, one dude in particular, who will go unnamed—would carry a kind of toxic energy into the gym with him and how quickly that would infuse everything and everyone therein. What was up with all that? It just seemed like there was more to explore.

Thank you to David Patterson—with assists from Aemilia Phillips and Chandler Wickers—at the Stuart Krichevsky Literary Agency, who not only took the idea seriously, but also agreed that trash talk was a worthy avenue of investigation. Y'all found this book a perfect home. Thank you to Ben Adams at PublicAffairs for seeing the project's potential from the beginning. And thank you to Katie Adams—an editor who will never be rid of me, it seems—for helping find the book's final form.

Thank you to the rest of the team at PublicAffairs who played key roles in bringing this book to life. Thanks to Melissa Raymond, Olivia Loperfido, and Kelly Lenkevich for keeping the production wheels turning; to Kate Mueller for the careful copyediting; to Pete Garceau for the amazing cover design; and to Johanna Dickson for helping this book cut through the noise.

Thanks to Jon Fell, Matt Goldman, Jordan Chamberlain, Tom Souhlas, and Jared Joiner, who weighed in at key moments with important opinions of taste and aesthetic. To Brendan Flaherty, Adam Rubin, Patrick Hruby, Eric Nusbaum, and Stayton Bonner, for the conversation, pep talks, and offers to help. To Eric Sobel, Dave Levin, Scott Eden, Keith Newton, Ben Ryder Howe, Paul Winner, and Luke Zaleski, good dudes all. To my attorneys, Seth Klein and Marina Salguero. And to my rabbi, Rachel Greengrass.

I couldn't have done this without support and encouragement from so many other friends—too many to name here—or without hands-on help from my family in Atlanta, New Jersey, and beyond. Thank you to my parents, Marilyn and Allen; my Atlanta in-laws, Marianne, Stephen, Jed, Isla, and Doris; and especially to Arielle, Azalea, and Elliott, who had to deal with me more than anyone else as I grappled with increasing loads of book-related stress, which was never just my own. Finally, thank you to Aubrey Wasilewsky, who, throughout her nearly two-year battle with triple-negative breast cancer, demonstrated a level of emotional resilience and mental toughness to which everyone—athlete or otherwise—ought to aspire. I certainly do. Your memory will always be a blessing.

Credit: Wesley Flowers

Rafi Kohan is an Atlanta-based writer and editor. His first book, *The Arena*, was a finalist for the 2018 PEN/ESPN Award for Literary Sports Writing. Previously, he has served as deputy editor at the *New York Observer* and as executive editorial director for the *Atlantic*'s creative studio, Re:think. His writing has appeared in numerous publications, including *GQ*, *Men's Journal*, *Rolling Stone*, The Ringer, and the *Wall Street Journal*.

PublicAffairs is a publishing house founded in 1997. It is a tribute to the standards, values, and flair of three persons who have served as mentors to countless reporters, writers, editors, and book people of all kinds, including me.

I. F. STONE, proprietor of *I. F. Stone's Weekly*, combined a commitment to the First Amendment with entrepreneurial zeal and reporting skill and became one of the great independent journalists in American history. At the age of eighty, Izzy published *The Trial of Socrates*, which was a national bestseller. He wrote the book after he taught himself ancient Greek.

BENJAMIN C. BRADLEE was for nearly thirty years the charismatic editorial leader of *The Washington Post*. It was Ben who gave the *Post* the range and courage to pursue such historic issues as Watergate. He supported his reporters with a tenacity that made them fearless and it is no accident that so many became authors of influential, best-selling books.

ROBERT L. BERNSTEIN, the chief executive of Random House for more than a quarter century, guided one of the nation's premier publishing houses. Bob was personally responsible for many books of political dissent and argument that challenged tyranny around the globe. He is also the founder and longtime chair of Human Rights Watch, one of the most respected human rights organizations in the world.

· · ·

For fifty years, the banner of Public Affairs Press was carried by its owner Morris B. Schnapper, who published Gandhi, Nasser, Toynbee, Truman, and about 1,500 other authors. In 1983, Schnapper was described by *The Washington Post* as "a redoubtable gadfly." His legacy will endure in the books to come.

Peter Osnos, *Founder*